The Sociolinguistics of Identity

Advances in Sociolinguistics

Series Editor: Professor Sally Johnson, University of Leeds

Since the emergence of sociolinguistics as a new field of enquiry in the late 1960s, research into the relationship between language and society has advanced almost beyond recognition. In particular, the past decade has witnessed the considerable influence of theories drawn from outside of sociolinguistics itself. Thus rather than see language as a mere reflection of society, recent work has been increasingly inspired by ideas drawn from social, cultural and political theory that have emphasized the constitutive role played by language/discourse in all areas of social life. The Advances in Sociolinguistics series seeks to provide a snapshot of the current diversity of the field of sociolinguistics and the blurring of the boundaries between sociolinguistics and other domains of study concerned with the role of language in society.

Forthcoming titles in the series:

Language, Society and Social Identity
Philip Riley

Language, Power and Institutions
An Introduction to Institutional Discourse
Andrea Mayr and Bob Holland

Discourses of Endangerment
Ideology and Interest in Defence of Languages
Edited by Monica Heller and Alexandre Duchêne

Linguistic Minorities and Modernity, 2nd Edition
A Sociolinguistic Ethnography
Monica Heller

Multilingualism
A Critical Perspective
Adrian Blackledge and Angela Creese

Sociolinguistics of the Media
Helen Kelly-Holmes

Language Ideologies
A Critical Approach to Sociolinguistics
Sally Johnson and Tommaso M. Milani

Language in the Media
Representations, Identities, Ideologies
Edited by Sally Johnson and Astrid Ensslin

The Sociolinguistics of Identity

Edited by Tope Omoniyi and Goodith White

continuum

Continuum
The Tower Building
11 York Road
London SE1 7NX

80 Maiden Lane
Suite 704
New York NY 10038

British Library Cataloguing-in-Publication Data
A catalogue record for this book is available from the British Library.

ISBN: 978-1-8470-6332-8 (PB)

Typeset by Free Range Book Design & Production Limited
Printed and bound in Great Britain by Biddles Ltd, King's Lynn, Norfolk

To the memory of Robert Brock Le Page (1920–2006)

... sounds, words, signs
acts in a complex grammar
of identity inscribe us
in the moments of our becoming.

Contents

Contributors

David Block
University of London

Katherine Richardson Bruna
Iowa State University

Lourdes Burbano-Elizondo
University of Sheffield

Moises D. Perales Escudero
Universidad Juārez Autonoma

Jennifer Jenkins
King's College London

Carmen Llamas
University of Aberdeen

Louise Mullany
University of Nottingham

Tope Omoniyi
Roehampton University

Siân Preece
University of Westminster

Julia Sallabank
Lancaster University

Massimiliano Spotti
Tilburg University

Yasir Suleiman
University of Cambridge

Roberta J. Vann
Iowa State University

Goodith White
Leeds University

1   Introduction

Tope Omoniyi and Goodith White

Across the social and behavioural sciences in general there has been an increased interest in identity as a subject of inquiry and, as a result, a growing body of literature in the area (see Lavie and Swedenburg (eds) 1996; Jega 2000). In particular, as a dimension of linguistic enquiry, identity has moved to the fore as a priority subject for investigation (see for example Torres *et al.* (eds) 1999; Wodak *et al.* 1999; Norton 2000; Omoniyi 2000, 2004; Dent 2004; Joseph 2004; Pavlenko and Blackledge (eds) 2004; and Block 2005 among numerous others). In spite of these efforts, there still remain questions which confront researchers. Additionally, researchers feel compelled to challenge older paradigms of analysis in order to continue to expand the frontiers of knowledge in this research domain. Identity is a problematic and complex concept inasmuch as we recognize it now as non-fixed, non-rigid and always being (co-) constructed by individuals of themselves (or ascribed by others), or by people who share certain core values or perceive another group as having such values.

So what is *the sociolinguistics of identity*? Sociolinguistics may be said to have entered its golden age in late modernity. As a discipline it has incorporated into its agenda an applications dimension so that sociolinguistic theories rise beyond just describing or explaining social phenomena but also have the capacity to impact human development positively. The significance of sociolinguistics and that of its offshoot disciplines is being acknowledged in practical applications of the interventionist strategies it offers in areas such as forensic linguistics, minority education, literacy and development and medical linguistics. With these advances in mind then, the sociolinguistics of identity focuses on the ways in which people position or construct themselves and are positioned or constructed by others in socio-cultural situations through the instrumentality of language and with reference to all of those variables that are identity markers for each society in the speech of its members.

Therefore the challenge that we attempt to take up in putting this volume together is to re-examine the analytical tools employed in the sociolinguistic research of 'identity' in order to either assess and comment on their efficiency or demonstrate their applicability in specific research contexts, establish the roles of language in the identity claims of specific communities of people, and determine the place of identity in a variety of social contexts, including workplaces and language classrooms. What then does 'the sociolinguistics of identity' entail in this volume? We have witnessed the tremendous growth of sociolinguistics as a discipline from a modest variationist beginning that was more or less limited to a determination of social identity based on the distribution of specific social and linguistic variables among a given population into a discipline that now engages with various aspects of social theory (see Coupland 2003) and sees language as playing the central role in both interpreting and proclaiming identity (Joseph 2004). In the light of this expansion to the field, volumes such as this which attempt a multidisciplinary coverage become not only useful but absolutely essential as an appropriate reflection of the state of affairs.

Although the original idea of putting together a volume on contemporary sociolinguistic positions on the conceptualization and processing of the complex subject of identity, as well as the initial list of contributors to it, sprung from the seminar on 'Language and Identity' at the University of Reading (5–6 July 2004) jointly sponsored by the British Association for Applied Linguistics (BAAL) and Cambridge University Press (CUP), this volume in its final shape reflects coverage of a much wider sociolinguistic terrain and researchers who had not attended the seminar were therefore invited to contribute to the volume: Suleiman's and Vann *et al.*'s chapters are based on plenary and colloquium presentations respectively at the 2005 AILA Congress in Madison, Wisconsin. We have as contributors attempted to achieve a reasonable degree of cohesion by considering the following common positions and articulating these in relation to our individual issues and contexts of interest:

1. that identity is not fixed;
2. that identity is constructed within established contexts and may vary from one context to another;
3. that these contexts are moderated and defined by intervening social variables and expressed through language(s);
4. that identity is a salient factor in every communicative context whether given prominence or not;
5. that identity informs social relationships and therefore also informs the communicative exchanges that characterize them;
6. that more than one identity may be articulated in a given context in which case there will be a dynamic of identities management.

Chapters 2, 3 and 4 of this volume (Omoniyi, Block and Suleiman) focus on the analytical tools which are currently employed by sociolinguists to research identity and explore their potential for revealing the role played by language in expressing or interpreting identity in a wide variety of social contexts. These writers are not uncritical of the six common positions on identity which we have cited above, while recognizing that they offer richer ways of researching the relationship between language and identity than earlier structuralist/essentialist approaches, which perceived individuals and groups as having fixed identities which could be explained by universal laws of behaviour. Omoniyi tackles the problems for researchers inherent in point 6, that is, the challenge of analysing how the multiple identities present in social action are managed by individuals and groups. He proposes and illustrates the application of a fluid 'hierarchy of identities' model which is a more effective tool and paradigm for analysing multiple identification. He complexifies the notion of the situation or context in which processes of identification take place, redefining social actions as separable into a series of 'moments'. These 'moments' are potential units of identification, each containing repertoires of multiple identities which may be complementary to or in conflict with other identities present in the same 'moment'. He shows how this model may be applied, not only to social interactions where decoder and encoder are present, but to moments of representation when individuals are engaged in interpreting cultural texts such as road signs, notices, advertisements and so forth, in which the encoder is absent. He points out that this concep- tualization of social action is different from the more restricted application in discursive psychology. The model accommodates the notion that identity is fluid and that people negotiate between several identity categories or 'selves' in different 'moments' of identification.

Block focuses on some of the problems associated with our first position on identity cited above, i.e. that it is not fixed, but unstable, fluid and fragmented. He agrees in principle with this poststructuralist approach to identity, but feels that too many researchers may have uncritically accepted this stance, which tends to marginalize considerations of the self and underestimates the influence of social structures in constraining individual agency and choice. While he does not wish to argue against the notion that the identities which an individual assumes are at least in part those s/he chooses to assume: 'a self-conscious, reflexive project of individual agency'; Block finds a way of describing the influence of social structures on individuals, not in terms of essentialized social constructs such as ethnicity and gender, but as participation in communities of practice, such as family, colleagues at work, social activities and so on. By participating in a number of different communities of practice, each with their own goals and patterns of behaviour, individuals construct identities in their relationships within these communities. Identity thus becomes something which is a mixture of individual agency and the influence of social structures of various types. However, Block also points out that this view of identity, while focusing on the individual as a social being, subject to the influences of the environment within which s/he is located, leaves out any notion of the individual's core 'psychological self' which directs interaction with the outside world. He cites evidence from language learning of the workings of this stable core 'self', namely in the areas of silence and conflict between internal and external worlds. He concludes that the researcher needs to find ways of reconciling structure and agency, but also needs to be aware that the core self, 'the subconscious deep inner workings of the mind', might impact on an individual's sense of identity. He acknowledges the fact that this inner self poses considerable problems for investigation.

Suleiman takes on the difficult task of discussing national identity, which as a group identity, composed in turn of members of different ethnic, cultural, economic, territorial and linguistic groups, poses problems for investigation, particularly in terms of points 1 and 6 above, which posit that identity is not fixed and that more than one identity may be articulated in a given context. Can one talk of a national identity given the disparity of the individuals who might claim membership of a given national group? Suleiman prefers to use poly-centricity rather than hierarchy as a paradigm for describing the relationships between individuals within the national group. He describes how language plays an important part in creating national identity, and conversely how language is constructed as part of the ideological work of nation building. In particular he focuses on two roles which language plays in the construction and expression of national identity. The first is the use of language as a 'proxy'; a means of indirectly articulating issues to do with politics and identity which would cause problems if expressed too openly in the public sphere. The second is the use of names and ethnic labels as expressions of ethnic and national identity in situations where conflict or contestation about aspects of national identity exist.

Chapters 5, 6 and 7 (Jenkins, Llamas and Burbano-Elizondo) examine points 2 and 3 above, i.e. that identity is constructed within established contexts and may vary from one context to another; and that these contexts are moderated and defined by intervening social variables and expressed through language. All three chapters describe the role of language choice in establishing and maintaining identity within small communities (although in the chapter by Jenkins perhaps this should be redefined as a community which shares particular characteristics, since the community of speakers of English as a second language is extremely widely distributed geographically and also very numerous). The studies reported in these three chapters focus on specific linguistic forms (pronunciation features, grammatical and lexical items) and discuss the links which language users make between these micro-analytical variables and social categories.

Jenkins focuses on the issue of identity in language learning and takes as her starting point the ambivalent responses of many non-native speakers (NNS) of English to her proposal that a core of pronunciation features of English crucial in promoting intelligibility in interactions where English is used as a lingua franca (ELF) could form the basis of a much more realistic set of targets for learners of English than trying to achieve a completely 'native-like' pronunciation. She found that many NNS teachers and learners were strongly opposed to the idea of abandoning native speaker norms for pronunciation. While some of the opposition was due to misunderstandings about the nature of what she was proposing, she argues that some of the support for native-like accents springs from the desire of NNS to claim membership of the group who use the dominant discourse – and this is still perceived to be first language (L1) speakers of English rather than a worldwide community of ELF speakers. Her investigations led her to problematize the relationship between NNS and their membership of a community of English speakers. On the one hand they desired a native-speaker pronunciation of English, especially where that would lead to economic and social benefit, but on the other hand they retained an attachment to their mother tongue which led them to wish to retain some pronunciation features of their mother tongue when speaking English. She argues that the relationship between accent and affiliation to a particular group is affected by a complex set of factors which require further investigation.

Llamas considers practices of categorization, self-making and 'othering' in the identity construction processes of speakers of English in the town of Middlesborough in the North of England. Middlesborough is a transitional town, situated between two major geographical regions, the North-East and Yorkshire, but not wholly belonging to or identifying with either. Llamas studies two phonological features, glottalized /p/ and TH-fronting, and speakers' attitudes towards their use. She focuses on the ways in which such language forms index the social identities of speakers, and elicits the associations which speakers make between such forms and meaningful social groupings. Drawing on Tajfel's work on social categorization, cited in Turner 1999, she describes community identity as springing from the individual's desire to belong to a group which is distinct from and perceived in a more positive sense than other groups. This community identity may be to some extent fluid and 'imagined' (Anderson 1991). Using an innovative method of data elicitation (SuRE) which included questionnaires to elicit attitudes towards both language use and geographical area, and an Affiliation Score Index designed to test in-group preference, she discovers that some speakers are less oriented towards membership of a local community than others, and that local geographical orientation towards Yorkshire or the North-East also appears to differ according to the age of the speaker.

Burbano-Elizondo's study also describes linguistic variation in a town in the North-East of England, in this case Sunderland, which is more firmly situated within a major geographical region than Middlesborough. Nevertheless, as Burbano-Elizondo writes: 'Despite the compactness of the North-Eastern community, within its boundaries we can identify various strong and distinct local identities'. She, like Llamas, makes use of the ideological framework proposed by Silverstein (1992) which identifies two orders of indexicality in language – first-order indexicality, which refers to the links which speakers establish between linguistic forms and social categories, and second-order indexicality, which considers the ways in which speakers rationalize the link between linguistic form and social category. Different communities will interpret and justify the links in different ways. Burbano-Elizondo makes use of the SuRE analytical tools to identify some of the local ideologies which surround the local Sunderland dialect and which emerge from the links made between language and social meaning. She finds that her informants not only felt that there was a distinct Sunderland or 'Mackem' identity, but that they were also able to identify linguistic forms which differentiated the Sunderland dialect from Tyneside English.

Chapters 8–13 (Sallabank, Mullany, Preece, Spotti, Vann *et al.* and White) focus on contexts in which participants have to choose between languages or varieties of a language and in which an individual's identity orientation may shift from 'moment' to 'moment' (see Omoniyi, this volume). In this sense, many of the papers articulate views on point 6 above, that is, that more than one identity may be articulated in a given context, in which case there will be a dynamic of identity shifts and possible conflicts between 'competing' identities.

Sallabank investigates attitudes towards Guernsey French, which is now spoken fluently by only 2.26 per cent of the population of Guernsey, an ageing and dwindling group of speakers. She points out that language is only one amongst a number of potential markers of identity, such as gender, religion, job, personality, social class, etc., and that feelings of ethnic identity can survive total language loss. She finds that much of the existing literature on language loss and endangerment takes a rather essentialist view of identity and tends to assume that if a language dies, a particular ethnic identity disappears. She points out, for example, that it is possible to retain a strong attachment and identification with Jersey Norman French and 'Jerseyness' without being able to necessarily speak the language. She follows Block's compromise of seeing individuals as capable of choice and change, but also shaped to some extent by the social context in which they find themselves. She concludes that younger people now see Guernsey French as something interesting and 'cool', 'a secret language of our own', and that Guernsey people are beginning to realize what they could lose if the language dies out, but it is likely that the older generation will be the last fluent native speakers.

Mullany uses narratives of personal experience to explore conflicts between gender and professional identities, pointing out that in the process of telling a story 'the self is evaluated in the light of cultural meanings, beliefs and normative practices' (Schiffrin 1996: 168). She finds evidence that some of the women in her study feel that professional identity is constrained by the gender identity that they perceive others in the company have imposed on them. Dominant discourses of femininity often appear to be incompatible with the social and cultural expectations which are seen as constituting the identity of a successful manager.

Preece writes about a group of male undergraduates and their processes of identification with new social and academic communities on entry to university. For these young men, there were difficulties in reconciling their existing membership of a multi-ethnic masculine peer group (with its own variety of English) and negotiating membership of an academic community of practice (which involves acquiring skills such as academic writing). Preece argues that acquiring academic literacy is not just a matter of gaining new competencies in the language but also involves individuals in profound changes in their sense of their own identity. She illustrates how the undergraduates resist being positioned as 'deficient' in terms of their membership of the academic community by performing a kind of laddish masculinity.

Spotti's chapter reports his investigation of the linguistic and cultural affiliations of immigrant pupils in a Dutch primary school, and the role which these affiliations may play in their construction of identity inside and outside the classroom. He considers how individuals combine dominant, residual and emergent cultural elements to express changing affiliations in contexts where a number of cultures overlap. He finds that the pupils opted for Dutch because it promoted a sense of in-group cohesion with the 'host community' and possibly also a form of resistance to parental authority. At the same time, a strong affiliation remained to the land they had come from. Spotti sees these pupils as active in creating new ways of affiliating with their new country, in which they 'redefine what it means to belong to a certain nation'.

Vann *et al.* also focus on classrooms as places in which new socio-academic identities are forged by immigrant children. They analyse face-to-face exchanges between teachers and students in a secondary school multilingual classroom in Iowa and examine the linguistic means which students use for negotiating identity while in class. They take the position that identities are fluid and created and recreated through interaction, and demonstrate how teacher–student discourse is used to negotiate multi-layered and multi-faceted identities as students, Spanish speakers, boys or girls, individuals with different personality traits and so on. They also highlight the role of frames in influencing interaction and the identity work that results from those interactions.

White attempts to prove that Irish identity, traditionally linked to the Irish language, might now be more appropriately expressed through an emerging standard variety of Irish English. She, like Suleiman, emphasizes the role which language plays in forming, promoting and maintaining national identity, and argues that in a post-nationalist, globalizing world, standard Irish English allows its speakers to express Irish identity while at the same time permitting international communication. By means of a corpus, questionnaire and map task, she explores the distinctive features of this variety of English and attitudes towards its use.

While we are confident that the discussions in the chapters in this volume contribute to identity research in general, and in particular to its application in the specific communities or contexts that some of the authors have studied and reported on, we are also aware that the dynamics of social change and political-cum-cultural realignments that are always present ensure that the claims we make can only be valid for the context that they represent. Moreover, these communities or contexts are hardly representative of all others with which they co-exist in the same geopolitical camp. The implication of this then is that these studies ought to serve as encouragement for the investigation of other communities in a bid to ascertain if the findings reported here hold true for them and, if not, to advance sociolinguistic knowledge by proffering an alternative conceptualization or paradigm of analysis.

The classroom identity construction activities that Vann *et al.* report would ordinarily provide useful allusions in looking at other immigrant groups and/or border communities around the world in order to articulate a theory of classroom identity that may have universal application with such populations. However, we must ask if it is reasonable to refer to universal essentialist categories such as 'immigrants', 'refugees' and 'borderlanders' if Spotti's Dutch, Vann *et al.*'s Mexican and Preece's British classroom populations are not only diverse but also need to be viewed in relation to the contiguous social groups outside the classroom with which they form a polity and within which their identities are structurally negotiated. This is worth debating because of the implications it has, for instance, for new and emergent diasporas as well as the intricacy of the new social reality that globalization has authored (Coupland 2003).

Finally, the issues and questions about theory and methodology in identity research that were raised in some of the chapters, especially those by Omoniyi, Block and Suleiman, essentially keep the debate going by presenting new paradigms and tools that hopefully will be subjected subsequently to critical scrutiny in future research in order to test their efficacy. For instance, the classroom identity studies reported in this volume may have validated Norton's (2000) recommendation of the poststructuralist claim that identity is multiple, and a site of struggle, but it remains to be articulated whether or how the nature of struggle which is variable may impact identity research in classrooms differently. These are only a few obvious suggestions as to how researchers may take forward the debates we have started or contributed to in the chapters that follow. There may be many other less apparent ones that contextual interpretation or application of some of the claims may also throw up. Nevertheless, we hope that the individual chapters and discussions provide sufficiently engaging matter to sustain the interest of all readers.

References

Anderson, B. (1991), *Imagined Communities: Reflections on the Origin and Spread of Nationalism*. London: Verso.

Block, D. (2005), *Multilingual Identities in a Global City: London Stories*. Basingstoke: Palgrave Macmillan.

Coupland, N. (2003), 'Introduction: sociolinguistics and globalization', *Journal of Sociolinguistics*, 7, (4), 465–72.

Dent, M. J. (2004), *Identity Politics: Filling the Gap Between Federalism and Independence*. Burlington: Ashgate.

Jega, A. (ed.) (2000), *Identity Transformation and Identity Politics under Structural Adjustment in Nigeria*. Uppsala: Nordiska Africa Institute.

Joseph, J. (2004), *Language and Identity: National, Ethnic, Religious*. Basingstoke: Palgrave Macmillan.

Lavie, S. and Swedenburg, T. (eds) (1996), *Displacement, Diaspora and Geographies of Identity*. London: Duke University Press.

Norton, B. (2000), *Identity and Language Learning: Gender, Ethnicity and Educational Change*. London: Longman/Pearson Education.

Omoniyi, T. (2000), 'Islands and identity in sociolinguistics: a theoretical perspective', in T. Omoniyi (ed.), *Islands and Identity in Sociolinguistics*. Berlin: Mouton de Gruyter, pp. 1–13.

— (2004), *The Sociolinguistics of Borderlands: Two Nations, One Community*. Trenton, NJ: Africa World Press.

Pavlenko, A. and Blackledge, A. (eds) (2004), Negotiation of Identities in Multilingual Settings. Clevedon: Multilingual Matters Ltd.

Torres, R. D., Mirón, L. F. and Inda, J. X. (eds) (1999), *Race, Identity, and Citizenship: A Reader*. Oxford: Blackwell.

Schiffrin, D. (1996), 'Narrative as self-portrait: sociolinguistic constructions of identity', *Language in Society*, 25, (2), 167–203.

Silverstein, M. (1992), 'The uses and utility of ideology: some reflections'. *Pragmatics*, 2, (3), 311–23.

Turner, J. C. (1999), 'Some current issues in research on social identity and self-categorization theories', in N. Ellemers, R. Spears and B. Doosje (eds), *Social Identity: Context, Commitment, Content*. Oxford: Blackwell, pp. 6–34

Wodak, R., de Cillia, R., Reisigl, M., and Liebhart, K. (1999), *The Discursive Construction of National Identity* (trans. by A. Irsch and R. Mitten).

Part I

Identity and Sociolinguistic Theory and Methods

2 Hierarchy of identities[1]

Tope Omoniyi

Identity is generated through culture – especially language – and it can invest itself in various meanings: an individual can have an identity as a woman, a Briton, a Black, a Muslim. Herein lies the facility of identity politics: it is dynamic, contested, and complex.

(Harrison 1998: 248)

Introduction

In their outline proposal, the managers of the UK's ESRC-funded interdisciplinary research programme 'Identities and Choice in the 21st Century' noted that 'issues of identity have moved to centre stage in the 21st century' and set as an objective bridging the gap between theory and empirical research. This chapter is intended as a contribution towards that broader goal. The association between language and identity is well established in research in the fields of applied linguistics (Ivanič 1998), sociolinguistics (Labov 1966), sociology of language (Fishman 1999, Omoniyi 2000) and the social psychology of language (Giles and Bourhis 1976) among others. These studies have been carried out among varying populations, including individuals and groups, in classrooms, communities and other contexts of identification. They have explored issues such as ethnolinguistic vitality, class-based language behaviour, language and social capital, gender, power, access and control, and other ideological concerns in contemporary social theory. The latter includes the issue of the growing significance of religion as an identity variable in global politics (see Modood 1998, Omoniyi and Fishman 2006). Much of the earlier work done in this line of research focused on the end-product (identity categories), rather than the production process, identification. In other words, the goal was often to define and categorize an individual or group. My intention in this chapter therefore is to refocus so that the significance of identification as a process is brought to the fore and we can engage with how the process creates and manages a hierarchy of identities (HoI). I shall demonstrate how such a theoretical paradigm might work as well as the methodology of setting it up.

Broadly, in pursuit of my stated intent above, I have two tasks. The first is to review recent approaches and developments in language and identity research and address what I perceive to be a movement away from primordialist models such as sex, ethnicity and territory (cf. Balibar and Wallerstein, 1991) to more dynamic models, which locate identity and identification as product and process respectively in constructed social action. This is necessary because the HoI model that I shall present exemplifies the latter. The second task I have is to present the model for scrutiny as a theoretical option for explaining the negotiation of multiple identities and most importantly make a case for *moments* as the focus of analysis in identity research. The logic of this is that contexts and acts are constituted of different moments within a stretch of social action. I shall explore the application of HoI in a number of contexts including non-interactional ones. A variety of data types will be used to demonstrate how the model works with conversations, monologues and public symbols.

The very nature of identity, what Joseph (2004: 1) called 'identity of identity', is contentious. One of the purposes served by identity as a concept is that of constituting a frame of reference within which our recognition of an entity takes place. There are two dimensions to the recognition process: the physical visual (normative, social, behavioural) and the cognitive (abstract, mental). Even though these dimensions are not discontinuous entities (cf. Joseph 2004: 5), the former is 'directly observable' while the latter can only be inferred from other phenomena such as behaviours and actions. This distinction is between a kind of objective reality that we *name* from convention, and the imagined or perceived that we *describe*.

Joseph (2004) adapts Saussure's semiotic model which he described as 'supremely elegant in construction' in discussing the role or place of names in identity construction. He suggests that examinations of the linguistic aspects of identity need not engage with 'questions of consciousness or cognitive processes' (2004: 5). Both naming and describing as dimensions of identity are complicated when culture is factored into the equation. Wagner (forthcoming) demonstrates the usefulness of the Saussurean paradigm for the analysis of identity in her application of it to the interpretation of road signage. I shall return to this later with some illustrative data.

According to Tabouret-Keller (1997: 315), 'language acts are acts of identity'. He identified four key areas of identity research – self-identity, collective identity, institutional identity and global identity. It is also established that people and organizations possess multiple identities on the basis of the multiple roles they are capable of fulfilling or representing in the socio-cultural relationships in which they participate.

The base assumption I shall work with is that all social actions are separable into moments which make up the stretch of time it takes to accomplish them. There are in such moments competing as well as complementary multiple identities or in Blommaert's terms 'identity repertoires' (2004). I use multiple identities in the first of two senses that Joseph (2004: 8) describes, i.e. in terms of the multiple roles that human beings have. His second sense of the multiplicity of identity, which he credits to Jan Christiaan Smuts, concerns the 'consciousness of other selves'. This does not lend itself easily to the sort of measurement and scrutiny that I shall attempt later, for reasons that will be self-evident shortly. I should also point out from the outset that my discussion of identity here excludes contexts in which institutional structures impose identities and therefore restrict or obstruct options and/or choice. For instance, speaking as an accused person, counsel or judge in a courtroom, a prisoner in a prison yard or an asylum-seeker in a holding centre almost permanently privilege these identities to the exclusion of any others that the persons may have.

The identity category that is perceived from, or projected through, language behaviour is the consequence of moment-by-moment factor-driven decisions about appropriateness and position of that category in a hierarchy of identities. In other words, the configuration of factors may change from one moment to another, consequently leading to different decisions being made and altering the structure of the hierarchy. For my purposes here, I conceptualize social action as not confined to contexts of face-to-face interaction, or in fact any kind of communicative negotiation within dyads, triads or larger groups. Social action may also be an instance of reflective engagement when people are confronted by situations of which they seek to make sense.

Dialogic or polylogic encounters are a prerequisite for analysis using the discursive psychology paradigm (see Edwards and Potter 1992). Potter and Edwards (1999: 448) for instance note that discursive psychology conceptualizes action 'in terms of the enormous range of practical, technical and *interpersonal* tasks that people perform while living their relationships, doing their jobs, and engaging in varied cultural domains' (my emphasis). However, to interpersonal contexts we must add action in those moments of representation and interpretation of codes involving individuals confronted by advertisements, plaques, road signs, car number plates and other cultural texts in a liberal and inclusive sense of the term. These texts are invested with properties that are laden with meaning within established social systems. As social actors and members of these social systems we are able to read concepts, people, places and objects. After all, as Joseph (2004: 36) suggests, '"reading" in the sense of interpreting identity fulfils the criteria for an evolutionary basis to language. It also underpins both representation and communication'. Differences between the lived experiences of people account for variation between the versions of identity constructed, particularly their constructions or representations of 'Self'. The process is broadly interactional in nature and involves the encoder (who may [not] be present) and the decoder (always present). Both encoding and decoding have more or less equal significance in the identification process. However, when encoders are not physically present as an entity during decoding, they still exist in the decoder's perception of social reality and any interpretation is projected upon or anchored to them.

Review of approaches

There has been a movement away from structuralism's notions of identity as 'static' or 'essential' in the sense in which variationists such as Labov (1966) and Trudgill (1974) used it with reference, for instance, to the distribution of individuals and groups into social classes. In 1985, Le Page and Tabouret-Keller published their seminal volume, which may be said to have triggered the wave of sociolinguistic research that began to view identity as produced within social action rather than as pre-existing categories to which people and things are assigned. At about the same time, social constructionism became the preferred approach in social psychology as we find in the work of Kenneth Gergen (1985, 1999) and others. Post-structural sociolinguistics evidenced in contemporary studies such as Rampton (1995), Butler (1997), Coupland (2003) and Pennycook (2003) has effected change in identity research practice. I shall identify three such changes as key. First, identity research has become multitheoretical and multidisciplinary. Language remains central to this tradition, for as Joseph (2004) notes, language and identity are inseparable. Secondly, there has been a change in conceptualization from traditional essentialist categories to individual performers in late modernity. That shift has marked the progression from 'acts of identity' (LePage and Tabouret-Keller 1985) to 'styling the other' (Rampton 1995), 'performativity' (Butler 1997 and Pennycook 2003). Thirdly, identification is a multilayered process and a hierarchy of identities model brings this out clearly. Now let us look more closely at each of the changes above to establish the exact manner of their impact upon identity research.

Multitheoretical and multidisciplinary

Race and identity

Diversity programmes in multiracial and multicultural societies reflect the organization and management of social structures in pretty much essentialist terms, such as the distribution of resources to reflect the demographic composition of state. Some of the issues emanating from racial identity considerations include inclusion/exclusion in schools in the UK, institutional(ized) racism discourse in the public sphere, racially-defined medical conditions such as hypertension, anaemia, HIV/AIDS, etc. From the perspective of ideology, poststructuralists have summarized the debates in this framework as focusing on DIFFERENCE and OTHERNESS. This includes largely a resistance discourse that tackles the hegemony inherent in global social formations. For example, in articulating disapproval of total European integration and 'protecting' UK sovereignty, Robert Kilroy-Silk, Member of the European Parliament (MEP) on the platform of the United Kingdom Independent Party (UKIP) said in a television interview 'I like Spain and Portugal. I spend a lot of my time in *those countries* every year. But do I want to be *governed by those people*? No. I want to be *governed by my own people*' (June 2004, my emphasis).[2] Kilroy-Silk constructs his membership of an exclusive identity cohort. This is realized through the use of deixis as an 'othering' device as exemplified by the italicized phrases/clauses. Included in the same framework are the discourses generated around and about the North-South dialogue, colonial and postcolonial discourses on issues such as fair trade, the New World Information & Communication Order, etc.

Ethnicity and identity

Much of the early work on ethnicity in language research was carried out within paradigms in anthropological enquiry. They identified communities of people by describing their language and cultural practices (Gumperz and Hymes 1972). Fishman (1999) and Conversi (2003) give an indication of the directions in which debates of ethnicity have moved recently. However, for my purposes here I want to draw attention to two contrasting contexts for the investigation of ethnicity and the identities associated with them. The first context is a consequence of social and political events in the previous sphere (race and identity). For instance, the scramble for and partition of Africa in the last quarter of the nineteenth century brought an end to homogeneous ethnic kingdoms as a sociological fact in sub-Saharan Africa. Africa's new ethnically diverse prefabricated nation states became the locus of competition for resources, status and control. The conflicts in Rwanda, Liberia, Cote d'Ivoire, Sierra Leone and Sudan have all sprung from within the framework of ethnic diversity or ethno-nationalist sentiments and agendas.

The second and contrasting context may be said to result from events orchestrated by competition and distrust between diverse ethnic groups with defined territorial affiliations and histories. Migration, for instance, from Africa's zones of crisis and the creation of immigrant communities in the heartland of the West gave birth to the 'ethnic minority' identity phenomenon, which is relative to a racially white mainstream in European cities and in North America. Culture and the notion of the originary are at the core of these debates. Projects on the management of diversity and multiculturalism are prime factors in defining the new nation. It is in order to mention Vigoroux's (2005: 238) alternative articulation of 'territoriality' as located in an 'interactional and dynamic model' rather than in a primordial paradigm of analysis.

Social classes

Early sociolinguistic research as evidenced in the works of Labov (1966) and Trudgill (1974) established a social perspective on identity research that differentiated between the language behaviours of members of different social groups. Social identities are defined on the basis of membership of social classes which reflect differences in distribution of social roles and statuses, and access to and control of the means of production. Membership of these social divisions is hereditary. In societies without a traditional social class structure, socioeconomic groups are discernible which more or less parallel the social class categories, but membership of these is open to all and attainable by competition. At the top of the socio-economic hierarchy is an elite class. Research in World Englishes, English as a Second Language (ESL), English as a Foreign Language (EFL) and Teaching of English to Speakers of Other Languages (TESOL) complements research in discourse and social theory in investigating issues about language as symbolic power (Bourdieu 1991).

What comes across rather strongly from the discussions of the paradigms presented above with their varied foci is the fact that identity research is complex, multitheoretical and increasingly multidisciplinary. The next task, then, is to engage with the contrast or conflict between essentialist notions of identity and the more recent preference for viewing identity as performed and constructed.

From essentialism to performativity

As Kamwangamalu noted (personal communication), 'recent literature on identity (and on issues in mother tongue education) has made extensive use of the term "essentialism". It (the literature) says what essentialism does but not what it is or is not. That is, very little or no effort at all has been made to explain or contextualize the term'. So to begin with, what is essentialism? For our purposes in this chapter, essentialism is the philosophy behind labelling any number of normative characteristics or practices as constituting the core of an individual or group which are then used to define them and held to be true of all members of the group. Conversi (2003: 271) cites as an illustration of this the 'reiterated and totalizing use of ethnonyms: entire groups are hypostatized as cohesive entities'. These in turn provide the frame for conceptualizing identity as static.

Bucholtz (2003: 400) anchors her 'authentication of identity' theory to a distinction she makes between essentialism and strategic essentialism. She argues that essentialism actually serves a positive end in the way that it enables researchers to 'identify a previously undescribed group and offer a preliminary description'. According to Bucholtz, essentialism, for group members, 'promotes a shared identity, often in opposition to other, equally essentialized social groups', while the latter 'may be a deliberate move to enable scholarly activity, to forge a political alliance through the creation of common identity, or to otherwise provide a temporarily stable ground for further social action' (2003: 401). These perspectives on essentialism are a departure from the more conventional negative representation associated with it in identity research (see Conversi 2003).

Obviously the contexts in which identification plays out are diverse and may put up different demands that may or may not support Bucholtz's perspective on essentialism. However, the use of *strategic essentialism* in language and gender studies and research on African American vernacular English in the 1970s 'to recognise and legitimate their widely devalued linguistic practices' (Bucholtz 2003: 401) was both radical and positive. But Bucholtz remarks that changes in the political and intellectual climate today make the essentialist strategy 'no longer necessarily most effective or productive' (2003: 402).

Coincidentally, as I was preparing the final draft of this chapter, riots raged through France, the circumstances of which could not be entirely disentangled from essentialism (see *Le Figaro*, 7 November 2005).[3] The riots in Northern England in 2000, the fact that governments must make conscious efforts not to encourage racial or religious profiling in the aftermath of the terrorist bombings in New York City (11 September 2001), Madrid (September 2004) and London (July 2005), the murder of Black teenager Stephen Lawrence in 1993 resonating in the murder of another Black teenager, Anthony Walker, in

Liverpool in September 2005, or in fact the media and public opinions expressed after Hurricane Katrina's devastation of New Orleans in 2005 all suggest that some aspects of social reality such as racism have not changed and as a result, Bucholtz's dismissal of the essentialist strategy as outdated in identity research is arguably a 'mainstream' perspective that must be tempered with caution. Globalization has not completely erased territories, hence it is difficult to disengage references to these in the identification process, as Sallabank's and Burbano-Elizondo's chapters (Chapters 8 and 7, respectively) in this volume demonstrate.

Rather than choose between contrasting perspectives on essentialism I shall propose the Hierarchy of Identities model (HoI) which in my opinion harmonizes these views. The core assumption of HoI is that there may be moments for which recourse to essentialism is both adequate and unavoidable such as in the conflict situations that I referred to above. However, I shall further complicate my task of framing the discussion of essentialism by making two other references to specific literature in sociolinguistics and applied linguistics. First, Fasold (1984: 240) says 'Language shift will only occur if, and to the extent that, *a community desires to give up its identity as an identifiable sociocultural group* in favour of an identity as a part of some other community' (my emphasis). In doing so, he invokes an essentialist notion of identity as whole, fixed, conclusive and tangible, and sees identity as a basis of community formation.

Secondly, the idea that English, Spanish, Finnish or any other language for that matter represents the identities of speakers of particular languages that are territorially fixed in England, Spain and Finland respectively raises some fundamental problems. For instance, how are the bilinguals and trilinguals in these groups to be identified? Is it appropriate to lump together in the same identity category native speakers of English who exhibit varying bilingual patterns? As identity tags, English as a Second Language, Spanish as a Second Language and Finnish as a Second Language speakers carry a stigma of partial foreignness and implicitly challenge claims of attainable competence in a second language. Following from these we can infer the following problems with essentialist notions of identity, at least in language research:

- they are incapable of adequately accommodating the creativity that may mark the reality of the moment of identification in the future because identity is rigidly fixed and exists outside of action: product rather than process; being rather than becoming;
- they don't often recognise identity as constructed and co-constructed;
- they do not accommodate hybridity convincingly – dual citizenship, bilingualism, biracial types/Metis remain unproblematized;
- they are incapable of explaining the translocal and transnational which straddle traditional borders both in a physical and conceptual sense;
- identity is other-ascribed, ascribed to a group/community;
- it is difficult if not impossible to determine group boundaries based on language use behaviour – accommodation, convergence, divergence, dialect-levelling, etc. There are no rigid cohorts, not even on Martha's Vineyard (Labov 1972; Josey 2004)!

- social class identities are defined by phonological variables – contradicted or challenged by the non-conformist middle-class youths in Trudgill's (1974) Norwich study – stressing that identity is constructed within action and it is ongoing: we are in the process of becoming (Hall 1992).

Identity is multiple and multilayered

Goffman's (1959) notion of the 'presentation of self' implies the possibility of several presentations in the course of an interaction. These presentations are all acts of identity. The situating of identity within social action reaffirms the significance of the relational factor. This breaking up of identity into contexts, acts and moments facilitates the conceptualization and articulation of multiple roles and identities that may not have equal salience. This approach defines the frame for studies that consider identity as fluid and that the individual is able to move in and out of identity categories by varying their acts in response to demands and needs within particular moments of identification. The framework recognizes multiple positioning, multiple selves and challenges binary identity oppositions which the other frameworks accommodate – black versus white, Pakistani versus Indian, Christian versus Muslim, middle class versus working class, natives versus immigrants, etc. Goffman (1981: 128) remarks that:

> A *change in footing* implies a *change in the alignment we take up to ourselves and the others present* as expressed in the way we manage the production or reception of an utterance. A change in our footing is another way of talking about a *change in our frame for events*. This paper is largely concerned with pointing out that participants over the course of their speaking constantly change their footing, these changes being a persistent feature of natural talk. [...] In this paper I want to make a pass at analyzing the *structural underpinnings of changes in footing*. The task will be approached by reexamining the primitive notion of speaker and hearer, and some of our unstated presuppositions about spoken interaction. (See also Goffman's [1981] 'participation status' and 'participation frameworks'.)

If we think of *alignments* as positionings of self in relation to a set of social images or characteristics that are value-rated within a framework of community norms and conventions, then we can understand how the same person from one moment to another is able, and may need, to project various 'selves' as they deem appropriate. I shall include here an argument that I have made slightly more elaborately elsewhere for an expanded meaning of codes in order to re-theorize the concept of codeswitching in sociolinguistics (see Omoniyi 2005: 730). I have suggested the expansion of 'code' so that 'all other signifying, representing, and expressive codes that we read and interpret ... such as dress, dance, costume, religion, gender, youth, ethnicity, nation, music, talk, walk, and so on are accommodated'. Within and between social systems these variables are known to be indexical of certain essentialist identity categories that are laden with socio-cultural values. In other words, codeswitching may serve as a tool in producing 'appropriate' alignments and stances or positionings for example as a conscious survival strategy when one traverses a supposed zone of danger such as urban ghettos socially constructed as 'troubled'. The wise ethnographer may modify 'characteristic actions' that define them (van Dijk 1998: 124) such as dress style and style of walk to index in-group membership and identity or to converge towards the dominant subculture norm to claim terrain rights, and reduce the chances of being perceived or constructed as 'other' with grave consequences. Alternatively, the orientation may take the form of divergence in order to index membership of a competing identity cohort if the intention was to mark or stress difference.

Both voice (Bakhtin 1981) and positioning (Davies and Harre 1990) like Goffman's 'presentation of self' are established concepts in the management of multiple identities. Bilinguals may simply by an act of codeswitching reposition or align themselves with another group different from the one they had seemed to claim leading up to the moment of switching. Recently, Pavlenko and Blackledge (2004) have invoked these concepts in their discussion of negotiation of identities in multilingual contexts. While their idea of negotiation rightly conveys a sense of acknowledgement of the existence of multiple identities, it seems to subscribe implicitly and ultimately to the idea of one-or-the-other identity where a preferred identity emerges at the conclusion of negotiation. They conceptualize identities as 'social, discursive, and narrative options offered by a particular society in a specific time and place to which individuals and groups appeal in an attempt to self-name, to self-characterize, and to claim social spaces and social prerogatives' (2004: 19). I would argue that although this claim portrays what societies 'offer' to the constitution of individual selves, it is silent on what the various selves offer to shape the identity of society, particularly in complex multilingual environments. In contrast to Pavlenko and Blackledge's claim, the relationship between the individual and society may be best articulated with Kendra Wallace's application of James Gee's Discourse Theory to the life histories of mixed heritage college students in arguing that multiethnic identity is a 'situated phenomenon emerging at the intersection of the individual and the collective' (Wallace 2004: 195). However, I take Pavlenko and Blackledge's reference to 'specific time and place' as my point of departure in articulating the hierarchy of identities as a theoretical model.

HoI, the model

Identity negotiation must be construed not as an end in itself but as a tool in the service of hierarchization. An individual's various identity options are co-present at all times but each of those options is allocated a position on a hierarchy based on the degree of salience it claims in a moment of identification. And since degree of salience is variable from one moment to another as a result of changes of socio-situational factors, position on the hierarchy for any identity option is equally variable. In other words, the location of an identity option on the hierarchy fluctuates as the amount of salience associated with it fluctuates between moments.

The idea of hierarchization is not exactly new even though the articulation of it here is more elaborate. In my investigation of identity among inhabitants of Idiroko/Igolo and Woodlands/Johor Bahru borderland communities between

Nigeria and Benin (1991) and Singapore and Malaysia (1996) respectively, I had found that among the Yoruba and Malay who straddle these international boundaries, participants in interactions constantly hierarchized nationality, ethnicity and other identities depending on their assessment of the context and the goals they sought to achieve (see Omoniyi 2004: 30). Van Dijk (1998: 119) notes:

> Similarly, social members may share in several social identities that are more or less stable across personal contexts, and thus defining a personal self, but in concrete situations some of these identities may become more salient than others. Thus in each situation, the salience, hierarchy or relevance of group identification will monitor the actual social practices (e.g. the action priorities or 'motivation') of social actors.

In essence then the agenda I am pushing here is for a re-examination of how we conceptualize 'situation' which I believe is more complex than we have acknowledged in the literature so far. An identification context may comprise one or more actions with one or more performance moments. Thus each situation is potentially characterized by multiple positioning acts in which a cluster of identities are invoked and read but each varying in salience. The most salient identity option in any one moment of performance within a given interactional context is foregrounded through talk and located therefore at the top of a hierarchy of identities.

Language choice presupposes the existence of alternatives. Language is an acceptable identity marker (Le Page and Tabouret-Keller 1985; see also White, this volume, Chapter 13) so that the alternative languages not chosen in a given moment within an interaction would be alternative identities that are backgrounded or that are less invoked. But the process is a lot more intricate, I would argue. In other words, one identity isn't simply chosen from an array of possibilities over the others which are discarded; there is on the contrary a cluster of co-present identities but with varying degrees of salience. The latter depends on the most preferred presentation of self in a given moment. We must bear in mind though that identity is the consequence of both production and reception.

I shall further claim that in any identification context, all of the participants' co-present identity options are hierarchized with great dynamism based on decisions of appropriateness in the moments of choosing between identity options in relation to evaluations of the state of affairs in terms of relationships and dispositions. Within a more materialist framework, choice is based on the potential of options to achieve the specific goal we pursue in a moment of production. The most appropriate or lucrative identity option is foregrounded or shunted to the top of the hierarchy while the others fall into place behind or beneath it in order of their relevance to the moment of identification. This, I would suggest, is the reason that we are able to detect strains of other identities different from the one declared or foregrounded in particular moments. Thus Pavlenko and Blackledge's (2004) reference to 'a specific time and place' can be made more specific and thus better conceptualized in terms of moments.

Moments of identification

Before I offer a formal definition for moment of identification as a conceptual construct, I want to show first that the groundwork for it has been done in previous studies in which it was evident that within a single social activity it is possible to articulate more than one identity. For example, in an interview, 'participants were found to imply that they were both engaged in regular and reflective consumption of political news and current affairs and that they were relatively uninterested in such matters' (Dickerson 1996: 62). Dickerson comments that:

> This tension between an identity of engagement and disengagement with the consumption of politics in the mass media is illustrated within a single interview; in extract 1 the interviewee, L, produced an identity of being relatively uninterested in watching politics whereas in extract 2 L displayed that he consumed a wide range of televised politics. This variation in the identity which was produced may create problems if we wished to use the interviews to categorize interviewees in terms of their level of interest in televised politics. However, the occurrence of this inconsistency suggests that we can fruitfully attend to the specific turn-by-turn context in which the different identities are produced.
>
> (1996: 62)

Dickerson's suggestion that resolution lies in the utterance turn rather than the activity as a whole however does not resolve the problem in those situations in which multiple identities are articulated within the same utterance turn. It is this that proves the usefulness of the moment of identification concept, because several moments may reside within an utterance turn.

Pennycook (2003: 516) also lends voice to the notion of moment when he asks in his discussion of the creation of English-based words *saido* (side) and *furiikii* (freaky) in Japanese rap 'what sort of identity is being fashioned in the performance and reception of such lyrics? What type of Japaneseness, global citizenry, and rap identities are produced in these *moments of global English*?' (my emphasis). Similarly, Vann *et al.* (this volume, Chapter 12) in their analysis of students' classroom talk activity that parallels the remunerative world of work, note that 'other students show their appreciation of his [a student's] wit with their laughter, *thus co-constructing his identity at this moment*' (my emphasis). What these claims demonstrate is that identity is located in the moment within a stretch of utterance, or thought in a non-interactional context, when the specific signifying communicative action is performed and/or perceived (see also Ibrahim's *Use of Moments of Identification*, 2003: 173).

At this juncture, we can formally define 'moment' as a tool in the conceptual framing of hierarchy of identities. A moment is a temporal unit of measurement and/or monitoring in the identification process. Moments are points in time in performance and perception at which verbal and non-verbal communicative codes (e.g. advertisements, clothes, walk style and song lyrics, among others) are deployed to flag up an image of self or perspectives of it. From a methodological point of view, these moments are indeed measurable and this can be done in the following ways:

1. Counting and setting out the numerical order in which several identities are foregrounded in the course of action – similar to event structure as espoused by Bell (1991). Determine the identity in sections of spoken or written text. All of the identities encoded are co-present in the entire situation but the sections illustrate where particular identities are foregrounded. Some texts may suggest more than one identity – a function of different interpretive cultures. Such situations may produce a cluster of identities which in our discussion we then attempt to proffer an explanation for, such as a performer's deliberate attempt to create a complex or ambiguous self.
2. Dividing action up on a timescale on to which identities are then mapped – so, if an event lasts 10 minutes, divide the timescale up such that we not only know what identities are foregrounded but we also know which ones were sustained for longer periods. The scale starts from 0 (zero) time and is graded for the duration of talk delivery (or performance) with markings to indicate where a particular identity is first foregrounded and where it is displaced or backgrounded in order to give prominence to another. Again, there could be a cluster of identities to a stretch of time on the scale.
3. Showing by shading when two identities occupy the same moment. Select a different colour or pattern for each identity invoked and shade the time slots as appropriate.

Model application

Now let us explore the extent to which the claims that I have made above can be empirically substantiated. For this purpose I shall present five pieces of data: a newspaper extract, public symbols (a road sign, a facility locator), vehicle registration number plate, a monologue and a piece of conversational data. The first piece of illustrative data is an extract from a free London commuter newspaper – *Metro*, which is circulated on the London Underground (*Metro*, 24 October 2003, p. 14).

Example 1: Newspaper extract

Sir Michael Caine in 60 Second Interview by Harry Scott:

> **HS:** How did you get that *Texan twang*?
> **MC:** A *Texan dialect coach* recorded all my dialogue for me three months before the picture started and sent me a cassette. I played it everyday. Then when I got to Austin where we were filming he wasn't too thrilled about what I was doing. He said: 'You've got the accent right but not the rhythm. You're speaking like *an Englishman with a Texan accent.' English people* speak each word separately. *Texans* are lazy. Each word leans onto the next one.'

To begin with, this extract contains an interaction within an interaction. Thus there are two levels at which identity and identification may be playing out. The embedding interaction is an interview between Michael Caine and Harry Scott of the Metro. The embedded interaction is a discussion between the Texan coach and Michael Caine reported by the latter to Harry Scott. When Harry Scott asks

'How did you get that Texan twang?' the implicit unstated is an exclusion of Michael Caine from Texan identity as a natural category, while 'get' situationally inferences Caine's 'actor' identity. This represents what Joseph (2004) described as fictional rather than real identities. However, the references are fashioned on established cultural practices.

Example 2: Public symbols

The images in Figures 1a and 1b are photographs I took on a trip to Morocco in October 2004. Figure 1a is a plaque showing direction to a female ablution room in the sprawling King Hassan II Mosque in Casablanca. Figure 1b is a road sign by the National Defence Administration building also in Casablanca.

Figure 1a Ablutions for Women

Figure 1b Private. National Defence Administration

When I showed these images to a sample of friends back in England who were not literate in Arabic, a number of interesting responses were offered which exemplify the nature and process of construction and ascription of identity. The respondents were not told where the images had come from. Some of the responses elicited included:

- they are from an Islamic country;
- they're from an Arabic-speaking country;
- something is in this direction (Figure 1a);
- no entry (Figure 1b);
- your hand may be chopped off if you break this law (said jokingly);
- I have no idea.

In the first response, some respondents had inferred a religious and national identity from the Arabic text. The road sign however is secular in that it has nothing to do with religion. I would argue therefore that in ascribing an 'Islamic' identity to the country from which the signs derive, the respondents constructed themselves as people who perceive the Arabic language as coterminous with Islamic identity. The orientation of the respondents who gave the second response is different. They do not perceive Arabic as indicative of an Islamic identity. This is especially significant post-September 11 particularly in relation to stemming religious profiling. The point to be made here in relation to HoI is that in my discussions with the respondents it was established that they had all thought of both these options yet the choices they declared revealed differences of ordering in their perception.

The road sign is a universal symbol (see Wagner forthcoming) and was correctly identified by most of the respondents, all of whom happened to be holders of a driver's licence. We could consider the semiotics of road signs and motoring regulations as something accessible to members of a particular discourse community – thus constituting an identity marker in a sense. What is however most interesting here is the fact that all of the respondents immediately oriented to the visual rather than the textual signage; the Arabic text required skills in a literacy mode they couldn't identify with. The text actually says 'Private' and 'National Defence Administration' rather than 'No Entry' as my respondents suggested based on the visual prompt.

The next response must be situated within the context of humour deriving from extra-contextual knowledge of judicial practice in the Middle East, even though it may not have been politically correct. In this particular case, the respondent noticed my unease with the intended joke and immediately dropped the humour frame for a more serious and intellectual stance thus affirming the co-constructedness of identities and more significantly indicating the manner in which an interlocutor may influence the structure of the hierarchy of identities that a speaker constructs in an encounter.

One more point to make here and which ties in well with the reservation I expressed earlier about confining identity construction, or as a matter of fact influences upon the process, to interactions as in discursive psychology is the role of what Bell (1992) called the 'absent referee'. I contend then that apart from the possibility of the kind of monologues in Example 2 above, there is also the possibility of a third person 'not physically present at an interaction but possessing such salience for the speaker that they influence language choice even in their absence' (Bell 1992: 328) and therefore being the more significant influence on foregrounding an identity option.

Example 3: Number plates and identity

My next example is drawn from a relatively popular pastime on the roads, deciphering identity from vehicle number plates. Number plates are inscribed with a unique vehicular identity that is assigned by a licensing authority such as the Driver and Vehicle Licensing Agency (DVLA) in the United Kingdom. The current practice of vehicle registration which is in synchrony with the European Union format consists of two letters (local memory tag), two numbers (age *identifier*) and finally three random letters (for instance, RV05 ABC). This numbering system makes it possible to determine with certainty the regional as well as the age 'identity' of a vehicle. In the old numbering system of one letter, number(s) followed by three letters (for example, P1 OET, L1 ZZY, K4 REN, B16 GUY, V3 GAN), the age of the vehicle, i.e. year of registration, was indicated by the first letter. In addition to conventional registration marks, the DVLA sells personalized marks at competitive commercial rates. Car owners may purchase registration numbers that spell their names as in the examples above: Poet, Lizzy (Elizabeth), Karen, Big Guy and Vegan.

Figure 1c Vehicle number plate

The picture in Figure 1c was used to elicit reactions from third-year university undergraduates. Individual students engage in a reflective task that requires them to read the registration mark and construct a context of interpretation that enables them to access the probable communicative intent of the vehicle owner. They figure out the probable word or name within the set of values that define an identity in a given socio-cultural context. This is a broadening of the definition of social interaction to include sole actor activities that do not require co-presence of sender and receiver. The interlocutor (reader) is an open category and includes anyone who reads and attempts to decipher the intended name or message. The students in the survey were required to study the photograph carefully and write anything that it suggested to them on identity. They made comments about the identity of the vehicle owner using descriptors such as affluent, middle class, proud, English, show off, businessman. In relation to HoI, the students constructed a hierarchy of these identities in the order in which they presented the options.

Let us now attempt to problematize my students' action described above. When we see a personalized registration on the number plate of a car, something about its configuration triggers our curiosity and we try to unravel the communication or information that the owner of the vehicle intended to convey by the personalized code. Greenall's (2002: 24) concept of *socialized interpretational drive* itself anchored to assumptions in traditional theories of discourse (see Bach and Harnish 1979; Kiefer 1979; Brown and Yule 1983) provides an explanatory frame for this practice. We make guesses about the name, personality or social circumstance of the owner. The process of interpreting registration codes generates options about the identity of the owner or the particular vehicle in our minds. The interpretation of codes is contextualized within a set of shared values specific to a social system. Individuals bring to the interpretation process the sum total of their lived experiences in a community. In this regard, the application of Conversation Analysis in discursive psychology may be too straitjacketed and exclusionary and therefore incapable of handling identity and identification located outside conventional interaction.[4]

Example 4: Identity and Irish Music [5]

The extract below is an unscripted monologue taken from the ICE-Ireland corpus of Irish English. It is a sample of academic discourse in which the speaker (MC) is delivering a lecture on Irish Music. I specifically chose this to illustrate a dimension of identity construction that is both not located within conventional two-party or multi-party interaction and one in which the object of identification is not a person or group per se, but a cultural property or practice, in this case music.

> Er, now generally speaking, when we hear the expression 'Irish music' being used today, people tend to be thinking of traditional music, er even though strictly speaking I suppose that if we talk about Irish music, you can talk about er the classical music, let's say written by Sean O'Riordan, you can talk about [2 sylls] music, you can talk about a wide range of music if you're talking about Irish music. However it's generally accepted that when people talk about Irish music, they mean traditional music. And if you turn on the radio and hear

De Dannan, or hear the Chieftains, you'll say 'that's Irish music'. If you hear U2, you'll say 'that's rock and roll', you don't say it's Irish music. Er, I know that we could dwell for a long time on the semantics and definitions of those expressions, but for our purpose here today I think we'll just use the expressions as they're used normally by people. Er, in the case of Irish music, as we now call it, it's convenient, I think, for our purpose, to divide it into two categories. Now there are many ways in which we could divide it, but for simplicity we can divide it into the categories of instrumental music and what we call the shan nos er singing which is the er old Gaelic style singing. I'll come back to that later and I'll I'll give you the er the Gaelic expression for it. The instrumental tradition. Er for many people this is the first introduction to what we call 'Irish music'. Peop(as I said a while ago, you turn on the radio, and you'll hear the Chieftains, you'll hear De Dannan or something and you'll say 'well look, that's Irish music', or if you don't know what it is, you'll say 'look, what's that?'. And somebody'll tell you, 'it's Irish music'. And in ninety-nine per cent of the cases, it's going to be instrumental music, dance music. Okay. Er so it's not surprising then that we dwell quite a lot on the instrumental music, and specifically er on the dance music, and again when people talk about Irish music, they generally mean the instrumental dance music. Okay, so if people talk about Irish music, they certainly won't mean U2, they may not mean the shan nos singing, but almost certainly they'll mean the er er the instrumental dance music, okay.

So how would the HoI model handle the analysis of identity here? Let us begin by establishing the indexicalities contained in the monologue. Directly or indirectly, the following signs are all indexical of Irishness or at least a degree of it: Irish music, Sean O'Riordan, Gaelic, De Dannan, The Chieftains and U2. In the diagram below I present 'Irish music' as an identity type based on the argument in MC's monologue above by a presentation of what it is and what it isn't.

Irish Music	≠	**Rock and Roll**
↕		
Traditional Music		↕
↕		
Instrumental/Dance		↕
↕ ↕		
De Dannan The Chieftains		U2

According to MC, Irish music is not rock and roll but one that is synonymous with traditional music which may be either instrumental or dance music. The bands De Dannan and The Chieftains are described as symbolizing Irish music. In the diagram above, the category De Dannan, The Chieftains and U2 index all of the preceding identity categories in the strata above them. Identity arises partially out of distinctions to others. MC uses '*that be/it be*–constructions' to separate Irish music from rock and roll: 'well, look that's Irish music' and 'it's Irish music'. These constructions have an essentialist tone to them in the way that they suggest exclusiveness or absolutism. What are unresolved in these claims are the possibility of fusion and the adaptation of instrumentation across genres so that strains of one may be present in another.

Example 5: Identity by association through visas

S1 : Well, there won't be any time now before Christmas.

S2 : No, no, what are you doing for Christmas?

S1 : Erm. Well last week's *Guardian* was, had a very interesting trip to the Holy Land and Jordan

S2 : Yeah, oh right, how nice

S1 : And erm I was just telling Liam about it at lunch and he said it sounded very good. A very full six-day trip

S2 : yes

S1 : with something organised for every day

S2 : Right

S1 : including midnight ceremonies in Jerusalem on Christmas Eve

S2 : Yes, oh how lovely, yes

S1 : And Christmas dinner

S2 : Yes

S1 : And erm, I thought six hundred and something sterling

S2 : That's OK

S1 : That's very good, wasn't it

S2 : Yeah, it is. Have you *booked it?*

S1 : *No, it only crossed* my mind, no I haven't booked it, but I *just thought well*

S2 : *Yes, It's getting very* late by the hour

S1 : Yeah, and you see, Israel and getting a visa

S2 : Yeah

S1 : You know [and]I have a visa for Damascus on my visa so I don't know if
      S2 : [yeah]

S2 : Well yeah, it's a group, you don't need a visa for Israel, *you need a visa for*
                                   S1 : yes, *you need a visa for*
Jordan

Jordan, yes, and a group visa does, if they have more than twenty people,
'cos I was supposed to be going [last]
                                 S1 : [Really] ?
Christmas, yes, yeah yeah, and then the [friend] I was going with, her sister
                                 S1 : [Mmm]
had to be, her sister died [so] it was cancelled and erm, but we were travelling
                           S1 : [Mm]
on a group visa 'cos we were more than twenty [people] to Jordan and you
                                   S1 : [Right]   S1 : [Oh
don't need one for [Israel] but you just have to see to it I think that the Israelis
I see]   S1 : [Mm]
don't stamp your passport

S1 : That they don't, or I'd never get back somewhere *else again, yeah*

S2 : *That's right*

S1 : I think that the Damascan, yeah there's just a lot of er writing on my passport at the moment

S2 : Yes

The identity inferences in the conversational extract are indexical of national and/or religious affiliations and cultural practices: Christmas, Holy Land, visa, Jordan, Israelis, Damascan. The nature of hierarchization inherent in the presentation of these identities has to do with managing the impact of the politics of the Middle East conflict. S1 has a visa for Damascus (Syria) and because she would be travelling in a group doesn't need a visa for Israel. However, they needed a visa for Jordan. We must understand the comments within the framework of our knowledge of international relations in the region. It is in that regard that the advice to ensure that 'the Israelis don't stamp your passport otherwise I'd never get back somewhere else again' must be interpreted. The moment of hierarchization in the conversational exchange is the point at which this utterance was made in line with basic international travel wisdom. Implicitly, this arguably locates association with Israeli national identity conveyed through the immigration department's endorsement in a passport on a lower rung of the ladder than association with the Arab national identities in the region. Let us wrap up this section with a cursory look at some of the discourse tools employed in the design of a hierarchy of identities.

Strategies employed in hierarchizing identities

I shall present a number of identification contexts in order to examine the discourse tools that are used to achieve hierarchization:

- In conversations, *footing shifts* (Goffman 1979) may be used to renegotiate how or who one is perceived to be from moment to moment as we find with politicians in media interviews. They continuously shift between the personal self and the public selves. 'We as a government', 'As a nation, we ...', and 'In my opinion, ...', etc. The reconfiguration of the hierarchy to replace a previously foregrounded identity option is not solely up to the person performing an identifying act but rather: (a) the consequence of or reaction to the interlocutor's previous stance; (b) the result of the current speaker's evaluation of previous speaker and sense of appropriate self-image derived from their performance; or (c) the result of speakers' positioning of self within the context of a larger sociocultural unit.
- In personal narratives, *change of orientation* (Labov and Waletsky 1967) define 'orientation' in narrative in terms of positioning – location – who, where and when. Autobiographies, life histories (Pavlenko 2004; Wallace 2004, etc.) are tools of performance here.
- In political speeches, *use of embedded structures* in which the subject is repositioned in contrast to its existing identity – President George Bush's Iraqi Ultimatum in 2003 – the opening invokes Mr Bush's American identity and his identities as US President and Commander-in-Chief, all of which are needed in order for such a speech to fulfil the appropriate felicity conditions to carry the illocutionary force intended.
- In commentaries, *use of marked solidarity forms* in media and sports commentaries in which objectivity and neutrality are expected, identities may be renegotiated momentarily – either intentionally or through a slip; *use of negative comparisons* (Pavlenko 2004: 40), for instance 'old' versus 'new' immigrants, 'old versus new Europeans' in the expanding discourses of EU expansion.
- In transactions, *switch from Language A to B* for haggling in multilingual contexts which excludes the customer but includes a third party from whom

the trader seeks advice or an opinion; *switch to a shared indigenous language* from a shared official ex-colonial language (Omoniyi 1987, 2004).

- In song lyrics, in the contexts of (re)appropriation, postcolonial subjects reposition themselves by performing transcultural identities (Pennycook 2003) *using established Western forms mixed with African forms to create fusion music* – this is exemplified by diaspora musical groups like London-based JJC & 419 Squad (see Omoniyi 2005).
- In community narratives and claims, especially in postcolonial nations, ethnic identities are articulated in oral narratives and folk tales and songs. Sometimes narratives become an indirect weapon of conflict when they are used to construct legitimacy and ownership, especially in disputes such as the Bakassi Peninsula between Nigeria and Cameroon on which the International Court of Justice at The Hague adjudicated in October 2002 (see Omoniyi and Salami 2004).

The contexts used above to illustrate the hierarchization of identities are in no way exhaustive but they at least represent a spread sufficient to give indication that HoI as a theoretical and methodological construct enjoys extensive applicability.

Concluding remarks

In the foregoing sections I have made and hopefully defended a number of claims that potentially could change the way we think about identity. Identity and identification are certainly more complex conceptually than had been reflected in traditional sociolinguistic literature. In order to realistically capture this complexity we need to acknowledge that the distinct identity categories which we often talk about only exist as discrete units that we imagine for convenience of reckoning. In reality, people, places and things may be constructed and projected in multiple and dynamic ways.

I have also argued that identification is not exclusive to conventional interactions, but that on the contrary the process may be contained within a monologue or include a moment of reflective activity such as an individual's encounter with a sign of which they try to make sense. All interpretations are done within recognizable frames built on established norms and conventions of a social system. These processes generate a cluster of identity options that are then distributed on a hierarchy based on ratings from least salient to most salient. Other non-interaction-based identification processes include reading and locating self in relation to billboards, reading the 'other' (community) through its signs, etc.

In addition, I argued that in interactions, salience of identity options is determined by the interplay of several social factors as well as the response of participants to these factors. Identity options are always co-present, the difference between them being in the degree of salience that they command which determines their position on a hierarchy of identities. Finally and equally importantly, I have made a case for the recognition of moments as a unit of measurement within utterances or any other activity that constitutes identification.

Notes

1 A version of the discussion that is the nucleus of my chapter was given as a keynote at the
   BAAL/CUP Seminar on 'Language and Identity' at the University of Reading, 5–6 July
   2004. First, I thank students on my Discourse and Conversation Analysis module in the
   Autumn of 2005 at Roehampton University for participating in the interpretation of my
   data. Next, I thank Professor Nkonko Kamwagamalu (Howard), Dr Heidi Armbruster
   (Southampton), Dr Annabelle Mooney (Roehampton) and my co-editor Dr Goodith White
   (Leeds) for comments and advice on various drafts of this chapter. I completely absolve
   them of any residual flaws for which I take sole responsibility.
2 This is an interesting indication of the significant role that 'difference' plays in identity and
   identification.
3 ABC News – Reuters, 6 November 2005: 'Rioting began 10 days ago with the accidental
   electrocution of two youths of African origin apparently fleeing police. Their deaths ignited
   anger among ethnic minorities over unemployment, racism, police treatment and their
   marginal role in France' – '*Chirac vows order as French riots spread*' (www.abcnews.
   go.com/International/wireStory?id=1286831, accessed November 2005).
4 Discursive psychology will have a problem with analysing identity and identification
   around one actor grappling with a code (car number plate) rather than two interactors
   co-constructing a notion of reality.
5 Dr Goodith White generously offered me the extracts in Examples 4 and 5 from her contribution to the ICE-Ireland corpus.

References

Bach, K. and Harnish, R. M. (1979), *Linguistic Communication and Speech Acts*. Cambridge:
   The MIT Press.
Bakhtin, M. (1981), *The Dialogic Imagination: Four Essays*. (ed. M. Holquist, trans. C.
   Emerson and M. Holquist) Austin: University of Texas Press.
Balibar, E. and Wallerstein, I. (eds) (1991), *Race, Nation, Class: Ambiguous Identities*.
   London: Verso.
Bell, A. (1991), *The Language of News Media*. Oxford: Blackwell.
— (1992), 'Hit and miss: Referee design in the dialects of New Zealand television advertise-
   ments', *Language and Communication*, Vol. 12:3-4, 327-340.
Blommaert, J. (2005), *Discourse: A Critical Introduction*. Cambridge: Cambridge University
   Press.
Bourdieu, P. (1991), *Language and Symbolic Power*. (ed. and introduced by J. B. Thompson,
   trans. G. Raymond and M. Adamson) Cambridge: Polity in association with Basil
   Blackwell.
Brown, G. and Yule, G. (1983), *Discourse Analysis*. Cambridge: Cambridge University
   Press.
Bucholtz, M. (2003), 'Sociolinguistic nostalgia and the authentication of identity', *Journal of
   Sociolinguistics*, 7, (3), 398-416.
Butler, J. (1997), *Excitable Speech: A Politics of the Performative*. London: Routledge.
Conversi, D. (2003), 'Resisting primordialism (and other -isms)', in D. Conversi (ed.)
   *Ethnonationalism in the Contemporary World: Walker Connor and the Study of
   Nationalism*. London: Routledge, pp. 269-90.
Coupland, N. (2003), 'Introduction: sociolinguistics and globalization', *Journal of
   Sociolinguistics*, 7, (4), 465-72.
Davies, B. and Harre, R. (1990), 'Positioning: the discursive production of selves', *Journal of
   the Theory of Social Behaviour*, 20, 43-65.
Dickerson, P. (1996), 'Let me tell us who I am: The discursive construction of viewer identity',
   European Journal of Communication, 11, (1), 57-82.

Edwards, D. and Potter, J. (1992), *Discursive Psychology*. London: Sage.

Fasold, R. (1984), *The Sociolinguistics of Society*. Oxford: Blackwell.

Fishman, J. (ed.) (1999), *Handbook of Language and Ethnic Identity*. New York: Oxford University Press.

Gergen, K. (1985), 'The social constructionist movement in modern psychology', *American Psychologist*, 40, 226–75.

— (1999), *An Invitation to Social Constructionism*. London: Sage Pub.

Giles, H. and Bourhis, R. (1976), Methodological issues in dialect perception: A social psychological perspective, *Anthropological Linguistics*, 19, 294–304.

Goffman, E. (1959), *The Presentation of Self in Everyday Life*. New York: Doubleday.

— (1979), 'Footing', *Semiotica* 25, 1–29.

— (1981), *Forms of Talk*. Oxford: Blackwell.

Greenall, A. J. K. (2002), '*Towards a Socio-cognitive Account of Flouting and Flout-based Meaning*'. Unpublished doctoral thesis submitted to the Department of English of the Norwegian University of Science and Technology.

Gumperz, J. and Hymes, D. (eds) (1972), *Directions in Sociolinguistics: The Ethnography of Communication*. New York: Holt, Rhinehart and Winston.

Hall, S. (1992), 'The question of cultural identity', in S. Hall and T. McGrew (eds) *Modernity and its Futures*. Buckingham: Open University Press.

Harrison, G. (1998), 'Political identities and social struggle in Africa', in A. J. Kershen (ed.) *A Question of Identity*. Aldershot: Ashgate, pp. 248–70.

Ibrahim, A. (2003), '"Whassup, homeboy?" Joining the African Diaspora', in S. Makoni, G. Smitherman, A. Ball and A. K. Spears (eds), *Black Linguistics: Language, Society, and Politics in Africa and the Americas*. London: Routledge, pp. 169–85.

Ivanič, R. (1998), *Writing and Identity: the Discoursal Construction of Identity in Academic Writing*. Amsterdam: John Benjamins.

Joseph, J. (2004), *Language and Identity: National, Ethnic, Religious*. Basingstoke: Palgrave Macmillan.

Josey, M. (2004), 'A Sociolinguistic Study of Phonetic Variation and Change on the Island of Martha's Vineyard'. Unpublished doctoral dissertation submitted to New York University.

Kiefer, F. (1979), 'What do conversational maxims explain?', *Linguisticae Investigationes*, 3, 57–74.

Krims, A. (2000), *Rap Music and the Poetics of Identity*. Cambridge: Cambridge University Press.

Labov, W. (1966), *The Social Stratification of English in New York City*. Washington DC: Centre for Applied Linguistics.

— (1972), *Sociolinguistic Patterns*. Philadelphia: University of Pennsylvania Press.

Labov, W. and Waletsky, J. (1967), 'Narrative analysis: oral versions of personal experience', in J. Helm (ed.), *Essays on the Verbal and Visual Arts*. Seattle: University of Washington Press, pp. 12–44.

LePage, R. and Tabouret-Keller, A. (1985), *Acts of Identity: Creole-based Approaches to Language and Ethnicity*. Cambridge: Cambridge University Press.

Modood, T. (1998), 'New Forms of Britishness: Post-immigration Ethnicity and Hybridity in Britain.' Paper presented at the Trinity College Dublin conference *Expanding the Nation: Towards a Multi-Ethnic Ireland*, 22–24 September.

Omoniyi, T. (1987), 'The market value of code alternation and switching: socio-economic implications of aspects of sociolinguistic variation', *IFE Studies in English Language*, 1, (1–2), 45–54.

— (2000), 'Islands and identity in sociolinguistics: a theoretical perspective', in T. Omoniyi (ed.), *Islands and Identity in Sociolinguistics: Hong Kong, Singapore, and Taiwan*. International Journal of the Sociology of Language 143. Berlin: Mouton de Gruyter, pp. 1–13.

— (2004), *The Sociolinguistics of Borderlands: Two Nations, One Community*. Trenton, NJ: Africa World Press.

— (2005), 'Toward a re-theorization of codeswitching', in "Toward a More Inclusive Applied Linguistic English Language Teaching: A Symposium", *TESOL Quarterly*, 39, (4), 729–34.

Omoniyi, T. and Salami, L. O. (2004), 'Identity constructs in a contested borderland: The Bakassi Peninsula', in D. Oni, S. Gupta, T. Omoniyi, E. Adegbija and V. Awonusi (eds), *Nigeria in the Era of Globalization: Contemporary Discourses and Texts*. Lagos: CBAAC, pp. 171–93.

Omoniyi, T. and Fishman, J. A. (eds) (2006), *Explorations in the Sociology of Language and Religion*. Amsterdam: John Benjamins.

Pavlenko, A. (2004), 'The making of an American: negotiation of identities at the turn of the twentieth century', in A. Pavlenko and A. Blackledge (eds), pp. 34–67.

Pavlenko, A. and Blackledge, A. (2004), (eds) *Negotiation of Identities in Multilingual Contexts*. Clevedon: Multilingual Matters Ltd.

Pennycook, A. (2003), 'Global Englishes, Rip Slyme, and performativity', *Journal of Sociolinguistics*, 7, (4), 513–33.

Potter, J. and Edwards, D. (1999), 'Social representations and discursive psychology: from cognition to action,' *Culture & Psychology*, 5, (4), 447–58.

Rampton, B. (1995), *Crossing: Language and Ethnicity among Adolescents*. London: Longman.

Tabouret-Keller, A. (1997), 'Language and identity', in F. Coulmas (ed.), *The Handbook of Sociolinguistics*. Oxford: Blackwell, 315–26.

Trudgill, P. (1974), *The Social Differentiation of English in Norwich*. Cambridge: Cambridge University Press.

Van Dijk, T. (1998), *Ideology: A Multidisciplinary Approach*. London: Sage.

Vigouroux, C. (2005), 'There are no whites in Africa: territoriality, language and identity among Francophone Africans in Cape Town', *Language & Communication*, 25, 237–55.

Wagner, A. (forthcoming), 'The rules of the road: a universal visual semiotics', *International Journal for the Semiotics of Law*.

Wallace, K. R. (2004), 'Situating multiethnic identity: contributions of discourse theory to the study of mixed heritage students', *Journal of Language, Identity, and Education*, 3, (3), 195–213.

3 Identity in applied linguistics

David Block

Introduction

There has been a veritable explosion in recent years as regards the number of researchers in the social sciences who are putting identity at the centre of their work, prompting Zygmuut Bauman to observe that identity is 'today's talk of the town and the most commonly played game in town' (Bauman 2001: 16). Social theorists and sociologists, such as Stuart Hall, Anthony Giddens, Manuel Castells, Chris Weedon and Bauman himself, have all contributed to the development of a general poststructuralist/constructivist take on identity, situated at the forefront of discussions of the current state of late modern/postmodern societies. This poststructuralist approach to identity supersedes structuralist approaches, which seek to establish universal laws of psychology or social structure to explain individuals' fixed identities. Specifically, as Smart (1999) notes, poststructuralism is about a 'critical concern' with issues, such as:

> (i) the crisis of representation and associated instability of meaning; (ii) the absence of secure foundations for knowledge; (iii) the analytic centrality of language, discourses and texts; and (iv) the inappropriateness of the Enlightenment assumption of the rational autonomous subject and a counter, contrasting concentration on the ways in which individuals are constituted as subjects.
>
> (Smart 1999: 38)

Importantly, poststructuralists reject anything that smacks of essentialism, defined by Mary Bucholtz as follows:

> Essentialism is the position that the attributes and behavior of socially defined groups can be determined and explained by reference to cultural and/or biological characteristics believed to be inherent to the group. As an ideology, essentialism rests on two assumptions: (1) that groups can be clearly delimited; and (2) that group members are more or less alike.
>
> (Bucholtz 2003: 400)

What I have written thus far refers to the social sciences in general, but it also rings true for applied linguistics, where poststructuralism seems to be the default epistemological stance for sociolinguists and second language learning researchers who focus on identity as a key construct in their work. Though I agree in principle with this poststructuralist approach to identity, a perverse scepticism inside me makes me think that in a relatively uncritical manner, too many researchers are signing up to a kind of official protocol, based above all on the work of social theorists such as Castells, Giddens, Hall and Weedon, whereby it is taken as axiomatic that identity is unstable, fragmented, ongoing, discursively constructed and so on.

This paper, then, is a short reflection on this poststructuralist take on identity: what it is, a critique of it and what the critique means to me. I begin with a definition of the poststructuralist approach to identity and then consider a well articulated critique of this approach by Mervyn Bendle (2002). I explore how the poststructuralist approach to identity might be problematic, in particular in how it marginalizes the traditional interests of psychologists in the self. I then move to examine the example of one second language learning researcher, Colette Granger (2004), who has attempted to bring the self into second language learning research by drawing on work in psychoanalysis. I also consider how her approach might be applied to some of my own data, before concluding with some thoughts on this work and how seriously I should take Bendle's critique.

Poststructuralist identity

First and foremost, poststructuralists see identity not as something fixed for life, but as an ongoing lifelong project in which individuals constantly attempt to maintain a sense of balance, what Giddens (1991) has called 'ontological security', that is the possession of '"answers" to fundamental questions which all human life in some way addresses' (Giddens 1991: 47). This ongoing search for ontological security takes place at the crossroads of the past, present and future, as in their day-to-day interactions with their environments, individuals are constantly reconciling their current sense of self and their accumulated past, with a view to dealing with what awaits them in the future. This process is necessarily conflictive in nature: metaphorically, it involves a dialectic whereby often-contradictory forces must be synthesized. It is not, therefore, about the simple accumulation of experiences and knowledge.

The outcome of the conflictive struggle for ontological security is not generally neat and tidy, and it often leads to feelings of ambivalence. Ambivalence emerges from the uncertainty of feeling a part of activities or collectives of individuals and feeling apart from them (Bauman 1991). It involves the conflicting feelings of love and hate and it is the simultaneous affirmation and negation of such feelings. For Anthony Elliot, 'the *ambivalence* of identity ... [is] the tension between self and other, desire and lack, life and death, consciousness and unconsciousness' (Elliot 1996: 8). Papastergiadis (2000) relates ambivalence to the notions of 'nearness' and 'farness' put forward by Simmel (1950) in his discussion of the 'stranger', that is the state of being intimate with one's surroundings while remaining, metaphorically, outside them.

Ambivalence is thus the natural state of human beings who are forced by their individual life trajectories to make choices where choices are not always

easy to make and to develop syntheses. However, this process of synthesizing is
not a simple half-and-half proposition whereby the individual becomes half of
what he/she was and half of what he/she has been exposed to. Rather, the result
is emergent in that it arises in a not-altogether predictable way and it cannot
be reduced to the constituent parts which make it up. It occupies a 'third place'
(Bhabha 1994; Hall 1996), which results from the 'negotiation of difference ...
within which ... elements encounter and transform each other' (Papastergiadis
2000: 170).

This mention of negotiation of difference and the idea that individuals strive
for a coherent life narrative, seeking to resolve conflicts and assuage their
ambivalent feelings, raises the issue of the extent to which identity is a self-
conscious, reflexive project of individual agency, created and maintained by
individuals. Surely, in the work of some authors, there is perhaps too much talk
about individuals making choices, in other words, an overemphasis on individual
agency. Giddens, for example, has suggested that even in the most extreme
of life conditions, there is some space for individual choice and the 'reflexive
constitution of self-identity' (Giddens 1991: 86). Elsewhere, the cultural anthro-
pologist, Mathews (2000), argues that identities are not entities into which one
is 'raised'; rather, one 'assumes' an identity and then works on it. Identity is thus
seen to develop in what Mathews (2000) calls the *cultural supermarket*: just
as the modern supermarket offers foods from all over the world, in all shapes
and sizes, so the international media and advanced technology together make
available to individuals around the world a range of identities to be assumed.
However, the cultural supermarket is not a completely free market where any
self-identity under the sun can be assumed; nor is it a reality in an equal way for
all of the inhabitants of this planet. In the former case, there are social structures within which individuals exist (be these state governments, peer groups or
educational systems) which constrain the amount and scope of choice available
to individuals. In the latter case, there are individuals living within social structures that do not allow them to make as many choices (e.g. societies where the
roles of men and women are circumscribed by tradition).

Discussing language and minority rights, May (2001) argues that much of the
work around the concept of hybridity and third places is 'overstatement' and
'[i]f taken to an extreme, for example, all choices become possible; a position
represented by the methodological individualism of rational choice theory' (May
2001: 39). In making his criticism, May echoes the views of social theorists such
as Layder (1997) who defend the notion that social constructs such as ethnic
affiliation, while not fixed for life, do nevertheless provide a grounding for much
of one's day-to-day activity. What May writes is also in line with current discussions on the role of consciousness in the construction of subjectivities in cultural
anthropology, where authors such as Ortner take the following stance:

> At the individual level, I will assume that, with Giddens, that actors are always at least
> partially 'knowing subjects', that they have some degree of reflexivity about themselves
> and their desires, and that they have some 'penetration' into the ways in which they are
> formed by circumstances. They are, in short, conscious in the conventional psychological
> sense, something that needs to be emphasized as a complement to, though not a replacement
> of, Bourdieu's insistence on the inaccessibility to actors of the underlying logic of their

practices. ... I will be addressing subjectivity in the more psychological sense, in terms of inner feelings, desires, anxieties, intentions and so on, of individuals, but at other times I will be focusing on large scale cultural formations.

(Ortner 2005: 34)

Despite his concern about the limits of agency, May accepts a degree of instability in social constructs such as ethnicity in the form of ongoing negotiation (as argued by Papastergiadis), but, in agreement with Layder and Ortner, he does not want to throw away all notions of structure which condition lives. May explains his position as follows:

Negotiation is a key element here to the ongoing construction of ethnicity, but there are limits to it. Individual and collective choices are circumscribed by the ethnic categories available at any given time and place. These categories are, in turn, socially and politically defined and have varying degrees of advantage or stigma attached to them. ... Moreover, the range of choices available to particular individuals and groups varies widely.

(May 2001: 40)

I agree with May that it is probably wrong to take concepts such as hybridity, third places and choice to the extreme of arguing that social phenomena such as ethnic affiliation cease to have any meaning. Indeed, I see parallels to his views in current discussion and debates about gender (e.g. Alsop *et al.* 2002; Eckert and McConnell-Ginet 2003), where there is disagreement about whether or not poststructuralism, associated with arguments against fixed and 'essentialized' notions of femininity and masculinity, offers a way forward, or simply serves to drain debate of any foundation from which to argue. As authors such as Spivak (1999) have observed, there may be strategic reasons for engaging in essentialized community politics. However, such strategic activity takes place at the level of *praxis*, that is in people's day-to-day activities, and while essentializing group and cultural traits and practices might work at this level as a tool to get things done, it does not seem a good strategy to adopt when working as a researcher, trying to construct understandings and explanations of observed phenomena. Working as a researcher, I think that hybridity and third places work far better than essentialized notions of identity when it comes to making sense of the cases of individuals who have moved between and among qualitatively different sociocultural contexts.

One way to take on board May's concerns about abandoning structure in favour of agency is to frame identity work in terms of individual participation in 'communities of practice' (e.g. Lave and Wenger 1991; Eckert and McConnell-Ginet 1992; Wenger 1998). Eckert and McConnell-Ginet define a community of practice as 'an aggregate of people who come together around mutual engagement in an endeavour'(Eckert and McConnell-Ginet 1992: 464). Emerging from this mutual engagement in an endeavour are '[w]ays of doing things, ways of thinking, ways of talking, beliefs, values, power relations – in short practices ...' (Eckert and McConnell-Ginet 1992: 464). Such a framework starts with the assumption that learning is situated 'in the context of our lived experience of participation in the world ... [and] is a fundamentally social phenomenon, reflecting our own deeply social nature as human beings capable of knowing

...' (Wenger 1998: 3). There is also the belief that the relationship between social participation and communities of practice is crucial. Social participation refers 'not just to local events of engagement in certain activities with certain people, but to a more encompassing process of being active participants in the *practices* of social communities and constructing *identities* in relationship to these communities' (Wenger 1998: 3). Communities of practice correspond to the different subject positions people adopt on a moment-to-moment and day-to-day basis, and indeed throughout their lifetimes, depending on who they are with: family, colleagues at work, social groups at schools and so on.

Reference to communities of practice and individual participation relates directly back to the idea that identity is an emergent process, taking place at the crossroads of structure and agency. This means that while identity is conditioned by social interaction and social structure, it at the same time conditions social interaction and social structure. It is, in short, constitutive of and constituted by the social environment. This is the two-way action of 'structuration theory', as outlined by Giddens (1984). Giddens rejects the structuralist approach to social phenomena whereby the actions of individuals are determined by structures; however, at the same time, he does not want to account for human activity by solely depending on agency. Thus, for Giddens, individuals do not develop their sense of self, working exclusively from the inside out or from the outside in; rather, their environments provide conditions and impose constraints whilst they act on that same environment, continuously altering and recreating it.[1]

Structuration theory and other poststructuralist models of identity share the view of identity as process as opposed to essentialized fixed product. One consequence of this view is that very term 'identity' might well be seen as too static in its nominal form. Thus, some authors (e.g. Hall 1995), prefer to use 'identification' in an attempt to capture this processual angle. Elsewhere, Weedon (1997) does not even mention 'identity' in her discussion of poststructuralist constructions of the self. Weedon rejects '[h]umanist discourses [that] presuppose an essence at the heart of the individual which is unique, fixed and coherent'. Instead, she refers to 'subjectivities', which she defines as the 'the conscious and unconscious thoughts and emotions of the individual, her sense of herself and her ways of understanding her relation in the world.' (Weedon 1997: 32). Finally, for authors such as Harré, identity is about the constant and ongoing positioning of individuals in interactions with others. The key concept of 'positioning' is defined as 'the discursive process whereby people are located in conversations as observably and subjectively coherent participants in jointly produced storylines' (Davies and Harré 1999: 37). This plurality of terms notwithstanding, 'identity' is still the most often-used term, as witnessed by its appearance in recent book titles by Pavlenko and Blackledge (2004), Joseph (2004), Block (2006; 2007) and Benwell and Stokoe (2006).

Finally, theorists and researchers adopting a generally poststructuralist approach to identity have tended to emphasize one or more social variables which include ethnicity, race, nationality, gender, social class and language, all glossed in Table 1 below. This table, however, requires several qualifications and clarifications. First, all of the identities listed and glossed in the table are about positionings by others and self-positionings, about ascriptions from without and affiliations from within, what Blommaert (2005) calls 'ascribed' and 'achieved' (or 'inhabited') identities. The different identity types are, therefore, co-constructed and furthermore, simultaneously individual and collective in nature. Secondly, although I list and gloss these different identity types separately, I in no way wish to suggest that they stand independent of one another in the larger general identity of a person. As I explain elsewhere (Block 2006, 2007), when discussing race, ethnicity, nationality, gender, social class and language, it is indeed difficult to discuss one type of identity without mentioning others. Thus, masculinities and femininities must be understood in terms of language positioning (Eckert and McConnnell-Ginet 2003); race and ethnicity are interrelated in many people's minds (Pilkington 2003); language and social class are tightly linked (e.g. Eckert 2000); and so on. Thirdly and finally, there obviously are other angles on identity not listed or glossed. For example, in recent years, there has been a growing attention to sexual identity (e.g. Cameron and Kulic 2003) and given the recent rise in high-profile religious activity in the world (e.g. Christian fundamentalism in the US, Islamic fundamentalism in Iran), religious identity promises to become a key area of inquiry in coming years (e.g. Modood 2005).

Table 1 Individual/collective identity types (based on Block 2006: 37)

Ascription/affiliation	Based on
Ethnic	A sense of a shared history, descent, belief systems, practices, language and religion, all associated with a cultural group
Racial	Biological/genetic make-up, i.e. racial phenotype (NB often conflated with ethnicity)
National	A sense of a shared history, descent, belief systems, practices, language and religion associated with a nation state
Gendered	Nature and degree of conformity to socially constructed notions of femininities and masculinities
Social Class	Associated with income level, occupation, education and symbolic behaviour
Language	The relationship between one's sense of self and different means of communication: language, a dialect or sociolect. Could be understood in terms of Leung *et al.*'s (1997) *inheritance, affiliation* and *expertise*

To conclude this discussion, a poststructuralist approach to identity frames identity as socially constructed, a self-conscious, ongoing narrative an individual performs, interprets and projects in dress, bodily movements, actions and language. All of this occurs in the company of others – either face to face or electronically mediated – with whom to varying degrees the individual shares beliefs and motives and activities and practices. Identity is about negotiating new subject positions at the crossroads of the past, present and future. The individual is shaped by his/her sociohistory but also shapes his/her sociohistory as life goes on. The entire process is conflictive as opposed to harmonious. The individual often feels ambivalence and there are unequal power relations to deal with, around the different educational resources and assets, that is, social capital, possessed by participants.

As I have made clear thus far, it is my view that this approach to identity has become dominant among theorists and researchers interested in how individuals 'do' themselves in different social contexts: a casual perusal of recent works in sociology and anthropology journals, research monographs, edited collections and texts bears this claim out. However, with so many social scientists adopting this poststructuralist framework, some voices have begun to emerge critiquing the foundations on which the research boom is based. One such voice is Mervyn Bendle (2002), to whom I now turn.

Bendle's critique

Bendle (2002) discusses the rise of identity as a key concept in the social sciences and how its current dominance in the social sciences is problematic. Bendle begins with the notion that both theorists and the focus of their enquiries change over time, citing several reasons why the focus on the self, in particular, has come about. First, there is the late nineteenth- and early twentieth-century psychology and psychiatry, with the likes of William James and Sigmund Freud at the forefront. For the first time, theorists put the self at the centre of research, as something worthy of empirical study, requiring expert knowledge. Secondly, Bendle notes that during the nineteenth and twentieth centuries there was a slow process of secularization in Europe. This secularization led to a greater valuing of life on earth and self-fulfilment via worldly activity as opposed to other-worldly activity (i.e. religion). A third reason for the rise of identity relates to certain human rights advances in the advanced industrialized nations, particularly in the twentieth century. These advances took place concurrently with the rise of secularism and this is no accident, as the latter phenomenon meant the eroding of traditional institutions blocking social mobility, be this across social class, ethnic or gender lines. Finally, as was observed above, social scientists themselves have changed the way they see the world. According to Bendle, there has been movement from a structuralist preoccupation with stability, function and structure to a priming of individual agency, a movement from fixed, essentialized notions of race, ethnicity, gender and so on, to a poststructuralist, constructivist perspective which sees these categories as more fluid and unstable.

For Bendle, the rise of identity as a key concept in so much recent and current work in the social sciences is 'indicative of [a] crisis', which manifests itself in two ways. On the one hand, there is now a widespread belief, and even an assumption among many social scientists, that the formation, maintenance and projection of identity has changed in recent years. This is most of all the case in the post-industrial and industrialized world where decisions about what is important to study are made. This realization that identity is something worthy of study has, in turn, led to a notable increase in the amount of research aimed at investigating it. However, more research has led to a second way in which the rise of identity is indicative of crisis, namely, it has shown how ill prepared so many researchers have been for the new reality to which they have turned their attention. In other words, identity as a concept is often under-theorized and therefore unable to work as a framework for the target of study. Of course a big problem is how identity has come to be framed as an ongoing process as opposed to a single set product. Bendle wonders how social scientists can see it as so important yet so ungraspable. He writes:

> There is an inherent contradiction between a valuing of identity as something so funda-mental that it is crucial to personal well-being and collective action, and a theorization of 'identity' that sees it as something constructed, fluid, multiple, impermanent and fragmentary. The contemporary crisis of identity thus expresses itself as both a crisis of society, and a crisis of theory. The crisis of identity involves a crisis of 'identity'.
> (Bendle 2002: 1–2)

This crisis of identity is more pronounced in sociology, in particular among those who examine globalizing forces and flows related to the movement of peoples, money and culture around the world. And the crisis arises no doubt because of the newness of the ontology which has become the focus. However, the crisis also results from having borrowed the concept of identity from an already established field, which many would see as its rightful home: psychiatry. Bendle constructs an effective deconstruction of the work of Giddens and Castells, two of the better known globalization and identity theorists in recent years. He makes the point that they have, in effect, superficialized identity, focusing on surface malleability and change in the self in response to an ever more complex set of stimuli served up by the environment. And, he notes that they have not explained '[u]pon what psychological substrate such a transient construction rests and how it mobilizes the energies that are observably necessary to maintain an integrated personality in dynamic conditions of social change' (Bendle 2002: 8).

Bendle agues that there is need to move from 'surface' models of analysis put forth by so many today to more 'depth' models and from overly optimistic and romanticized approaches to more pessimistic and 'dark' ones. For Bendle such a move means looking more carefully at ego psychology and so called 'left' psychoanalytic theories of identity. This should be done in the name of balance and the healthy consideration that there just might be an inner core self, not entirely stable and surely conflicted, which acts as a constraint on human devel-opment. There is, therefore, more to the fluid and fragmented identity than a response to the environment. In addition, the notions of multiple identities and fragmentation, so important to poststructuralists and constructivists, would be seen by psychoanalysts as something to be treated. While the former seem to put conflict out there as something that can be resolved, the latter see conflict as evasively retiring into the inner recesses of the mind.

For Bendle, Giddens is one of the few general poststructuralist/constructivist theorists who try to engage with psychoanalysis. In Giddens' 1991 book there are references to Freud, Lacan and others. Unfortunately, Bendle thinks that Giddens has either not fully understood the work of these authors, and therefore has misrepresented it, or that he simply has not been able to convey his understandings to readers in a coherent fashion. While Giddens brings in terminology such as 'ontological security' and 'existential anxiety', he soon takes the more optimistic tack that human beings manage to adapt to social change around them leaving to the side the inner self of paranoia, schizophrenia, false self, disorder and so on. He therefore does not address how all of these inner-self phenomena might hold individuals back and act as a check on their self-realization, self-identity projects. Indeed, the very term self-identity seems to be at the crossroads of psychological and sociologically informed versions of who people are. However, Giddens, and many, many others who hold similar views on identity, have systematically failed to address the psychological while emphasizing the social.

Applied linguistics and identity

What is a trend in the social sciences generally comes to be a trend in applied linguistics, and the interest in poststructuralist approaches to identity has been no exception. In the past six years alone (2000–present), there have been at least ten monographs, textbooks and collections, published in English, which highlight identity and draw on this protocol. These publications include: Norton's (2000) study of immigrant women in Canada; Toohey's (2000) study of the relationship between the communication activities of language minority children in primary education in Canada and their socialization processes; Pavlenko et al.'s (2001) edited collection on language learning and gender; Schechter and Bayley's (2002) study of the language practices and language affiliations of Mexican American families in the US; Hall's (2002) textbook on culture and research; Bayley and Schechter's (2003) collection of papers on language socialization and multilingualism; Kanno's (2003) study of the life stories of Japanese returnees; Miller's (2003) account of the language and socialization processes of immigrant children in Australia; Pavlenko and Blackledge's (2004) collection of papers on the negotiation of identities in different language, cultural and political contexts; and Block's (2006) discussion of multilingual identities in London.

The last publication cited above shows how in my own work, I have also accepted the poststructuralist take on identity. However, I cannot help but wonder if many authors (myself included) are perhaps signing up to it in a relatively uncritical manner. I also wonder if, as Bendle argues, these authors are to varying degrees guilty of adopting a model of identity which is 'radically under-theorised and incapable of bearing the analytical load that the contemporary situation requires' (Bendle 2002: 1). In particular, I wonder what has happened to the psychological self in the publications that I read.

Granger, psychoanalysis and second language learning

Colette Granger is one applied linguist, who has at least to some extent taken up Bendle's call for a more psychologically informed approach to identity.[2] Focusing on the phenomenon of silence in second language learning, she laments that it has traditionally been seen either as a sign that language learners do not comprehend or as a period during which they gather the linguistic knowledge necessary to be able to speak. For Granger, such interpretations of silence ignore a third possibility, namely that silence is a part of an internal identity struggle as individuals sort out feelings of loss (of the L1) and anxiety at the prospects of an uncertain future in a new language. She draws on Freudian psychology and Lacanian psychoanalytic theory (primarily via Fink 1995) and develops a theory of identity that seems to be, at first glance, somewhat in line with what Bendle has in mind.

Granger mines Freudian and Lacanian psychoanalysis for concepts which she then uses to make sense of two databases: published memoirs written by individuals who have experienced language and culture border crossing in their lifetimes and diary studies of language learners, produced by applied linguists. She discusses the ego as 'a kind of overseeing intermediary, negotiating relations between internal and external worlds' (Granger 2004: 42), where the medium of this negotiation is language. There is talk of anxiety, conflict, projection and avoidance, all of which arise in relation to experiences of destabilization and loss. Parallels are drawn between what the infant experiences and what child, adolescent and adult L2 learners experience. Above all, ambivalence and liminality (i.e. existing at the threshold) are the emotional and physical metaphors, respectively, that arise from destabilization and the loss of the 'love object', in this case what Granger calls 'the first language self'. The latter is 'the self that could make itself known, to the world and to itself, in its first language' (Granger 2004: 56). Thus, in Granger there is a discourse of psychoanalysis which the author aims to draw on in her attempt to make sense of silence in second language learning. However, what I note in her database, and the subsequent analysis of it, is that she is dealing less with silenced learners than with conflicted learners. I now turn to an example of how she 'psychoanalyses' a particular case.

In a seminal and oft cited article, Bailey (1983) reviews diary studies carried out during the late 1970s by nine language teachers/applied linguists (including Bailey herself) and two 'non teachers'. Bailey focuses on two key constructs – competitiveness and anxiety – charting how they manifest themselves in diary entries. In one example, Walsleben (1976) describes her experience of learning Farsi as foreign language. In her account there is open conflict between the diarist and the teacher and this leads to Walsleben eventually to give up the learning of Farsi. One point of conflict with the teacher is the practice of administering frequent vocabulary tests to students unprepared to take them and who view them as a waste of time. Walsleben tells the story of how on one particular day, matters came to a head:

> After the break (the teacher) announced that he would give the vocabulary test, 'If that's OK.' Shirley stated again her difficulty in studying uncontextualized words for a vocabulary tests, and (the teacher) explained that he nonetheless felt that it was a justifiable way of building up our vocabularies. When he repeated that he was going to give the test and he looked at me when he said, 'If that's okay.' I responded tersely, 'You're the professor, but in my opinion it's a poor use of time.' That was the proverbial last straw. For the next hour and a half the whole class was embroiled in a very emotional exchange of opinions dealing with what the class was and was not, what it could and should be, who would let whom do what.
>
> (Bailey 1983: 87 [Walsleben 1976: 34–5]).

As Bailey puts it, in this case it seems that the diarist is not competing with her classmates; rather, she 'is struggling with the instructor for control of her language learning experience' (Bailey 1983: 87). A week after the blow-up with the teacher, Walsleben dropped out of the class.

For Granger, Walsleben's experience might be seen as a struggle with the teacher for control of her language learning, as Bailey suggests; however, there is another way, based in psychoanalysis, of framing Walsleben's experience. According to this line of analysis, Walsleben is involved in a struggle between the inside and outside, between Freud's' 'I should like to eat this' and 'I should like to spit it out' (Freud 1925: 439). Granger sums up Walsleben's state and that of other diarists in Bailey's survey who mention conflicts with their teachers as follows:

> This conflict between 'taking in' a second language and rejecting it is rooted in the ambiva-
> lence of the learner's desire both to learn and to refuse learning that accompanies learning's
> perpetual state of emergency ... It is articulated ... in frequent analogies that the diarists
> make between the relationships of teachers and students and those of aprons and children.
> These analogies also call to mind once again the Freudian concept of family romance ...
> entailing, in part, motives of sibling rivalry, among which is a sense in which the child
> may imagine herself as the product of a clandestine love affair between her mother and a
> man other than her actual father, or alternatively as the only 'legitimate' child among her
> siblings.
>
> (Granger 2004: 99)

The kind of ambivalence described by Granger, revisiting Walsleben, can also be found among students participating in research I carried out over ten years ago, as I now explain.

The case of Silvia

The small database I will examine here is a part of a larger case study I developed over ten years ago in Barcelona, around a highly motivated upper intermediate level learner of English named Silvia.[3] I interviewed Silvia on a more or less weekly basis over a ten-week course she was attending. My interest at the time was in what she would cite as salient in her lessons and how she would evaluate these salient items. Examining the data now, I would say that Silvia adopted different subject positions as she provided accounts of her lessons. For example, there was one ongoing narrative which involved Silvia's relationships with her fellow students. Another involved her contesting the way the teacher corrected her written work. Here I will look at two excerpts, produced in two different interviews which relate to Silvia's construction of relationship with her teacher. The interviews originally took place in Spanish, but here I present English trans-lations. I have used a simplified form of transcription to aid readability.

In excerpt 1, Silvia (S) is talking to me (D) about her relationship with her teacher, a topic that she herself had brought up:

> S: The only thing is that sometimes I think that teachers, because they speak English and
> you don't, they are above you. And this infuriates me, actually because ... I don't know,

but you get this feeling a little and I've mentioned it to other people and they've told me I'm right. I mean it's not just my thing, I'm not going to have any kind of inferiority complex.

D: What? That I have something you don't have?

S: That I don't have and it's costing me a lot to have it and for this reason [they] look down on [you].

D: I've never thought about that. But don't you think that it's also mixed up with the power relation that might exist between teacher and student?

S: Yes, of course, there is always a power relation between the teacher and the student. At times, it has bothered me.

D: It's the feeling that the person ... yeah, I understand.

S: And you say: 'Well who do you think you are? You're just a teacher'. It's true. You might know a lot of English but I know a lot of other things.

(Silvia, 2 June 1993)

On the surface, the important thing in this exchange is how Silvia, a well-educated upper-middle class woman, announces that there are things that she does not have to take from someone who is 'just a teacher'. She expresses certain resentment at the power inherent in the position of teacher and she does not accept the fact that the classroom situation puts her in a less powerful position, albeit for only four hours a week. And all of this, because the teacher has English, the object of her desire and efforts.

From the kind of psychoanalytic perspective that Granger has adopted, this exchange is chock-full of significance. There is the latterly mentioned object of desire – English – and how teachers flaunt the linguistic knowledge that the student is spending time and paying money to acquire. However, there is perhaps a degree of displacement going on here: is it English or the teacher herself that Silvia desires? There is also deciding how to interpret the end of intervention 1, when Silvia emphatically declares that she is 'not going to have any kind of inferiority complex'. This denial might well be seen as a de-projection of how she feels, that is, a statement meaning the opposite of what it appears to mean.

Two weeks later, after the final lesson, Silvia surprised me with an interesting statement about her relationship with teachers, which in a way seemed less than congruent with her remarks about teachers being 'just teachers':

I like talking to teachers. I don't know why, but I like it a lot. And besides, we went to the bar and had a glass of *cava*. But of course since we had never gone to the bar with her, you never get to know her very well. So we were asking her where she was from and how she had ended up here and everything. I don't know, you situate people more when you know a little about their past because if not ...

(Silvia, 16 June 1993)

Here Silvia celebrates how she finally was able to talk to her teacher away from the pressures of the course. She confesses that she likes talking to teachers.

However, following Granger's psychoanalytical methodology, what sense can one make of Silvia's comments?

Taking the two excerpts together, there seems to be a parallel structure at work here. For Granger, there is a 'conflict between "taking in" [a teacher] and rejecting [her] [which] is rooted in the ambivalence of the learner's desire both to [align with the teacher] and to refuse [aligning with the teacher]'. Taking into account that Silvia in effect has studied several different languages in her lifetime and that at the time of the study she was in the middle of two years of uninterrupted enrolment, the psychoanalyst would likely wonder about the object of her desire: As I queried previously, is it the language or contact with teachers?

The short answer to this question is: I do not know. Here, I am engaging with psychoanalysis in an attempt to make sense of Silvia's words. However, I should make clear that I do not see myself as a competent psychoanalyst of learner accounts of their language learning experiences. Indeed, I am concerned that I might be seen to be trivializing theoretical frameworks, taken up on the spur of the moment by a researcher wishing to vary his approach to data. Surely, taking up the subject position of psychoanalyst requires more of the individual than having read a couple of books about Lacan.

There is also the issue of how data match up with claims made by the researchers about the inner lives of informants. In Granger (2004), I think that revisiting Bailey's data is problematic for two reasons: first, because Granger is working with data collected by diarists/researchers with other purposes in mind, and secondly, because she only has access to a small part of the total database. As Fink (1997) notes, good psychoanalysis involves sustained contact between a trained psychoanalyst and an individual positioned as 'patient' and not the kind of secondary analysis that Granger has carried out.

So, where does all of this leave us as regards the poststructuralist approach to identity and Bendle's critique? I attempt an answer to this question in the final section.

Conclusion

On the one hand, I find Bendle's comments and suggestions about the poststructuralist approach to identity thought provoking. I can easily see his point about the inherent contradiction in valuing identity as such an important construct while saying that it is 'something constructed, fluid, multiple, impermanent and fragmentary'. In addition, my poststructuralist tendencies notwithstanding, I have always had niggling doubts about the apparent lack of any core self in publications that I read. Is there nothing stable deep inside, behind the different subject positions? However, taking on board Bendle's arguments puts me in a difficult situation: I still need to reconcile structure and agency – the ongoing problem *par excellence* for poststructuralists – but I also need to be attentive to the subconscious deeper inner workings of the mind and how they might impact on one's sense of self and identity. The question is: Can one take all of this on? Bendle seems to think that researchers and theorists can do so, and indeed are duty bound to do so, writing that 'an adequate response requires that critical and uncompromising analysis be conducted at the interface of sociology with the key underlying models of identity derived from constructionism, psychoanalysis and psychology' (Bendle 2002: 17). However, I am not so sure about this proposal for at least three good reasons.

First, there is the simple but basic rule of thumb that the right analysis for the questions being asked is always one carried out by a researcher knowledgeable and competent enough to ask and answer these questions. Perhaps psychoanalysis is not for social scientists who are interested in developing understandings of the identity work done by people living what Bauman (2005) has called 'liquid lives'. Liquid lives are lives in the fast lane, where 'the conditions under which ... [people] act change faster than it takes the ways of acting to consolidate into habits and routines' (Bauman 2005: 1). When researching the fast and furious world that Bauman describes, the right analytical framework may well be something that Bendle would find 'superficial'. In my recent research on migration (Block 2006), it has seemed far more appropriate to focus on the hurly burly of today's globalized world than the inner drives and desires of my informants.

Secondly, a move to include psychoanalysis in identity research might also be inappropriate if psychoanalysis is considered to be about *praxis*, an applied activity, as opposed to theory, a speculating activity (Fink 1997). In this case, a psychoanalytical framework might offer an effective way of explaining the inner recesses of the patient's mind, but it might not offer the best possible framework for understanding observed phenomena. There are obvious parallels here to what I said earlier in this paper about the possible benefits of essentializing ethnic identities. Research epistemologies are often very different from practical epistemologies.

Thirdly and finally, I note that as an analytical tool, psychoanalysis can be intrusive to those being studied. What I mean is that it focuses exclusively on individuals and their very personal inner lives. Thus a perusal of some of the publications cited previously in the discussion of identity in applied linguistics (e.g. Norton 2000; Kanno 2003; Block 2006), shows how these researchers are far less intrusive. In a sense, identity making is negotiated between the informant and the researcher and is not something that the latter must dig out of the former.

Notes

1 Not everyone would agree with my view that Giddens sees a strong role for social structure in his work. See Layder (1997) for a critical view.

2 This is not to say that Granger is the only applied linguist ever to mention language learning and psychology in the same breath: Guiora *et al.* (1972) carried out research around concepts like 'language ego' some 35 years ago. However, she is the only recent book-length analysis based on psychoanalysis that I have been able to find.

3 The case of Silvia is dealt with in a very different manner in Block (2000), where she is assigned the name 'GJ'.

References

Alsop, R., Fitzsimons, A. and Lennon, K. (2002), *Theorizing Gender*. Cambridge: Polity.
Bailey, K. (1983), 'Competitiveness and anxiety in adult second language learning: looking at and through the diary studies', in H. Seliger and M. Long (eds), *Classroom-oriented Research in Second Language Acquisition*. Rowley, MA: Newbury House, pp. 67–103.
Bauman, Z. (1991), *Modernity and Ambivalance*. Cambridge: Polity.
— (2001), *Community*. Cambridge: Polity.
— (2005), *Liquid Life*. Cambridge: Polity.
Bayley, R. and Schechter, S. R. (eds) (2003), *Language Socialization in Bilingual and Multilingual Societies*. Clevedon, UK: Multilingual Matters.
Bendle, M. (2002), 'The crisis of 'identity' in high modernity', *British Journal of Sociology*, 53 (1), 1–18.
Benwell, B. and Stokoe, E. (2006), *Discourse and Identity*. Edinburgh: Edinburgh University Press.
Bhabha, H. (1994), *The Location of Culture*. London: Routledge.
Block, D. (2006), *Multilingual Identities in a Global City: London Stories*. London: Palgrave.
— (2007), *Second Language Identities*. London: Continuum.
Blommaert, J. (2005), *Discourse*. Cambridge: Cambridge University Press.
Bucholtz, M. (2003), 'Sociolinguistic nostalgia and the authentication of identity', *Journal of Sociolinguistics*, 7, (3): 398–416.
Cameron, D. and Kulic, D. (2003), *Language and Sexuality*. Cambridge: Cambridge University Press.
Davies, B. and Harré, R. (1999), 'Positioning and personhood', in R. Harré and L. van Langenhove (eds) *Positioning Theory*. London: Sage, pp. 32–52.
Eckert, P. (2000), *Language Variation as Social Practice*. Oxford: Blackwell.
Eckert, P. and McConnell-Ginet, S. (1992), 'Think practically and look locally: language and gender as community-based practice', *Annual Review of Anthropology*, 21: 461–90.
— (2003), *Language and Gender*. Cambridge: Cambridge University Press.
Elliot, A. (1996), *Subject to Ourselves: Social Theory, Psychoanalysis and Postmodernity*. Cambridge: Polity.
Fink, B. (1995), *The Lacanian Subject: Between Language and Jouissance*. Princeton, NJ: Princeton University Press.
— (1997), *A Clinical Introduction to Lacanian Psychoanalysis: Theory and Technique*. Cambridge, MA: Harvard University Press.
Freud, S. (1925), 'Negation', in *The Penguin Freud Library*, Vol. 11. London: Penguin, pp. 435–42.
Giddens, A. (1984), *The Constitution of Society: Outline of the Theory of Structuration*. Cambridge: Polity.
— (1991), *Modernity and Self-Identity: Self and Society in the Late Modern Age*. Cambridge: Polity.
Granger, C. (2004), *Silence in Second Language Learning. A Psychoanalytic Reading*. Clevedon: Multilingual Matters.
Guiora, A., Beit-Hallahini, B., Brannon, R., Dull, C. and Scovel, T. (1972), 'The effects of experimentally induced changes in ego states on pronunciation ability in a second language: an exploratory study', *Comprehensive Psychiatry*, 13, 421–8.
Hall, J. K. (2002), *Teaching and Researching Language and Culture*. London: Longman.
Hall, S. (1995), 'Fantasy, identity and politics', in E. Carter, J. Donald and J. Squires (eds), *Cultural Remix: Theories of Politics and the Popula*. London: Lawrence and Wishart, pp. 63–9.
— (1996), 'The question of cultural identity', in S. Hall, D. Held, D. Hubert and K. Thompson (eds), *Modernity: An Introduction to Modern Societies*. Oxford: Oxford University Press.

Joseph, J. (2004), *Language and Identity*. London: Palgrave.

Kanno, Y. (2003), *Negotiating Bilingual and Bicultural Identities*. Clevedon: Multilingual Matters.

Lave, J. and Wenger, E, (1991), *Situated Learning: Legitimate Peripheral Participation*. Cambridge: Cambridge University Press.

Layder, D. (1997), *Modern Social Theory: Key Debates and New Directions*. London: Routledge.

Leung, C., Harris, R. and Rampton, B. (1997), 'The idealised native speaker, reified ethnicities and classroom realities', *TESOL Quarterly*, 31 (3), 543–60.

Mathews, G. (2000), *Global Culture/Individual Identity: Searching for a Home in the Cultural Supermarket*. London: Routledge.

May, S. (2001), *Language and Minority Rights*. London: Longman.

Miller, J. (2003), *Audible Differences: ESL and Social Identity in Schools*. Clevedon: Multilingual Matters

Modood, T. (2005), *Multicultural Politics: Racism, Ethnicity and Muslims in Britain*. Edinburgh: Edinburgh University Press.

Norton, B. (2000), *Identity in Language Learning: Gender, Ethnicity and Educational Change*. London: Longman.

Ortner, S. (2005), 'Subjectivity and cultural critique', *Anthropological Theory*, 5 (1), 31–52.

Papastergiadis, N. (2000), *The Turbulence of Migration*. Cambridge: Polity.

Pavlenko, A. and Blackledge, A. (eds) (2004), *Negotiation of Identities in Multilingual Settings*. Clevedon: Multilingual Matters.

Pavlenko, A., Blackledge, A., Piller, I. and Teutsch-Dwyer, M. (eds) (2001), *Multilingualism, Second Language Learning, and Gender*. New York: Mouton De Gruyter.

Pilkington, A. (2003), *Racial Disadvantage and Ethnic Diversity in Britain*. London: Palgrave.

Schechter, S. and Bayley, R. (2002), *Language as Cultural Practice : Mexicanos en el norte*. Mahwah, NJ: Lawrence Erlbaum.

Simmel, G. (1950), 'The Stranger', in K. Wolff (ed.), *The Sociology of Georg Simmel*. Glencoe, Ill: Free Press, pp. 401–8.

Smart, B. (1999), *Facing Modernity*. London: Sage.

Spivak, G. (1999), *A Critique of Postcolonial Reason: Toward a History of the Vanishing Present*. Cambridge, MA: Harvard University Press.

Toohey, K. (2000), *Learning English at School*. Clevedon: Multilingual Matters.

Walsleben, M. (1976), 'Cognitive and affective factors influencing a learner of Persian (Farsi) including a journal of second language acquisition'. Unpublished manuscript, University of California, Los Angeles.

Weedon, C. (1997), *Feminist Practice and Poststructuralist Theory* (2nd edn). Oxford: Blackwell.

Wenger, E. (1998), *Communities of Practice*. Cambridge: Cambridge University Press.

4 Constructing languages, constructing national identities[1]

Yasir Suleiman

Introduction

Each of the substantive terms in the title of this chapter is problematic, in that none is 'primitive' in the logical sense of being semantically irreducible and, in terms of practice, none is the locus of inter-subjective agreement among those whose scholarly interests converge on language and identity. And yet, the study of how language is deployed in the construction of identity, and how identity is used to construct language, has recently advanced in many disciplines without, it seems, 'let or hindrance', to use a stock phrase found on the inside cover of many passports, those ultimate authenticating symbols of identity in the popular imagination.

Let us look at identity first. Instead of using heavy-duty scholarly discourses on the topic, I will invoke a commonsense and self-reflective discussion of the concept by the Lebanese-French writer Maalouf, author of the best-selling novel *Leo the African* (1998), simply because elements of what he says resonate with me, with who I think I am. In his book *On Identity* (2000: 3), Maalouf begins as follows:

> How many times since I left Lebanon in 1976 to live in France have people asked me, with the best intention in the world, whether I felt 'more French' or 'more Lebanese'? And I always give the same answer: 'Both!'
>
> To those who ask the question, I patiently explain that I was born in Lebanon and lived there until I was 27; that Arabic is my mother tongue; and that it was in Arabic translation that I first read Dumas and Dickens and *Gulliver's Travels*; and that in my native village, the village of my ancestors, that I experienced the pleasures of childhood and heard some of the stories that were later to inspire my novels. How could I forget all that? How could I cast it aside? On the other hand, I have lived for 22 years on the soil of France; I drank her water and wine; every day my hands touch her ancient stones; I write my books in her language; never again will she be a foreign country to me.
>
> So am I half French and half Lebanese? Of course not. Identity can't be compartmentalized. You can't divide it up into halves or thirds or any other separate segments. I haven't got several identities: I have just got one, made up of many components combined together in a mixture that is unique to every individual.

Maalouf is primarily interested in personal identity, but he is aware that this identity is at the crossroads of many of life's currents and social categories of self-definition. Personal identities, according to Maalouf, are both complex and unique. They are not 'single malts' but 'blends' for which there is no single recipe. Identities also engage an assumption of alterity, the fact that it is not possible to posit identity without speaking of difference, of otherness. Personal identities, as Maalouf also tells us later in *On Identity*, are both stable and changeable. Maalouf emphasizes the potential for mutation, the fact that identity is always in a state of becoming, and he links it to different configurations in the 'hierarchy' of the elements making up an identity. Maalouf's use of the term 'hierarchy' in this context is not helpful, as I will explain later. I personally prefer to talk in terms of the poly-centricity of identity instead. Finally, Maalouf recognizes that the components of an identity may clash with each other under certain conditions. Yet these same components can exist in harmony under other, less inciting conditions. This is one of the paradoxes of identity: its capacity to combine the forces of relative harmony and fragmentation, of fusion and fission, into a single unit that manifests itself in different ways under different conditions. Owing to this, some scholars prefer to speak of an identity repertoire, rather than just 'identity' on its own.

As we shall see later, these features of personal identity apply to national identity, although their mode of operation may differ in each case. We may also add here that identities come to the fore under conditions of stress, conflict and lack of security, which is often the case in national identity at times of historical, social or political crisis. As Bauman states in a figurative turn of phrase, 'a battlefield is identity's natural home. Identity comes to life only in the tumult of battle; it falls asleep and silent the moment the noise of the battle dies down' (2004: 77). And, while recognizing that identities are negotiable, this study does not subscribe to the view that they are fleeting or easily discardable. Identities are categorially different from lifestyles, from the fact that people eat pizzas, drink French wine, holiday in Spain, wear designer clothes or drive BMWs.

Language – and this is the point of interest for us here – is an important ingredient of identity for Maalouf, both at the communicative and symbolic levels (see Edwards 1985 for these two functions). For some scholars – particularly linguists – writing about identity may in some sense be driven by personal concerns, even anxieties, about their own personal identity.[2] Writing about identity, a scholar may in fact use the occasion, knowingly or unknowingly, to grapple with issues of personal identity. In his book *Language and Identity*, Joseph (2004) – who alludes to himself as half Lebanese – is refreshingly open about this. In the 'Preface' to his book, Joseph tells us (*ibid.*: xii): 'I have dedicated this book to my two Lebanese grandparents because it was they who made it impossible for me not to think about identity and language every day of my life; and I have written it in part for my children ... who are bound to confront their own issues of language and identity one day.' Writing from my exilic position as a Palestinian living in Scotland, I too am open about this link of the personal with the professional in my work. In my book *A War of Words: Language and Conflict in the Middle East* (2004), I have put my identity on the line, so to speak, and used it as an anchor, to the best of my scholarly ability, to reflect on issues of language, identity and conflict in the Middle East, on both the theoretical and empirical levels. This theme of the link between professional and personal identity in relation to language in scholarly discourse is fronted by Baugh, an African American Professor of Education and Linguistics at Stanford, in his book *Beyond Ebonics: Linguistic Pride and Racial Prejudice* (2000). Baugh unapologetically writes (*ibid.*: 3):

> Readers of this book presumably seek an informed yet dispassionate survey of Ebonics, but it would be misleading to suggest that I approach this topic with complete linguistic objectivity. Although I bring more than twenty years of linguistic analyses to this subject, I spent my early childhood in inner-city communities where standard English is rare, and those experiences have shaped my life and professional work in ways that defy disengaged objectivity. Thus this topic is one that remains deeply personal.

Two things are interesting about the above examples. On the one hand, they signal that language, identity and liminality are linked to each other, in the sense that liminality seems to engender an acute interest in issues of language and identity. Baugh and Joseph assume this link in their work, as I do myself. On the other hand, the above examples show how the personal and the scholarly dimensions of a person's identity can interact with each other in discussions of language and identity. Constructing or deconstructing linguistic identity in scholarly discourses of this kind therefore has great significance because it engages and links that which is *interior* to the self in the realm of personal identity with what is *exterior* to it in the social domain of professional and collective identity. I wish to emphasize this double trajectory of *interiority* and *exteriority* here to draw attention to it as an aspect of construction that is rarely dealt with in studies of language and identity. I believe it is important to highlight this link because it raises questions about the nature of 'science as practice', in particular about the meaning and limits of 'objectivity' in scientific inquiry.[3]

Moving on to issues of language and collective identity, construction also looms large, but it is no more potent than when informed by ideological impulses of a subterranean kind. In my analysis of Spolsky and Cooper's pioneering book *The Languages of Jerusalem* (1991), I have tried to show how the seemingly objective construction of linguistic identity can be critically, albeit subconsciously, shaped by national ideology (see Suleiman 2004: 167–72). Investigating the major outlines of the architectural design of the book, what may be called its pre- or sub-text, I was able to show how the old city of Jerusalem in the 1980s (usually referred to as East Jerusalem), with its majority Arabic speaking population, somehow emerges as Hebrew-dominated in Spolsky and Cooper's work, not in the symbolic sense or in terms of power and linguistic vitality, but in terms of demography and the visibility of Arabic and Hebrew in the public sphere.[4] *The Languages of Jerusalem* thus presents another fascinating example of construction in relating language to identity, and this in turn raises further questions about the status of 'science as practice'.[5] We need not be coy about this, as Ivanić (1998) shows in her research on the discursive construction of identity in academic writing: there simply is no escaping construction in dealing with issues of language and identity, whether at the personal or collective level.

Let us examine this further by shifting the discussion to issues of language and national identity, which form the major topic in this chapter. In his book *National Identity*, Smith (1991: 15) – a leading scholar of nationalism – states, not unsurprisingly, that 'national identity and the nation are complex constructs composed of a number of interrelated components – ethnic, cultural, territorial, economic and legal-political'. Smith does not name language per se as a component of national identity, although we can assume from the arguments in the book that it is one of the most important constituents in the cultural component. In fact, language in this book is the *absent–present* of culture in definitional terms. Other scholars, for example Gellner (1983), Hobsbawm (1990) and Anderson (1991) highlight the role of language in national identity and nation building. However, for the most part, scholars of nationalism tend to treat language as a 'given' of nationalism, hardly ever discussing the 'constructedness' of this category of definition in sufficient detail or in a way that responds to the interests of professional linguists. In fact, I found myself slipping into this mode of thinking, and then correcting myself, in writing my book *The Arabic Language and National Identity: A Study in Ideology* (2003). The assumption in nationalism studies that languages are more or less self-evident categories must, therefore, be subjected to critical analysis. Referring to Anderson's well-known book *Imagined Communities* (1991), Gal points out that 'not only communities but also languages must be imagined before their unity can be socially accomplished' (1998: 325). As we shall see below, languages are constructed units of self-definition. Whether two or more varieties are established as different languages or as dialects of the same language will depend on a variety of contextual factors that are related to the history, politics, culture and demography of any given situation. The idea that languages are discursive projects, and that standard languages are the products of ideological processes will be guiding principles in this research (see Woolard and Schieffelin 1994: 64).

Constructing languages, constructing national identities

Starting with Scandinavia, we can talk about the constructed nature of Swedish, Danish and Norwegian as distinct national languages. These languages are historically related, exist on a continuum and are mutually intelligible, although each has its special linguistic characteristics and regional flavour (Vikør 2000). In purely linguistic terms, they can be treated as varieties of the same over-arching language. The differences between them seem to be less than those between the Arabic dialects at the end points of the Arabic language continuum from East to West, which, in contrast, are treated as varieties of the same language. Swedish, Danish and Norwegian are treated as three distinct languages for reasons that are intimately linked to political history, identity formation and nation building. In fact, the relative linguistic proximity of Danish and Swedish has been a factor in the conscious marking of their difference through selected orthographic symbols (*ibid.*: 109). Orthography is an effective way of making visible, of constructing, differences between languages.[6]

This constructing role of orthography/script as a political symbol is what, at one level, gives a strong expression to Urdu and Hindi as different languages,[7] in spite of the fact they are mutually intelligible in the spoken medium. The replacement of the Arabic script by the Roman and then Cyrillic scripts in the languages of the central Asian republics of the former Soviet Union, and the subsequent changes in script that have taken place since the dissolution of the USSR in the 1990s, are pieces of linguistic *constructioneering* that are closely tied to different conceptions of ethnic and national identity and to competing imperatives of nation building, regionally and internationally (see Gilson 1986 for Turkish script reform). In Germany in the nineteenth century and up to World War II, German was printed in Gothic type (Black Letter) to make it look different from French, which used the regular Roman type. In Ireland until the 1950s, a specific Irish type was used for Irish in print to make the language look different from English in print. These examples provide evidence of how the adoption of different types within one and the same script is used as a device to construct and symbolize different national identities (Kamusella 2001). No wonder that proposals for replacing one script by another in writing a language are sometimes perceived as an attack on a group's identity, its culture and its place in the full sweep of history. This is particularly true when the script in question is allied to religion, as in the case of Arabic.

China provides another example of how a common script can help forge a shared identity and maintain mutual intelligibility in writing among the speakers of different languages. Fusion, rather than fission, is the operative term here. In Taiwan, however, the suggestions for a distinct script for the native tongue Tai-yü are meant to signal difference from Mandarin as the dominant language (see Hsiau 1997: 311–12). These suggestions are, as we shall see later, a proxy for asserting a Hok-lo ethnicity in the face of the outsider 'wai-sheng-jen' (people from other provinces of China). Orthography, therefore, is not a neutral linguistic artefact, as is generally assumed in courses in linguistics. The debate over devising an orthography for kreyòl in Haiti thus revolved around 'competing representations of Haitianness at the national and international level – that is how speakers wish to define themselves to each other, as well as to represent themselves as a nation' (Schieffelin and Doucet 1998: 285). As Woolard and Schieffelin state, 'orthographic systems cannot be conceptualized simply as reducing speech to writing, but rather they are symbols that carry historical, cultural and political meanings' (1994: 65). This is an important observation: it highlights the need for an approach to language that transcends its communicative functionality to incorporate its symbolic meanings. Writing is more than just marks on paper that record speech: it is a cultural artefact with an enormous capacity to signify symbolically.

Returning to the Scandinavian sphere, Norway provides further elaboration of identity-driven linguistic construction, what I have called linguistic construc-tioneering above, to signal the largely conscious and target-oriented character of the process or – to continue with the constructioneering metaphor – the *operation* of fashioning the language–identity link. Now generally perceived as two standard varieties of the same language, although for a long time in the nineteenth and twentieth century they were construed and projected as distinct and competing standards, Nynorsk (New Norwegian) and Bokmål (Book or Literary Language) represent two different national imaginaries of Norwegian identity. Nynorsk, which was originally called Landsmål (the language of the countryside), sought to anchor Norwegian national identity to the dialects of the countryside, particularly those in the West and the mountains of the South-East, in the romantic conception that it is these dialects that link Norwegian to its authenticating traditions and folk culture, and, ultimately, through these to Old Norse. But, not unusually in nationalism, this was a hard-headed romanticism: it had the intention of putting sufficient distance between the emerging Norwegian 'language' and Danish, the old official language, by suggesting that Landsmål/Nynorsk belonged to a different Scandinavian sub-family (Old Norse) than Danish. The construction of Nynorsk is therefore part and parcel of an attempt to create a Norwegian national identity that is as different as possible from Danish. Alterity, or significant otherness, which we encountered in commenting on individual identity in Maalouf, was the main impulse here. Within the Norwegian body-politic, Nynorsk, as hinted above, was an expression of regional identity which, to this day, is a strong feature of the life and politics of modern Norway. In contrast, the construction of Bokmål sought to fashion a Norwegian national identity that is urban-based, and that sought to give expression to existing continuities with Danish to serve the interests of a class-based culture and elite. However, Bokmål, as can be expected, in turn gradually acquired Norwegian peculiarities of speech which marked it as different from Danish.

A similar situation occured in post-independence Greece of 1832, lasting until the second half of the twentieth century and involving Katharevousa (purifying Greek) and Dhimotiki (demotic) as the two variants of Greek (Trudgill 2000). Each of these varieties was constructed to respond to a different repertoire of national values and to express a particular vision of Greece as a national unit. In the popular imagination, Katharevousa accumulated symbolic meanings that linked it to the ancient past, Hellenism, Orthodox Christianity, the monarchy and to the zeal to purify the language from borrowed, especially Turkish, words to symbolize the eradication of centuries-long foreign domination. In contrast, Dhimotiki became associated with republicanism and democracy, with its origins firmly rooted in dialect-mixing in the Peleponnese, the area that formed the early nucleus of independent Greece. However, unlike in Norway where Bokmål seems to have gained the upper hand in education and the media, Dhimotiki in Greece seems to have won against Katharevousa, especially since 1976, following the overthrow of the military junta in 1974. Also, unlike in Norway, the struggle between Katharevousa and Dhimotiki led to open conflict on the streets. The translation of the gospels into Dhimotiki in 1901 led to riots in Athens and the deaths of eight people. In 1903, the performance of Aeschylus' *Orestia* in Dhimotiki led to further riots and to the death of one person (*ibid.*: 250). If this tells us anything, it tells us that in some cases people are prepared to pay with their lives for different constructions or visions of their linguistic-based identity.

Sadly, in some cases people pay with their lives for 'acts of linguistic transgression' not because they knowingly transgress, but because they unknowingly violate 'lexical border guards' that symbolically act as signs of belonging. In Lebanon, during the civil war in the 1970s and 1980s, the Arabic pronunciation for 'tomato' acted as a shibboleth, as a sign of belonging, which helped determine the speaker's identity as Palestinian or Lebanese. Literally, in some cases, pronouncing the word for 'tomato' as *'bandura'* in a Palestinian inflection, rather than *'banadura'*, which is the Lebanese pronunciation, was tantamount to signing one's death warrant.[8] The fact that a short vowel *'a'* inter-syllabically in the Arabic pronunciation of 'tomato' meant the difference between life and death is a damning judgement on nationalism. It is a chilling example of how lethal identity-politics can be when it really 'gets out of hand'. It also offers support to Kedouri's well-known condemnation of nationalism when he says that the 'attempt to refashion so much of the world on national lines has not led to greater peace or stability. On the contrary, it has created new conflicts, exacerbated tension, and brought catastrophe to numberless people innocent of all politics' (1966: 138).

In Scandinavia and in Greece, we have seen examples of how national or ethnic identities are used to construct language as a category of self-definition, and how language, in turn, is used to underpin, symbolize and promote these identities. This ideological constructedness of language along ethnic/national lines is found elsewhere, for example in the Balkans. Linguistically the Serbian, Montenegrin, Croatian and Bosnian varieties are similar enough to be classified as varieties of the same language, as reflected in their membership in Serbo-Croatian until the dissolution of Yugoslavia in 1991 (Greenberg 2004). In fact, at that point of dissolution the Serbian, Montenegrin, Croatian and Bosnian varieties were drawing closer and closer to each other, with lexical variation between them ranging between 3 per cent and 7 per cent (Carmichael 2000: 236). However, the dissolution of Yugoslavia marked a turning point in this process, particularly as far as Croatian and Serbian are concerned, which began to be promoted as distinct languages along nationalist lines. The fact that Croatian was written in Roman and Serbian in Cyrillic no doubt contributed to this process, but the main impetus for the new direction was national in character, and it lost no time in expressing itself in the public sphere. Thus, it is reported that, in the negotiations between the Serbs and the Croatians over the situation in Bosnia-Herzegovina in the 1990s, a member of the Croatian team demanded that translation services be provided, which led to huge laughter and consternation in the room and to one member on the Serbian side leaving the negotiations in disgust, never to be seen again. Similar expressions of Croatian identity were found in Yugoslavia before 1991, but these were kept in check through a number of coercive measures. Thus, in 1971, the Croatian [language] Society called for the use of 'Croatian' in commands in the Yugoslav navy on the grounds that 80 per cent of the navy operated in Croatian waters, the excuse or trigger for this being the use of 'Serbian' as the language of commands in the army (see *ibid*.: 237). But this, of course, was totally ignored.[9]

The Balkans, in the twentieth century, provide data on the coming together of mutually intelligible varieties to form a distinct language and, later, on the dissolution of these same varieties to form distinct languages, a phenomenon replicated in the relationship between Czech and Slovak in the modern period (see Coulmas 1994; Törnquist-Plewa 2000). Issues of ethnic/national identity lie at the heart of these two opposite processes of construction. We may talk here about *fusion* and *fission* in the nation-based linguistic construction of identity in the former Yugoslavia.

Moving the discussion forward, we can further point out that whether a language is constructed as a marker of national identity or not will to a great extent depend on the strategies of nation building adopted by the nationalist elite. These strategies are historically contingent and they depend on the objective features of a given situation and their potency. In Taiwan, Mandarin was promoted as the national language after the collapse of the Nationalist leadership in mainland China and the reconsolidation of its government in Taiwan in 1949. This policy was motivated by two objectives: fostering linguistic unity and ethnic harmony in Taiwan, and maintaining the claim that the Nationalists were the legitimate representatives of the whole of China (see Hsiau 1997). In Spain, Basque has traditionally been a weak marker of Basque ethnic/national identity, although the situation started to change towards the end of the nineteenth century (Urla 1988; 1993). When the stirrings of nationalism reached the Basque region in the nineteenth and early twentieth century, the language was mainly spoken in the countryside in a large number of dialects and sub-dialects, some of which were highly differentiated to the point of being mutually unintelligible. In addition, the urban population and middle class intellectuals had a poor command of the language, and the spoken Basque dialects in the country lacked a rich corpus of literary material to act as the norm or standard in writing. Race, not language, was therefore elected as the primary factor in the definition of the Basque national self (see Watson 1996; Mar-Molinero 2000). Italy provides another interesting example of the place of language in national self-definition. Ruzza (2000: 168) argues that language is a 'relatively weak indicator of national identity [in Italy], despite the substantial coincidence of linguistic, national and state boundaries.' To signal this, Ruzza describes Italian as a 'marker' of national identity rather than a 'source' of it (*ibid.*: 172); this is an interesting distinction. Strong regional identities, coupled with the existence of mutually unintelligible languages (German, Catalan, Franco-Provencal and Friulian/Romansh) and dialect groups, and the diglossic distance between written and spoken Italian have all conspired to turn standard Italian into a weak marker of the Italian national identity, except perhaps during the fascist period when a new emphasis on language emerged.

Dutch provides further insight into the construction of language and national identity. In the Netherlands, one of the early nation states in Europe, Dutch is a marker of national identity, but by no means the most important marker. In Belgium, the situation is very different: Dutch is the most important component or 'source', to use Ruzza's terminology, of Flemish national identity. Here we have an example of the same language being constructed or conceptualized in two different ways, in nationalist terms, owing to different historical factors, and this in spite of the fact that the areas where the language is spoken are compact and contiguous. In Belgium, the status of Flemish/Dutch as an instrument of national self-definition has always been constructed in relation to a 'significant other', the French language and its Walloon speakers (Howell 2000). For most of the nineteenth and twentieth centuries, Flemish/Dutch had to fight for equality with the French language in education and the public sphere. This struggle for equality has turned the language into a potent symbol of Flemish national identity. However, internally Flemish national identity manifested itself in two conceptions of the language. The first, Flemish-oriented, stressed the differences between the Dutch spoken in Flanders and that spoken in the Netherlands, and sought to establish the former as the norm. Proponents of this position espoused a view of Flanders as part of Belgium, but with strong ties to the Netherlands. The second, a Dutch-oriented movement, considered the Standard Dutch of the Netherlands as the norm, and espoused as its political objective a union with the Netherlands (Blommaert 1996).

As in Scandinavia and Greece, issues of language and national identity in the Netherlands and Belgium show the nuanced nature of construction. At one level, Dutch has different symbolic meanings in the Netherlands and Belgium. In the latter, it is highly ideologized as a component of national self-definition. This ideologization derives its meaning from the opposition of Dutch to French. Alterity is a prime force of definition here, with French and the Walloons being the 'significant others'. At another level, Dutch is ideologically differentiated in Flanders between the Flemish-oriented and the Dutch-oriented movements. I am sure that other differentiations do exist in Flanders, but the point I wish to emphasize here is that of the complex nature of construction. One may be tempted to describe this situation in terms of layers of self-definition, or by reference to an archaeology of construction, in line with Maalouf's use of the term 'hierarchy' mentioned above. As I have said at the beginning of this chapter, I prefer to talk about poly-centricity instead for three reasons: (1) the arbitrary ordering of the strata of definition in the archaeological model; (2) this arbitrariness is bound to be compounded when we factor in categories of individual and collective self-definition, for example those pertaining to gender, class, religion or lifestyle; and (3) an archaeological model would be ill-suited to account for the intersecting and context-dependent repertoire of identities, be they individual or collective in nature.

In the above discussion, I have dealt with a range of issues that are at the heart of the linguistic construction of national identity. These included the historically contingent nature of the construction of national identity, the role of the elites in formulating this identity, how alterity is invoked as an instrument of national self-definition, how orthography is used to mark difference between national identities, how language standardization is exploited as a site of conflict between different models of national identity in the same polity (urban-based versus countryside-based as in Greece and Norway; or civic versus cultural conceptions of the nation as in Flanders), how fission and fusion operate in constructing language-based national identities, and how language-based identity-politics can be enmeshed in strife in and between nations. These are not the only avenues for investigating the links between language and national identity. Others include how identity is marked in discourse (see Wodak *et al.* 1999; Chilton 2004), dictionary making (see Benson 2001), linguistic landscapes (see Landry and Bourhis 1997; Semmerling 2004; Suleiman 2004), language planning (Cooper 1989), bilingual education and minority rights (May 2001), language and post-coloniality (Ager 1996) and gender politics and codeswitching (Heller 1995; Suleiman 2004). In what follows I will deal with two issues to which I have alluded above: language as proxy; and personal names as texts of national identity.

Language as proxy

The above discussion shows the complex and contingent nature of construction in relating language to national identity. At times construction can take a convoluted route, using language as a *proxy*, what Coulmas calls 'harbinger of crisis' (1994: 36), to articulate issues of politics and identity that one would not, or could not, express openly or directly in the public sphere. The decisions in 1989 to establish Lithuanian, Estonian and Latvian as official languages before the break up of the Soviet Union was rightly interpreted in Moscow as a political and irredentist assertion of national identity, which, no doubt, was the spirit in which these decisions were made. Similar moves in other Soviet republics (for example Moldavia, Georgia and Armenia) were read in the same way. In an age of political correctness and anti-discrimination laws, language is sometimes pressed into service as a surrogate channel for expressing views about race, education, power and access to state resources. Schmid provides a well-documented study of how this is done in some circles in the US in her book *The Politics of Language: Conflict, Identity and Cultural Pluralism in Comparative Perspective* (2001). Dealing with the Americanization movement in the 1920s and the more recent English-Only movement, Schmid writes (*ibid.*: 4):

> Language alone has rarely been the major source of conflict in American society; instead it has been the proxy for other conditions that have challenged the power relations of the dominant group(s). [Thus] bilingual education and the usage of non-English languages in the public realm has become a substitute for tensions over demographic and cultural change, increased immigration from third world countries, new linguistic-based entitlements, and changing attitudes towards racial and ethnic assimilation.

The Toubon Law in France has been read in this vein too. Promulgated in 1994, the law sets out to regulate aspects of the use of French in the public sphere, in commerce and in scholarly output. The law makes French compulsory in the 'advertising, description and directions of use of products; it also demands that bills and receipts be couched in French ... that publications, journals and papers which benefit from public funds must at the very least include a summary in French if they have to be written in a foreign language, [and] that contracts must be in French, but a translation in the native language of the employee can be demanded by the latter' (Durand 1996: 82). While acknowledging that these are genuine concerns for the Toubon Law, Jacques Durand interprets it as a proxy, as an attempt to protect French against the onslaught of English, to help France maintain an influential position in the international arena in the face of the globalization and Americanization of culture. Another extra-legal aim of the law is said to be to signal French resistance to the creeping erosion of the power of the nation state within the EU, which manifested itself in the 'no' vote over the European constitution in May 2005; the fact that the Toubon Law coincided with French anxieties about the Maastricht treaty at the time gives credence to this interpretation. Finally, the law has been interpreted metonymically as an attempt to keep the French body politic free of foreign intrusions, whether they are foreign words or foreign bodies. Jacques Durand expresses this link as follows: 'Plans to send immigrants back to their homelands may well not be unconnected to the idea of cleansing a language of foreign elements' (ibid.: 84).

While I am not in a position to judge the veracity of the claims about the erosion of the power of the nation-state in the EU, or the metonymic, anti-immigration reading of the Toubon Law, there is it seems some truth in the claim about protecting 'Her Majesty the French language', as 'She' is sometimes referred to (Lodge 1998: 30), against the threat posed by English. This is ultimately an argument about identity, national worth and international standing in a changing world in which the political power of France and her culture have experienced attacks from the outside and creeping erosion from the inside. Anthony Lodge tells us that in France 'it is widely believed that to speak French badly, to break the rules of French grammar or to make frequent use of foreign words is to be in some way unpatriotic' (ibid.). Returning to Maalouf and his book *On Identity*, we can see a link between the Toboun Law and the French anxieties about the English linguistic invasion. In his characteristically astute manner, but with some exaggeration to drive his point home, Maalouf writes (2000: 112):

> In France, when I detect anxieties in some people about the way the world is going, or reservations about technological innovation, or some intellectual, verbal, musical or nutritional fashion; or when I see signs of oversensitivity, excessive nostalgia or even extreme attachment to the past – I realize that such reactions are often linked in one way or another to the resentment people feel about the continual advance of English and its present status as the predominant international language.
>
> This attitude seems in some ways peculiar to France. Because France herself had global ambitions as regards language, she was the first to suffer on account of the extraordinary rise of English. For countries that had no such hope, or had them no longer, the problem of relations with the predominant language doesn't arise in the same way.

Gramsci writes that 'every time the question of language surfaces, in one way or another, it means that a series of other problems are coming to the fore' (1985: 183). This applies to the above representations of English in America and French in France, which show how language can be constructed as a proxy to express ideas about issues of identity, politics, immigration and access to resources in education and other spheres. In Puerto Rico between 1898, when the country came under American sovereignty, and 1947, when it was granted self-government, talk about language policy was a proxy for talk about the political future of the country. The two have been so intertwined since then that one cannot talk about language policy without talking about politics and vice versa (see Morris 1996). In Taiwan, support for Tai-yü (Taiwanese language) is read as an assertion of a Hok-lo dominated ethnicity that is seeking to challenge the dominance of the Mandarin-based national identity, promoted by the ruling

Nationalist Party (KMT) and its 'wai-shen-jen' (Chinese mainlanders) ethnic base (see Hsiau 1997). In Senegal under French colonialism, support for the native language Wolof and Arabic by the Murid (Muslim) brotherhood in Touba was a mode of 'passive resistance' against the French Colonial language policy, to the extent that, to this day, the use of French is stigmatized in this community (see Ngom 2002).

In other cases, language is used as a proxy to avoid 'pressure' by the political authorities when talking about the taboo subject of national identity. Thus, discussions of the merits of teaching mathematics and science in Arabic or in English in Oman are bound up with issues of ethnicity and access to economic resources. In such discussions, the surface meaning is about language choice, but the deep structure meaning is about the politics of ethnicity and national identity, which Omanis broach with extreme care and normally speak about in code or in whispers because of their potentially divisive nature. Shelling Sarajevo in 1993, the Serbs declared that they were doing so to protect their culture and language against the Muslims in Bosnia-Herzegovina, although the Bosnians spoke the same language as the Serbs who were shelling them (Coulmas 1994). In Israel in the 1950s and 1960s, talk about language rights by the Arab Palestinian minority was a proxy for talk about the loss of land and other national rights, political discrimination and the right to resist (see Suleiman 2004: 146–9). An interesting repeat of this took place in the mid-1980s when the residents of Beit Hanina, an occupied Arab suburb outside Jerusalem, tried to recreate through street names in their neighbourhood a map of the 420 villages destroyed by the new state of Israel after 1948 (Cheshin *et al.* 1999: 146–7).

Names as signs of identity

I have argued elsewhere (Suleiman 2004) for the importance of names and ethnic labels as texts and semiotic practices that shed light on issues of ethnic and national identity, particularly in conflict situations. I was particularly interested in street names as cartographic texts that can be used to lay claims of ownership over the landscape and/or to recreate this landscape semiotically in the image of the nation, its history and aspirations. Ethnic labels are particularly interesting because of their ability to stereotype, inferiorize and exclude, as I have shown for Jordan through the use of the term *Beljik* (Belgians) to refer to Jordanians of Palestinian origin (*ibid.*: 116–19). In Lebanon, during the civil war (1975–90), the term *ghurabà'* (lit. strangers) was used to brand non-Lebanese Arabs, mainly Palestinian refugees and Syrian workers, as the 'Other' in spite of the fact that this 'Other' has thick ties of religion, language and culture with the Lebanese.[10] In some cases a group may not accept the name used to designate it. For example, in recent years the Greek Orthodox community in Palestine and Jordan has objected to the term 'Greek' in its name, arguing for it to be replaced by 'Arab' (al-Farah 2004). The voices calling for this change have become more and more vociferous in the past few years as a result of the sale or lease of Church land, by the Greek leadership of the Church, to the Israeli authorities in the Palestinian occupied territories and in Israel proper.

Names as signs of national or ethnic identity are also important in naming languages or varieties. Naming a variety or language gives it recognition and legitimacy and helps make it a site of identity formation in the ideological sphere, mainly through the exercise of alterity. In Flanders, it matters whether the language is called Dutch, Flemish or Flemish Dutch. Blommaert comments on this aspect of language ideology as follows: 'Naming the language(s) in Flanders is, in general, a very sensitive issue, and every option one may choose, however well-motivated sociolinguistically or anthropologically, quickly becomes the object of controversy' (1996: 254).[11] Following the demographic upheaval of the division of the Indian subcontinent in 1947, the Hindus of the Punjab called their language variety Hindi, not Punjabi, to differentiate themselves from the Sikhs, who spoke Punjabi (see Le Page and Tabouret-Keller 1982). However, the attempt to gain recognition and legitimacy tends to be undermined when a variety receives a multiplicity of names or goes by many 'aliases'. An example of this is African American English (AAE) which has been referred to by a variety of names (for example 'Black Talk', 'Black English Vernacular', 'Ebonics' and 'African American Vernacular English'). Wassink and Curzan argue that the use of multiple names for this variety has compromised its legitimacy as a marker of identity and has given 'potential ammunition for those who choose to disregard or denigrate AAE' (2004: 177). It is suggested that one step towards stopping this lack of recognition would be the adoption of one name/label to designate this variety.

Names of countries can also be a site of national identity contestation. One of the points of difference in the committee drafting the new Iraqi constitution in 2005 was the name of the country, with each of the proposed five names carrying its ideological and political meaning: (1) Federal Republic of Iraq (*jumhuriyyat al-'iraq al-ittihadi*); (2) Federal Iraqi Republic (*al-jumhuriyya al-'iraqiyya al-ittihadiyya*); (3) Federal Islamic Iraqi Republic (*al-jumhuriyya al-'iraqiyya al-ittihadiyya al-islamiyya*); (4) Iraqi Republic (*al-jumhuriyya al-'iraqiyya*); and (5) Republic of Iraq (*jumhuriyyat al-'iraq*).[12] In 1990, a debate took place in Czechoslovakia concerning the new name of the country. Known as the 'great hyphen debate', the Slovaks insisted on inserting a hyphen in the name of the newly re-formed country, *Czecho-Slovakia*, to give visibility to their national identity, which will be marked by an upper, rather than a lower-case 'S' in the proposed name. The proposal was rejected in the legislature in favour of a new name with two versions: Czechoslovak Federative Republic in Bohemia and Moravia (the Czech-speaking part), and Czecho-Slovak Federative Republic in Slovakia (see Coulmas 1994). The hyphen disappeared when the two parts of pre-1990 Czechoslovakia went their separate ways politically in January 1993. Greece provides another revealing example of the interest in names as signs of national identity. Coulmas reports how the Greek government was able to persuade other European Community members that the 'former Yugoslav republic of Macedonia would be granted EC recognition only on condition that it used another name' (1994: 39). Coulmas explains the reason behind this move as follows: 'Any association of [the republic of Macedonia] with the Macedonians of Northern Greece, whose language enjoys no official status, had to be avoided. Greece considers the name "Macedonian" to be part of its heritage and fears it would imply territorial claims by the new state on the Northern Greek province of Macedonia' (*ibid.*).

There is a vast body of literature on names, authored mainly by political geographers, anthropologists, ethnographers and, to a lesser extent, historians. Studies of language and national identity in different parts of the world underline the importance of names as texts of identity. In Israel, the act of giving or assuming a Hebrew name to replace the old diaspora name signals a process of self-transformation and initiation into Israeli Hebrew culture. In her book on *dugri* (talking straight) speech in Israeli *sabra* culture, Katriel (1986: 19) describes the adoption of the Hebrew name as a 'memorable moment' for the new immigrant, exemplifying this from her own experience.

Language purifiers have always recognized the symbolism of names as signs of belonging; this is the reason they include them in their linguistic culls and bans. In Greece in the 1930s, under the totalitarian regime of the time, Greek citizens of Slav-Macedonian origin were subjected to extremely harsh linguistic bans. Trudgill (2000: 256) reports how 'Anyone "caught" speaking Slavo-Macedonian was forced to drink castor-oil ...[and how] Slavonic family names were also compulsorily changed to Greek ones'. In Bulgaria between 1984 and 1990, the Turkish Bulgarian community was subjected to harsh laws which required them to adopt Bulgarian surnames and, even, to erase any Turkish and Arabic inscriptions from their tombstones (see Eminov 1997). Following the dissolution of Yugoslavia in 1991, some Croatian Serbs with un-Croat sounding names changed their names to Croatian-sounding ones, for example Jovanka and Jovan to Ivanka and Ivan to blend in linguistically, socially and politically (see Carmichael 2000: 238). Name culls provide another example of the intolerance that can characterize identity-politics in times of national stress or crisis.

The above are some of the ways that can be used to think about names in linking language to national identity. In what follows, I will deal with other examples that show how changes in personal name patterns correlate with changes in socio-political currents in the history of the nation. Here again, construction looms large, but it is, first and foremost, construction as practised by individuals in their capacity as 'free' agents and as members of their own communities. Names can also be extremely useful in establishing the constructions a community places on gender, modernization, religious affiliation, sectarianism and variations in inter-generational values and outlook, but this will not detain us here (for Arabic, see Abd-el-Jawad 1986; Gardner 1994; Borg and Kressel 2001).

Interesting research on Turkey by Richard Bulliet (1978) shows how the popularity of the three Islamic personal names Mehmet, Ahmet and Ali waxed and waned over almost a century and a half, starting in the 1820s. For reasons which I cannot go into here, Bulliet restricts his population to members of Parliament between 1828 and 1967, which calls for caution in interpreting his results. The nineteenth century witnessed a period of modernization in the Ottoman empire, linked to increasing secularization in what came to be known as the *tanzimat*. Charting the currency of the three names during the nineteenth century, Bulliet finds that their popularity dropped sharply from a peak of about 33 per cent in 1840 to less than 10 per cent in 1889, and he ascribes this to the 'formidable attack' which the modernization of the *tanzimat* mounted against the 'idea that Islam should be the basis of political life' (*ibid.*: 492). The names recovered in popularity slightly in 1895–99, to drop again to their lowest point in 1905–09. These upward and downward movements coincided respectively with the short-lived Islamic revival under Sultan Abdülhamit II and the coming to power of the Young Turks with their radical modernizing tendencies. Bulliet further finds that the recovery in the popularity of the three names in 1910–24 coincided with the Balkan Wars, the outbreak of World War I and the war against the Greek army that occupied parts of Turkey, when 'an increasing proportion of the populace seems to have experienced [these cataclysmic events] as years in which Islamic identity was threatened and needed reaffirmation in names' (*ibid.*). Following the establishment of the republic in 1924, with its strong secularizing tendencies, the popularity of the three names dropped again to about 12 per cent and had fluctuated around this figure to the end of the period of study in 1967. This steady popularity reveals the resilience of these names, but it also calls for further research to establish the reasons behind their resilience.

The other trend in naming-pattern changes in Turkey is the steady rise in the popularity of names of Turkish linguistic origin since the establishment of the republic. In 1885–89, the loss in popularity of the three Islamic names worked in favour of a dispersed group of personal names all of which were of Arabic origin. In 1910–14, 8 per cent of the new names ('previously un-encountered') were of Turkish linguistic origins. This figure rose to 32 per cent in 1925–29, and to 65 per cent in 1930–41. In 1959, the figure stood at 59 per cent. Bulliet interprets this phenomenon in changes in naming patterns as a reflection of 'a rise in Turkish national identity' (*ibid.*: 494). But he further points out that the fact that 'the new trend in Turkish naming seems to [have proceeded] quite slowly through the Atatürk period ... [suggests that] Turkish nationalism penetrated the population quite slowly' (*ibid.*). Some of Bulliet's conclusions may need calibration, but it would be interesting to build on his research to establish the popularity of the three names since 1967,[13] particularly to establish if the rise of the Islamist political parties in Turkey during the last two decades has had an impact on naming patterns.

A study of personal names in Hamadan, in midwestern Iran, offers similar conclusions about the coincidence of naming patterns with the socio-political currents operating in the country in 1963–88 (Habibi 1992). The study looks at three categories of names: Persian, Islamic and Arabic, and shows that, in 1963–73, Hamadan experienced a rise in Persian names among families belonging to the civil servant class, particularly female names. This increase is correlated with the White Revolution of 1963, the modernizing and secularizing tendencies of the Shah regime at the time, and the emphasis placed on pre-Islamic and old Persian values during this period. Later, these policies started to meet with resistance from the middle class and the intellectuals, a fact reflected in the rise of Islamic names for females among families belonging to the civil servant class in 1973–79, the years leading up to the Islamic Revolution. In 1979–83, the ratio of Persian names remained unchanged, although there was a slight drop in the ratio of Islamic names and a slight compensatory rise in the ratio of Arabic names. It is perhaps prudent not to read too much into these changes. What is interesting, however, is the rise of Persian names to their highest levels and the decline of Islamic names to their lowest levels in 1983–85. This coincides with the height of the Iran–Iraq war. It is possible that this swing in naming patterns marks a strengthening of Persian national identity, but this does not explain the drop in the popularity of Islamic names, or the fact that the popularity of Arabic names remained constant during this period.[14] Further work is needed to resolve this issue, but it seems pretty certain that names in Iran, like in Turkey,[15] can be an important source for constructing the relationship between language and national identity. In addition, changes in naming patterns act as an 'early warning system'; they signal changes in the socio-political currents at work in national or group identity.

I am not aware of similar studies for the Arabic-speaking countries. However, it would be surprising if the results of future studies for this part of the Middle East were any different. It is, therefore, certain that changes in naming patterns will be found to coincide with socio-political changes for any selected population. It is, for example, possible that a shift from non-Islamic to Islamic naming patterns would be exhibited for most Arabic-speaking countries during the last two decades as a result of the resurgence of Islam during this period. It is also possible that this shift would be marked more in male names than in female names. The text of the Qur'an has been recently mined to look for Islamic names. In a small circle of friends I know, there is one *Nồr* (light), two *ầyas* (sign from God or verse in the Qur'an), one *ầlà'* (favour from God) and a *Tasnầm* (name of a river in Paradise), all of which are female names. Also, one should not be surprised if, in some populations, the names of some modern leaders do make an appearance to express strongly held political views, for example Saddam.[16] And, finally, one would need to recognize that, when it comes to naming, the Arabic-speaking world is not a culturally homogenous area. Differences will exist according to country, region, class, education, tribal origin, religion, sect, education and many others.

Conclusion: re-constructing construction

In the literature on nationalism, construction is a loaded term. It is sometimes used to reject the antiquity of the nation (perennialism) or its organic conception as a 'social' given of the natural order of things (primordialism). Construction in this latter sense is a metaphor for saying that the nation is the outcome of modernity. This is the closest meaning to Gellner's understanding of the term (1983). However, some writers use 'construction' to argue that the nation is not just a product of modernity, but a discursive artefact, the result of a print community based on the vernacular, literature and the spread of journalism (Anderson 1991). Yet, others argue, more strongly, that the nation is an invention or creation that involves a high degree of social engineering and manipulation (Hobsbawm 1990).

In my own research on the Arabic language and national identity, I started as a convinced constructionist in Gellner's sense. In one way, I still subscribe to this view insofar as it rejects the perennialist and primordialist claims of the nation. But, in another way, I no longer agree with Gellner's view insofar as it claims that nations are *the* product of modernity. It is in my view possible to hold these two positions while still subscribing to a 'constructionist' view of the nation. But 'construction' here needs to be understood differently from the meanings outlined above. In particular, it needs to be distinguished from the notion of invention, which in the linguistic construction of the nation may be exemplified by the Sun-Language Theory, a concoction of fantasy and wishful thinking about the origins of Turkish.[17] This is a paradigm example of invention, manufacturing and pure myth-making. Discussing the role of myth in nationalist thinking, Schöpflin states that invention and imagination have 'clear and unavoidable limits' (1997: 26) which, he suggests, are determined by resonance. For a myth to resonate, we are told, it cannot be made out of 'false material' and it 'has to have some relationship with the memory of the collectivity that has fashioned it' (*ibid.*). Resonance is not empistemologically or methodologically problem free; however, by insisting that construction is not made out of material that is patently false or that lacks a basis in memory, we can put some limits on construction.

My research on the Arabic language and national identity has further led me to appreciate some of the merits of the ethno-symbolist conception of the nation. In particular, the fact that this paradigm allows one to talk about the modernity of the nation – with its socio-political and economic imperatives – while, at the same time, engaging the cultural and symbolic repertoire of a community to trace its continuity back in history. For a linguist who is interested in national identity, this ethno-symbolism provides a basis for moving the discussion of language from purely communicative functionality to include the rich terrain of symbolic meaning. It also allows for a fruitful articulation of synchrony with diachrony. But to do this we will need to release 'construction' from the attempts to box it terminologically. In other words, we need to rehabilitate 'construction' lexically to allow it to range over a wide semantic field.

Freed in this manner, construction can refer to the selection and shaping of data to support a particular view, position or interpretation. This will inevitably involve a degree of manipulation, even arbitrariness, as for example in the selection of script or forms of the standard language; but, to be successful, construction will also have to involve a commitment to resonance to commend the view, position or interpretation in question to the target audience, particularly when mobilization, as in nation building, is at stake.

Notes

1 This is a revised paper of a plenary talk delivered at the 14th AILA Triennial World Congress, University of Wisconsin-Madison, July 2005. The author wishes to thank the Leverholme Trust for their Major Research Fellowship, which enabled him to conduct this research.
2 Commenting on this aspect of identity, Smith writes: 'Perhaps the present widespread concern with identity is part of a broader trend of contemporary individualism; it may, equally, reflect the anxiety and alienation of many people in an increasingly fragmented world' (2001: 17).

3 In his study of ideology as discourse, Thompson asks, 'How can we pretend to stand above the fray, aloofly assessing the discourse of others, when our interpretation is but another interpretation, no different in principle from the interpretations of those whose discourse we seek to assess?' (1984: 12). This question is even more relevant when the target of interpretation is 'identity' and, in some cases, our own discourse on it.

4 See Ben-Rafael *et al.* (2004) in which Arabic is shown to be the dominant language in the linguistic landscape of East Jerusalem, with Hebrew coming as a distant third after English.

5 See Daston and Galison (1992) for an interesting discussion of the image of objectivity in scientific discourse.

6 Witness the fact that the Danish letters *œ* and *ø* were rendered as *ä* and *ö* in Swedish (see Vikør 2000: 109).

7 Urdu is written in a Persian form of the Arabic script. Hindi is written in Devanagari script.

8 The difference between the two pronunciations is less marked than the difference between the American and British English pronunciations of 'tomato'.

9 See Greenberg (2004) for the disintegration of Serbo-Croatian after the dissolution of Yugoslavia in 1991.

10 See Naùr (1996) for the social and political meanings of this term.

11 Blommaert adds: 'My own choice to identify the language of Flanders as "Flemish Dutch" would be seen by some to imply that Flemish is seen as a dialect (substandard, inferior) variety of Dutch. They would suggest ... "Flemish/Dutch", a term stressing the identity and equivalence of Flemish to Dutch' (1996: 254).

12 The term 'Federal' in the name of Iraq addresses Kurdish and, to a lesser extent, Shi'a aspiration for self-rule in the areas where they form a demographic majority. Sunni Iraqis oppose this. The use of the term 'Islamic' is supported mainly by Shi'a, who wish to make Islam the basic source of law in the new republic. The absence of the term 'Arab' from the name of the country is intended to address Kurdish fears of marginalization as a national group in the new republic.

13 For information on recent name-giving trends in Turkey see Başğöz (1985).

14 Bulliet has this to say about the decline in religious names in Iran which coincided with the reign of Reza Shah: 'The decline [in religious names in Iran] temporarily reverses in the pre-revolutionary years of the mid-1970s, when Islam became a rallying point for those opposed to the tyranny of Reza Shah's son, Mohammad Reza Shah. This brief resurgence of "Islamic" naming peaked around 1977. Then the decline resumed despite the creation of the Islamic Republic two years later and the great popularity of Ayatollah Khomeini. If this indicator should prove an accurate harbinger of future developments, the Iranian Revolution will ultimately be seen as the point of transition from tyranny to democracy, rather than from secularism to theocracy' (Bulliet 2004: 78).

15 Commenting on name-giving patterns in Massachusetts, Turkey and Iran, Bulliet reached the following conclusion: 'the beginning of a steady decline in the popularity of religious names coincides with a strong secular assertion of collective identity: the onset of republican revolutionary ferment in the 1770s in Massachusetts, the beginning of the *tanzimat* reform movement in 1939 in Turkey (the Ottoman Empire) and Reza Shah Pahlavi's of Persian nationalism and condemnation of traditional religious practices, such as the complete veiling of women, in Iran in the early the early 1930s' (Bulliet 2004: 77).

16 In Jordan, it is reported that 394 males were named Saddam after the first Gulf war in 1991. After the fall of Saddam in 2003, the government gave the parents the opportunity to change these names; a rare offer where name changes are extremely difficult.

17 Aytürk explains the genesis of this theory as follows: 'The rudiment of the Sun-Language Theory appeared ... in the last months of 1935 and the theory was proclaimed in its final form in 1936, receiving the blessings and active support of the Turkish government at the Third Language Congress in the late 1936. To put it briefly, the Sun-Language Theory was a bewildering combination of historical comparative philology, various elements from

psychological theories of the nineteenth century and psychoanalytical themes from ... Freud and ... Jung. ... In prehistoric times, the theory goes, the Turkic peoples of Central Asia had established an illustrious civilization; but as a result of climatic changes and a severe draught they started to emigrate in all directions, transmitting their Neolithic civilization to other peoples of the world. Naturally, it was assumed, the ancient form of the Turkish that these conquering emigrants spoke was also carried with them and contributed to every primitive language the most important concepts necessary for abstract thought as loanwords.

An interesting component of the Sun-Language Theory was the role of the sun in the birth of the language ... It was claimed that language was born as an act of worship, as part of an ancient Turkic ritual in the cult of the sun. Those Central Asian worshippers, who wanted to salute the omnipotence of the sun and its life-giving qualities, had done so by transforming their meaningless blabbering into a coherent set of ritual utterings' (2004: 16–17). See also Lewis (1999: 57–74).

References

Abd-el-Jawad, H. (1986), 'A linguistic and sociocultural study of personal names in Jordan', *Anthropological Linguistics*, 28, 80–94.

Ager, D. (1996), *'Francophonie' in the 1990s: Problems and Opportunities*. Cleveland: Multilingual Matters.

Anderson, B. (1991), *Imagined Communities: Reflections on the Origin and Spread of Nationalism*. London and New York: Verso.

Aytürk, İ. (2004), 'Turkish linguists against the west: the origins of linguistic nationalism in Ataturk's Turkey', *Middle Eastern Studies*, 40, 1–25.

Başgöz, İ. (1985), 'The name and society: a case study of personal names in Turkey', in G. Jarring and S. Rosén (eds), *Altaistic Studies* (Konferenser 12), 1–14, Stockholm.

Baugh, J. (2000), *Beyond Ebonics: Linguistic Pride and Racial Prejudice*. New York: Oxford University Press.

Bauman, Z. (2004), *Identity*. Cambridge: Polity.

Ben-Rafael, E., Shohamy, E., Amara, M. A. and Trumper-Hecht, N. (2004), Linguistic Landscape and Multiculturalism: A Jewish-Arab Comparative Study. Tel Aviv University: The Tami Steinmetz Centre for Peace Research.

Benson, P. (2001), *Ethnocentricism and the English Dictionary*. London and New York: Routledge.

Blommaert, J. (1996), 'Language and nationalism: comparing Flanders with Tanzania', *Nations and Nationalism*, 2, 235–56.

Borg, A. and Kressel, G. M. (2001), 'Bedouin names in the Negev and Sinai', *Zeitschrift für Arabische Linguistik*, 40, 32–70.

Bulliet, R. W. (1978), 'First names and political change in Turkey', *International Journal of Middle Eastern Studies*, 9, 489–95.

— (2004), *The Case for Islamo-Christian Civilization*. New York: Columbia University Press.

Carmichael, C. (2000), 'A people exit and that people has its language: language and nationalism in the Balkans', in S. Barbour and C. Carmichael (eds), *Language and Nationalism in Europe*. Oxford: Oxford University Press, pp. 221–39.

Cheshin, A. S., Hutman, B. and Melamed, A. (1999), *Separate an Unequal: The Inside Story of Israeli Rule in East Jerusalem*. Cambridge, MA: Harvard University Press.

Chilton, P. (2004), *Analysing Political Discourse: Theory and Practice*. London and New York: Routledge.

Cooper, R. (1989), *Language Planning and Social Change*. Cambridge: Cambridge University Press.

Coulmas, F. (1994), 'Language policy and language planning: political perspectives', *Annual*

Review of Applied Linguistics, 14, 34–52.

Daston, L. and Galison, P. (1992), 'The image of objectivity', *Representations*, 40, 81–128.

Durand, J. (1996), 'Linguistic purification, the French nation-state and the linguist', in C. Hoffmann (ed.), *Language, Culture and Communication in Contemporary Europe*. Clevedon: Multilingual Matters, pp. 75–92.

Edwards, J. (1985), *Language, Society and Identity*. Oxford and New York: Basil Blackwell in association with London: Andre Deutsch.

Eminov, A. (1997), *Turkish and Other Muslim Minorities in Bulgaria*. London: Hurst & Company.

al-Farah, W. (2004), 'A common mistake that must be corrected: why are we called Greek when we are Arab Orthodox? (Khaña' dàrij yajib taùþàþuh: li-màdhà kalimat al-râm wa-naþnu 'arab utrdhudux?)', *Al-Nashra*, Vol. 32: 30–2 (The Royal Institute of Religious Studies, Jordan).

Gal, S. (1998), 'Multiplicity and contention among language ideologies', in B. B. Schieffelin, K. A. Woolard and P. V. Kroskrity (eds), *Language Ideologies: Practice and Theory*. New York and Oxford: Oxford University Press, pp. 317–31.

Gardner, S. (1994), 'Generations of Change in Name-giving', in Y. Suleiman (ed.), *Arabic Sociolinguistics: Issues and Perspectives*. Richmond, Surrey: Curzon Press, pp. 101–25.

Gellner, E. (1983), *Nations and Nationalism*. Oxford: Basil Blackwell.

Gilson, E. H. (1986), 'Introduction of new writing systems: the Turkish case', in N. Schweda-Nicholson (ed.), *Languages in the International Perspective*. Norwood, New Jersey: Ablex Publishing Corporation, pp. 23–40.

Gramsci, A. (1985), *Selections from Cultural Writings*, translated from the Italian by W. Boelhower. London: Lawrence & Wishart.

Greenberg, R. D. (2004), *Language and Identity in the Balkans: Serbo-Croatian and its Disintegration*. Oxford: Oxford University Press.

Habibi, N. (1992), 'Popularity of Islamic and Persian names in Iran before and after the Islamic revolution', *International Journal of Middle Eastern Studies*, 24, 253–60.

Heller, M. (1995), 'Code-switching and the politics of language', in L. Milroy and P. Muysken (eds), *One Speaker, Two Languages: Cross-disciplinary Perspectives on Code-Switching*. Cambridge: Cambridge University Press, pp. 158–74.

Hobsbawm, E. (1990), *Nations and Nationalism since 1870*. Cambridge: Cambridge University Press.

Howell, R. B. (2000), 'The low countries: a study in sharply contrasting nationalisms', in S. Barbour and C. Carmichael (eds), *Language and Nationalism in Europe*. Oxford: Oxford University Press, pp. 130–50.

Hsiau, A. (1997), 'Language ideology in Taiwan: the KMT's language policy, the Tai-yü language movement, and ethnic politics', *Journal of Multilingual and Multicultural Development*, 18, 302–15.

Ivanić, R. (1998), *Writing and Identity: The Discoursal Construction of Identity in Academic Writing*. Amsterdam and Philadelphia: John Benjamins.

Joseph, J. E. (2004), *Language and Identity: National, Ethnic, Religious*. Houndmills, Basingstoke and New York: Palgrave Macmillan.

Kamusella, T. D. I. (2001), 'Language as an instrument of nationalism in central Europe', *Nations and Nationalism*, 7, 235–51.

Katriel, T. (1986), *Talking Straight: Dugri Speech in Israeli Sabra Culture*. Cambridge: Cambridge University Press.

Kedourie, E. (1966), *Nationalism*. London: Hutchinson University Library.

Landry, R. and Bourhis, R. Y. (1997), 'Linguistic landscape and ethnolinguistic vitality: an empirical study', *Journal of Language and Social Psychology*, Vol. 16, 23–49.

Le Page, R. B. and Tabouret-Keller, A. (1982), 'Models and stereotypes of ethnicity and language', *Journal of Multilingual and Multicultural Development*, Vol. 3, 161–92.

Lewis, G. (1999), *The Turkish Language Reform: A Catastrophic Success*. Oxford: Oxford University Press.

Lodge, A. (1998), 'French is a logical language', in L. Bauer and P. Trudgill (eds), *Language Myths*. London: Penguin Books, pp. 23–31.

Maalouf, A. (1998), *Leo the African*, translated from the French by Peter Sluglett. London: Quartet Books.

— (2000), *On Identity*, translated from the French by Barbara Bray. London: The Harvill Press.

Mar-Molinero, C. (2000), 'The Iberian peninsula: conflicting linguistic nationalisms', in S. Barbour and C. Carmichael (eds), *Language and Nationalism in Europe*. Oxford: Oxford University Press, pp. 83–104.

May, S. (2001), *Language and Minority Rights: Ethnicity, Nationalism and the Politics of Language*. Harlow, England: Longman.

Morris, N. (1996), 'Language and identity in twentieth century Puerto Rico', *Journal of Multilingual and Multicultural Development*, 17, 17–32.

Naùr, M. (1996), *The Term Strangers in the Discourse of Some Lebanese about the Civil War (al-Ghurabà' fã Khañàb' lubnàniyyãn 'an al-ḫarb al-ahliyya)*. Beirut: Dàr Al-Sàqã.

Ngom, F. (2002), 'Linguistic resistance in the Murid speech community in Senegal', *Journal of Multilingual and Multicultural Development*, 23, 214–26.

Ruzza, C. (2000), 'Language and nationalism in Italy: language as a weak marker of identity', in S. Barbour and C. Carmichael (eds), *Language and Nationalism in Europe*. Oxford: Oxford University Press, pp. 168–82.

Schieffelin, B. B. and Doucet, R. C. (1998), 'The "real" Haitian creole: ideology, metalinguistics and orthographic choices', in B. B. Schieffelin, K. A. Woolard and P. V. Kroskrity (eds), *Language Ideologies: Practice and Theory*. New York and Oxford: Oxford University Press, pp. 285–316.

Schmid, C. L. (2001), *The Politics of Language: Conflict, Identity and Cultural Pluralism in Comparative Perspective*. Oxford: Oxford University Press.

Schöpflin, G. (1997), 'The functions of myth and the taxonomy of myths', in G. Hosking and G. Schöpflin (eds), *Myths and Nationhood*. London: Hurst & Company, pp. 19–35.

Semmerling, T. J. (2004), *Israeli and Palestinian Postcards: Presentations of National Self*. Austin: University of Texas Press.

Smith, A. D. (1991), *National Identity*. London: Penguin.

— (2001), *Nationalism*. Cambridge: Polity.

Spolsky, B. and Cooper, R. (1991), *The Languages of Jerusalem*. Oxford: Clarendon Press.

Suleiman, Y. (2003), *The Arabic Language and National Identity: A Study in Ideology*. Washington DC: Georgetown University Press.

— (2004), *A War of Words: Language and Conflict in the Middle East*. Cambridge: Cambridge University Press.

Thompson, J. B. (1984), *Studies in the Theory of Ideology*. Cambridge: Polity Press.

Törnquist-Plewa, B. (2000), 'Contrasting ethnic nationalisms: eastern central Europe', in S. Barbour and C. Carmichael (eds), *Language and Nationalism in Europe*. Oxford: Oxford University Press, pp. 183–220.

Trudgill, P. (2000), 'Greece and European Turkey: from religious to ethnic identity', in S. Barbour and C. Carmichael (eds), *Language and Nationalism in Europe*. Oxford: Oxford University Press, pp. 240–63.

Urla, J. (1988), 'Ethnic protests and social planning: a look at Basque language revival', *Cultural Anthropology*, 1, 379–94.

— (1993), 'Contesting modernities: language standardization and the production of an ancient/modern Basque culture', *Critique of Anthropology*, 13, 101–18.

Vikør, L. S. (2000), 'Northern Europe: languages as prime markers of ethnic and national identity', in S. Barbour and C. Carmichael (eds), *Language and Nationalism in Europe*. Oxford: Oxford University Press, pp. 105–29.

Wassink, A. B. and Curzan, A. (2004), 'Addressing ideologies around African American English', *Journal of English Linguistics*, 32, 171–85.

Watson, C. (1996), 'Folklore and Basque nationalism: language, myth, reality', *Nations and*

Nationalism, 2, 17–34.

Wodak, R., de Cilla, R., Reisigl, M. and Liebhart, A. H. (1999), *The Discursive Construction of National Identity* (translated by Richard Mitten). Edinburgh: Edinburgh University Press.

Woolard, K. A. and Schieffelin, B. B. (1994), 'Language ideology', *Annual Review of Anthropology*, 32, 55–82.

Part II

Identity in Micro-sociolinguistics

5 English pronunciation and second language speaker identity

Jennifer Jenkins

Introduction

As a result of the spread of English across the countries of the Expanding Circle[1] (Kachru 1992) over the past three decades, the English language has become the world's principal lingua franca. Its non-native speakers now heavily outnumber its native speakers (Graddol 1997, 1999; Crystal 2003) and it has been estimated that 80 per cent of communication involving non-native speakers of English involves no native speakers at all (Benecke 1991: 54). Although some linguists consider the spread of English to pose a threat to the vitality of other languages (see, e.g. Phillipson 2003), the majority take an entirely positive view of the increasing number of functions that English performs in its role as the primary language of international communication.

The same cannot be said, on the other hand, of English forms. Non-native speaker (NNS) divergences from one or other of the two main Inner Circle native speaker (NS) varieties, American English or British English and their prestige accents, General American (GA) or Received Pronunciation (RP), continue to be regarded as signs of deficient learning. Suggestions that these divergent forms should be considered candidates for NNS-led features of emerging English as a Lingua Franca[2] (ELF) varieties rather than errors in English as a Native Language (ENL) are proving controversial (see Jenkins 2005a). Negative reactions have been particularly forthcoming in respect of pronunciation, although at present it is not clear whether this is because accent attitudes are more entrenched and resistant to change than attitudes towards the other language levels (see Lippi-Green 1997; Bonfiglio 2002), or because pronunciation is the first language level for which detailed ELF proposals have been made.

The issue, it seems, is one of the 'legitimacy' of ELF pronunciation. As Mauranen (2003) observes, the original causes of the spread of English, i.e. British colonialism and, later, the economic and political supremacy of the United States, 'have ceased to be the prime motivation for the continued spread of the language' (513). Meanwhile, internationally, the ownership of lingua franca English has shifted to its NNSs (Widdowson 1994; Ammon 2003). Nevertheless, legitimacy, it seems, is somewhat paradoxically still 'granted' by

NSs of English and their NNS admirers only to those English accents which originate with NSs (in particular, GA and RP).

In his discussion of the 'legitimate and illegitimate offspring of English', Mufwene (2001: 107) points out that both the indigenized Englishes of the Outer Circle and English-based Creoles are typically characterized as 'illegitimate' because of their contact with African languages. NS Englishes, by contrast, are considered 'legitimate' because of a mistaken belief in their evolution from Old English without 'contamination' by other languages. This same contamination metaphor obtains for current attitudes towards ELF accents, the only difference being that contamination here refers to influence from ELF speakers' first languages. In the second language acquisition literature, this influence is presented in deficit terms as either 'L1 transfer' or, more pejoratively, 'L1 interference'. It is considered an impediment to the acquisition of 'good' (i.e. nativelike) English. And in terms of pronunciation teaching, it is generally treated by means of 'accent reduction', an approach which aims to rid learners of L1 influence on their English accents in order to render their accents more intelligible and acceptable to NS listeners.

Whether a wholesale accent reduction approach is either desirable or likely to succeed is debatable and beyond the scope of this chapter, although for those learners who will be interacting in the future mainly with NSs, intelligibility for NS listeners is undoubtedly critical. ELF interaction contexts are, however, an altogether different matter. Here, learners will in the main be interacting with other NNSs from different L1s than their own, and the minority of NSs taking part in ELF interactions cannot expect the NNS majority to make pronunciation adjustments for their benefit. Now it is intelligibility for other NNSs that is paramount, and we cannot assume that what is critical for NS listeners is identical in respect of NNS listeners. Indeed, research carried out from the 1970s to the 1990s involving both NSs and NNSs (e.g. Smith and Rafiqzad 1979; Smith and Bisazza 1982; Smith and Nelson 1985; Smith 1992) has demonstrated that NS accents are by no means the most intelligible to NNS ears.

Building on the latter research, I investigated pronunciation intelligibility among NNSs from Expanding Circle contexts. From my findings, I proposed the Lingua Franca Core (LFC), a revised pronunciation syllabus which targets for production those features of GA and RP which were found in my studies to be crucial in promoting intelligible pronunciation in ELF interactions. The following section provides a brief outline of my ELF intelligibility research and of the proposed LFC. It is followed by a discussion of the ambivalent responses of many NNSs to the proposal. Finally, I consider some findings of my current research project, whose overall aim is to investigate the role of accent identity and accent attitudes in these responses, in order to weigh up the feasibility of an ELF approach to pronunciation.

Assessing ELF pronunciation intelligibility

The aim of the ELF pronunciation research was primarily to identify those pronunciation features, both segmental and suprasegmental, which obstruct mutual intelligibility in NNS–NNS interaction if they are not pronounced in a target-like (NS) manner. It also investigated the extent to which NNSs are aware of any such problematic features in their English accents, and able to accommodate to a given interlocutor by adjusting such features appropriately. The research, it was hoped, would enable those features that were regularly and systematically 'mispronounced', and were found *not* to obstruct intelligibility for another NNS, to be considered legitimate features of the respective NNS accent variety instead of errors. This would, in turn, I believed, resolve the conflict between the need for international intelligibility and respect for the (perceived) desire of many NNSs to project their L1 identity in their L2 English pronunciation (see for example, McKay 2002: 71).

Two main sets of data were collected over a period of four years: miscommunication data and accommodation data. The former were collected by means of field notes and recordings of exchanges in classroom and social settings. The latter were collected from recorded paired interactions where participants carried out two task types, namely a social interaction (in effect a casual chat) and an information exchange in which only the successful transfer of information would lead to the successful resolution of a problem. Both the miscommunication and accommodation data collection were followed up, where feasible, with questionnaires and interviews.

In the case of the miscommunication data, all breakdowns in communication were analysed – often by the participants as well as the researcher – in order to isolate those breakdowns that had been caused by divergences from the target pronunciation, and to distinguish these from divergences which had not impeded successful communication. In the case of the accommodation data, the degree and type of adjustments to pronunciation were compared across the two task types. Here the interest was in whether adjustments were made in the information exchange task in order to prevent pronunciation-based intelligibility problems for the interlocutor, and if so, whether these adjustments matched the items which had emerged in the miscommunication data as obstructing intelligibility (see Jenkins 2000 for full details).

From an analysis of all the data, the items found in a traditional pronunciation syllabus were assigned to 'core' and 'non-core' categories. The core category, subsequently called the 'Lingua Franca Core', consisted of those pronunciation features which emerged from the research as needing to be pronounced in a manner close to the NS target to ensure that pronunciation would be intelligible to another NNS from a different L1 (i.e. in ELF communication). These features are shown in Table 5.1 in which the core features in the right-hand column are compared with those traditionally taught for EFL/ESL (English as a Foreign/Second Language) in the middle column (i.e. for NNS-NS communication).

Table 5.1 EFL/ESL and ELF pronunciation targets: core features

	EFL/ESL target Traditional syllabus	ELF target Lingua Franca Core
1. The consonantal inventory	• all sounds	• all sounds except /θ/, /ð/ and [ɬ]
	• RP non-rhotic /r/ GA rhotic /r/	• rhotic /r/ only
	• RP intervocalic [t] GA intervocalic [r]	• intervocalic [t] only
2. Phonetic requirements	• rarely specified	• aspiration after /p/ /t/ /k/ • appropriate vowel length before fortis/lenis consonants
3. Consonant clusters	• all word positions	• word initially, word medially
4. Vowel quantity	• long-short contrast	• long-short contrast
5. Tonic (nuclear) stress	• important	• critical

Adapted from Jenkins 2002: 99

Those features designated non-core, it was argued, while remaining important in NS–NNS communication (both ESL and EFL), were not necessary in ELF contexts, and any systematic divergences from the NS target could (and should) be considered legitimate regional *L2* English pronunciation features. The features identified as non-core were those shown in Table 5.2, where the middle column indicates their importance in traditional pronunciation syllabuses and the right-hand column provides comments indicating why they are unimportant as targets in ELF. In effect, then, pronunciation error was being redefined for the purposes of ELF.

Table 5.2 EFL/ESL and ELF pronunciation targets: The non-core features

	EFL/ESL target Traditional syllabus	ELF target Lingua Franca Core
1. Vowel quality	• close to RP or GA	• L2 (consistent) regional qualities
2. Weak forms	• essential	• unhelpful to intelligibility
3. Features of connected speech	• all	• inconsequential or unhelpful
4. Stress-timed rhythm	• important	• unnecessary
5. Word stress	• critical	• can reduce flexibility / unteachable
6. Pitch movement	• essential for indicating attitudes and grammar	• unnecessary / unteachable

Adapted from Jenkins 2002: 99

In addition, a case was made for developing learners' accommodation skills so that they would be in a better position to adjust their pronunciation in accordance with the needs of a specific interlocutor. So, for example, an Italian speaker of English would need to acquire the sound /h/ and use it in words such as 'house' and 'head' when interacting with the majority of NNSs from other L1s. However, if he or she were communicating in English with another Italian or with, e.g. a French speaker of English (whose L1 likewise has no /h/ sound), then production of this sound would not be necessary for intelligibility, despite the fact that it is a core feature for ELF.

All this, it was argued, would render pronunciation teaching more relevant and realistic for those learners who intended to be ELF users, i.e. to communicate with other NNSs rather than with NSs. Classroom time for production could be focused on the LFC items (essentially the majority of consonant sounds, vowel length contrasts, word initial and medial consonant clusters and tonic stress placement and production). Meanwhile, the non-core items (certain consonants, vowel quality, weak forms and other features of connected speech, word stress, pitch movement and stress-timing) could be relegated to activities to promote reception only. In addition, it was argued, this approach would resolve the intelligibility–identity problem by enabling NNSs both to express their L1 identity and membership of the international ELF community in their pronunciation, while remaining secure in the knowledge that their accent was intelligible to their ELF interlocutor(s).

Reactions to the ELF pronunciation proposals

The ELF intelligibility principle per se (i.e. the notion of prioritizing mutual intelligibility for NNSs in NNS–NNS communication) has proved to be largely uncontroversial. A small number of NS scholars have questioned certain of the LFC's exemptions. Their concerns, however, have been based predominantly on their own (NS) intuitions and anecdote or, occasionally, on evidence drawn from experimental studies such as word recognition tests, or from research into NS–NNS interaction, rather than on empirical evidence drawn from authentic NNS–NNS interaction.[3]

A different picture emerges, however, when we turn to NNS reactions, especially among teachers, to the principle of redefining pronunciation error in order to embrace Expanding Circle speakers' accent varieties. Many NNS teachers and learners appear from their responses to be strongly opposed to the idea of abandoning NS pronunciation norms in order to identify accent-wise with their own L1 accent group, and rarely even consider identification with a more broadly-based international ELF speech community. The following are typical examples. The first response is from a German teacher of English who was taking part in an open forum discussion of my book, *The Phonology of English as an International Language* (2000) at the 2001 IATEFL[4] conference (recorded, transcribed and reported in Vaughan-Rees 2001):

I had a discussion with some of my adult students about global English before I came here and they're wondering which model they should follow in pronunciation. Well I told them that I'd very soon be going to the IATEFL conference and I'd learn much more about that.

> And next week, when I give them the good news you don't have to worry so much any more, these are the core features, I know exactly what they're going to say, almost all of them; they're going to say 'no, we want to know exactly how we have to pronounce it' (15).

The notion of RP as the 'correct' pronunciation for German learners of English is evidently so entrenched that the speaker does not feel it necessary to qualify 'exactly how we have to pronounce it' in any way. A teacher from Japan emailed me after the same conference. Her students expressed a similar view to the anticipated reaction of the German teacher's students, although like many others, she also sounds a note of ambivalence:

> Upon return, I immediately shared your ideas with my students. They were very interested. They still say they would try to acquire a native-like pronunciation, but they enjoy an acknowledgement of their 'human right' NOT to HAVE to sound native (emphasis in original).

The next example is from a Taiwanese teacher quoted in Holliday (2005):

> Although I did feel comfortable to be told that I did not have to be native-speaker like, I would definitely feel upset if I could not reach my own expectation in pronunciation. [...] I just wanted to draw attention to the psychological part, the feeling, how people feel about themselves in terms of speaking. [...] If we take Jenkins's view and tell them to stay where they are – you don't need to twist your tongue this way and that and it's perfectly all right to keep your accent – at some point, we would terribly upset the learners because they might want to. (9)

Similarly, two teachers of English in Austria (Hüttner and Kidd 2000), one an NNS, the other an NS, argue against the concept of an Austrian-English accent:

> The introduction of English as an international language in pronunciation teaching might encourage students to maintain – without any alterations – their current accent of English, which for the majority of our students will be 'Austrian English'. In our opinion, this would defeat the purpose of foreign language instruction. (76)

A noticeable feature of many reactions is that they reveal varying degrees of misinterpretation and misconception regarding what is being proposed. There is, for example, a widespread tendency to interpret the LFC as an invitation to teachers and learners to adopt an 'anything goes' approach to their pronunciation teaching and learning, and thus to promote pronunciation errors and fossilization. The Taiwanese teacher quoted above, for instance, interprets it to mean that her learners will 'stay where they are' rather than acquire an internationally intelligible Taiwanese-English accent. Likewise, the Austrian teachers fear that their students will retain their L1-influenced English 'without any alterations' (although they rightly go on to point out that one cause of this will be the current lack of adequate ELF descriptions and materials). This relates to a more fundamental misconception – the failure to grasp the essential distinction between EFL and ELF. An examination of the LFC's non-core features through an *English as a Foreign Language* lens inevitably leads to the conclusion that the LFC is promoting pronunciation errors rather than regional *English as a Lingua Franca* variants (see, for example, the confusions of these two targets by Sobkowiak 2003).

Another misconception is that the aim of the research underpinning the LCF was to simplify the learning process. In other words, my desire to provide a pronunciation syllabus that is more realistic and relevant in ELF contexts (by virtue of being grounded in NNSs' rather than NSs' needs) is mistakenly interpreted as an *a priori* intention to simplify the learning task. However, this was not so: any simplification is purely a welcome outcome of the research. So, for example, Szpyra-Kozlowska (2003) devotes an entire article to an analysis of the features of the LFC in terms of their difficulties for Polish learners. She then concludes that 'the LFC comprises many features which, on the one and [*sic*], diminish the teaching/learning load for Poles, but on the other hand, constitute no simplification of this task at all' (207). This may be true, but learning difficulty per se has never been the reason for teaching or not teaching specific L2 features.

A further misconception is that the LFC is a model for imitation, whereas it is in fact a core of pronunciation features which occur in much successful ELF (NNS–NNS) communication, and whose absence is likely to lead to miscommunication if L2 speakers do not share the same substituted form. Outside the core areas (see Table 5.1 above), speakers are free to transfer as they wish from their L1, with the resulting systematic forms (once described and codified) being variants of their local ELF accent (e.g. Korean English, Polish English) rather than errors in relation to an NS accent. Obviously, the role of accommodation is paramount here, but it tends to be overlooked by those who misunderstand the basis of the LFC in the first place. Other misconceptions include the claims that those who promote the LFC are prescribing it for all learners rather than offering a choice between the LFC and an NS accent, and that the LFC is an attempt to prevent L2 speakers of English being taken seriously (see Jenkins 2005c).

Clearly, then, the LFC proposals have caused a certain amount of anxiety and unease, part but not all of which has been fuelled by various misinterpretations of its intent. Even those NNSs who offer their support to the principle of local but internationally intelligible accents reveal a degree of ambivalence when it comes to putting their beliefs into practice in their classrooms (see, for example, the findings of Decke-Cornill 2003; Grau 2005). Although Timmis (2002) considers that NNS teachers are slowly moving away from native-speaker norms, the bulk of documented NNS teachers', learners and other users' responses to the LFC's principle of an internationally intelligible accent which shows the accent of their country, have so far been at best ambiguous. Their attachment to a native-like accent, at least above the level of consciousness, appears to remain largely intact. To this extent, little has changed in the 12 years since Andreasson (1994) argued that:

> [I]n the Expanding Circle...the ideal goal is to imitate the native speaker of the standard language as closely as possible... It would, therefore, be far from a compliment to tell a Spanish person that his or her variety is Spanish English. It would imply that his or her acquisition of the language left something to be desired. (402)

Despite the apparent strength of their support for native-like accents, however, teachers' and learners' levels of 'achievement' rarely match their attitude patterns. For example, in their study of the accent preferences of Austrian student teachers of English, Dalton-Puffer *et al.* (1997) found that while the stated preference of their participants was overwhelmingly for an RP or GA accent rather than for a local Austrian-English accent, it was the latter which they achieved. 'Clearly', the authors point out, 'there must be other factors exerting an influence on students' level of achievement'. They go on to argue that because pronunciation is 'the aspect of language that most obviously expresses social identity and group membership, further studies will also have to incorporate more deeply-seated socio-psychological factors connected to questions of "self"and identification with the target group' (126). It seems possible, then, that below the level of consciousness there may be a desire to express L1 group identity by means of retaining some aspects of the L1 accent in the L2, and that this may conflict with a conscious belief that a native-like accent is somehow better. It is with such 'questions of "self" and identification with the target group' that the rest of this paper is concerned.

Reappraisal

In his in-depth study of the linguistic situation in Hong Kong, Joseph (2004) makes a number of points that are of direct relevance to the current discussion. He points to the anxiety of its ethnic Chinese over Hong Kong English: '[w]ith few exceptions, it is linguists who talk about this language. Its speakers scoff at the notion that there is anything other than "good English" (represented by the overseas standard) and the "bad English" of their compatriots' (139). Joseph links the prevailing attitude with the emergence of distinctive Hong Kong features, and argues that its success as a separate variety will depend in part on the desire of its speakers for the variety to be recognized. The problem is that 'the "emergence of Hong Kong English" and the "decline of English standards in Hong Kong" are *one and the same thing*, looked at from two different points of view' (147; emphasis in original). On the one hand, then, ethnic Chinese English speakers in Hong Kong are producers of Hong Kong English; on the other hand, it seems that they are receptive deniers of its existence. In other words, there is a dichotomy between their identity as Hong Kong English *producers* and their identity as Hong Kong English *interpreters*. The same dichotomy, I will later argue, obtains for ELF and, in particular, for ELF accents.

Joseph hints at prestige and status as being implicated in the ethnic Chinese response to the existence of a distinctive Hong Kong English. In a similar vein, Miller (2004) discusses the notion of a 'politics of speaking which implicates speaker and hearer in ways that are ideologically loaded, and which may be the basis of empowerment or discrimination' (291). She appeals to the notion of 'audibility' in order to explain the way in which speakers are positioned or – more importantly for the present context – position themselves through the use of a second language. Miller defines audibility as 'the degree to which speakers sound like, and are legitimated by, users of the dominant discourse', and cites the work of both Lippi-Green (1997) and Bourdieu (1977) in support of her argument. According to Lippi-Green, there are rewards for speakers who lose their L1 accent in their L2 English and sound more like the dominant NS majority. Meanwhile, looking at the issue from the opposite perspective, Bourdieu contends that there can be negative consequences for speakers who speak the L2 with a non-native accent, and that they may be evaluated negatively in terms not only of their accent but also of their social identity. Miller concludes that being understood in the L2 is not sufficient: 'sounding right' is also important. Although she is referring specifically to migrant students in Australian schools, her argument has direct relevance to ELF contexts. For as was indicated in the introduction to this paper, even in Expanding Circle contexts of use, where NSs form a very small minority, legitimate English is still widely considered by native and non-native speaker alike to be that which adheres to the norms of educated NSs.

Joseph (2004) warns linguists that we 'risk having only a very partial understanding of the linguistic situation if we dismiss the popular perception outright because it is contradicted by our "scientific" data' (160). We cannot ignore, for example, that at present in Hong Kong, the use of the term 'Hong Kong English' is interpreted as being derogatory, as referring to L2 speakers' mistakes in respect of the native standard language. The same could equally be said of attitudes to ELF varieties (Spanish English, Japanese English and the like). The key to the recognition of the linguistic distinctiveness of Hong Kong English, Joseph argues, is English teachers themselves:

> only if and when teachers come to recognise that the 'errors' in Hong Kong students' English (at least the regularly occurring ones) are precisely the points at which a distinct Hong Kong identity is expressed in the language, will a Hong Kong English genuinely begin to emerge and to be taken as a version of Standard English rather than as a departure from it. (161)

Again, the same obtains for ELF varieties.

In the light of both arguments made in the language and identity literature and the responses to the ELF pronunciation proposals, I am in the process of reconsidering the original aims of the ELF pronunciation research. The primary aim had been to find a means of ensuring mutual pronunciation intelligibility in NNS–NNS interaction. It was assumed that if the intelligibility argument was well made, teachers would wish to incorporate the research findings into their pronunciation teaching. Meanwhile, the existence of an ELF speech community and desire for ELF group membership were taken for granted. In other words, defining the ELF speech community was a given rather than an aim of the original research. From the responses, however, it is evident that many NNSs do not regard themselves in this way, and that had self-categorization been considered, the outcome may have been different. Intelligibility alone, then, has proved insufficient, while L1 identity in L2 English and attitudes towards L2 accents have proved to be rather more complex than was originally anticipated.

Introducing identity into the equation

To illustrate the new phase of the research on which I have embarked, I report briefly here on a study which is part of a much larger project (Jenkins, forthcoming). The project as a whole is attempting to assess the feasibility of ELF pronunciation teaching by gaining insights into teachers' and learners' perceptions of NNS and NS English accents. As well as the collection and analysis of documentary evidence, the project involves both direct and indirect methods. In addition to a series of in-depth interviews with NNS and NS English language teachers and teacher trainers/educators, the direct methods being used are primarily drawn from the perceptual dialectology approaches of folk linguistics research, particularly those of Preston and his colleagues (e.g. Niedzielski and Preston 2003). These methods include map tasks, ranking ELF accents (e.g. for correctness, intelligibility and employability), and comments by participants on the tasks they have performed, in order to bring to the surface their beliefs and practices in relation to the ELF accents which they have been evaluating. Indirect methods include modified matched guise tests and personal construct psychology techniques (Kelly 1991).

For the study presented here,[5] the method selected was the in-depth interview as a means of enabling me to enter into the participants' worlds, and experience their lives as L2 English speakers and teachers from their own perspectives (cf. McLeod 1994). This, I believed, would provide valuable insights and indicate fruitful areas to follow up during the rest of the project.

The interviews lasted approximately 60 minutes, although the precise length was determined by each participant's desire to speak, and some were considerably longer. The final (unrecorded) part consisted of the interviewer's more detailed explanation to the participant of the purpose of the interview as a prelude to seeking consent to use the recorded data for academic study and publication. This elicited further, sometimes substantial commentary from the participants, and with hindsight it would have been wise to leave the recording equipment running to the very end of each session. The eight NNS teachers who participated were all female, and came from Italy (E and G), Japan (A and H), Malaysia (B), Poland (C and F) and Spain (D).[6] They were all proficient speakers of English, all had university first degrees (all except two also had master's degrees, and three were studying for doctorates). Their teaching experience ranged from pre-service in one case (A) to 17 years in another (H).

The interviews followed a rough pattern, with unscripted prompts being used flexibly to cover a range of issues based on responses to the ELF pronunciation proposals and the language and identity literature. These included the participants' attitudes to/beliefs about NNS and NS English accents, their level of identification with NNS and NS accents, their perceptions of others' attitudes and identifications, and any experiences they had had where they felt their accent was involved. My aim was to understand the situation from the participants' perspective and, in the process, uncover some of the subconscious causes of their attitudes. For this reason, I often returned to a topic several times with differently-worded prompts, which also had the effect of highlighting any contradictions which were emerging.

One further factor which I kept in mind was that it was important for the participants to gain some benefit from participating in a study that had such direct relevance to their own lives. From various comments at the end of the interview, this was the case for the majority. For example, participant H volunteered:

... I recognised before this interview I still have the native-like model [i.e. as goal], but now further recognition about the contradiction in terms of my view... So yeah, that's a good interview, and I can reflect on my idea in terms of EIL,[7] yeah.

The interviews were recorded, transcribed, coded and subsequently categorized on the basis of the main themes that emerged: the participants' accent attitudes, their perceived effects of 'accent experiences' on their attitudes/identity and their perspective on teaching ELF accents. Of these, the first and third themes are self-evident. The second theme, that of participants' perceived effects of their educational and social experiences on their ELF accent attitudes, might not seem to warrant the status of a main category. However, the data themselves proved otherwise.

Accent attitudes

Participants revealed considerable ambivalence in terms of their attitudes towards their own accents. Three were initially positive when asked if they liked their accents: 'Actually I'm quite happy with my pronunciation.' (A); 'Yeah, I think so, yeah.' (B); 'Two weeks ago I recorded my voice on the voice recorder. I quite liked it, and I'm still working on it.' (C). Four participants were negative or uncertain: 'I don't really know if I like it. I always try to do my best ... actually I wouldn't say I'm satisfied with my English.' (D); 'Erm, no. I think there are some problems that I have to solve.' (E); 'sometimes I do and sometimes I don't.' (G); 'No ... I want to improve my accent.' (H). One had no opinion: 'I don't really think of it, no, I mean I do not say I don't like it, I have no attitude as if I haven't been thinking about it.' (F).

Contradictions emerged when I asked how they would feel if someone mistook their accent for an NS accent. In all eight cases there was evidence of an attachment to an NS accent. Even participant A, the least attached, admitted that she would feel 'very mixed'. Those who had been negative or uncertain about their accents were more consistent with their original position. For example, D said she would be 'very happy', because '... if someone tells me that I speak good English and that you can't actually realise that I'm coming from Spain, for me would be good news like really feeling proud of it'. E responded: 'I suppose it would be a good thing because it's part of learning a new language ... to sound as much as the model'. In spite of this and the earlier claim that she did not like her accent, when I asked later which accent she would most like to have, she selected her own, saying 'I am comfortable about it. I'm proud of it... I don't want to be what I am not. I am Italian, I have my own culture, my roots are Italian'. Participant H responded to the question about an NS accent by saying: 'I'm seeking for that level'. Later in the interview she echoed this, saying that like all Japanese people, she 'worships' NS English pronunciation, wants to acquire it herself, and believes that a 'good' accent means an NS accent. However, she also claimed to be in favour of ELF, saying she would teach her students a Japanese-English accent and tell them that it is 'good'. Spotting the contradiction, she explained that an NS accent would give her a greater chance of success career-wise, while an NNS accent would lower her self-confidence.

Effects of 'accent experiences'

All eight participants remembered occasions, often many years earlier, when something had happened to them which they believed had affected their feelings about their own accents. For example, participant A described the way she had been ridiculed by a teacher in front of her classmates at the age of eleven because of her difficulty in pronouncing the word 'tree': '... I was a child and I had just started to learn English. I lost motivation actually, and many students started to laugh at me. It was quite a bad experience'.

Some of the negative experiences had taken place in Inner Circle contexts. Participant G, for example, recounts the way in which a London taxi driver responded when she had difficulty opening the taxi door:

> ...it was like two o'clock at night, and there was me struggling and he was telling me things that I didn't understand, and I was really tired so probably my Italian accent was much stronger than it usually is, and he was really bad to me, and I think he was really treating me badly because of my accent.

The extent to which these participants were able to summon such experiences in both number and detail leads me to conjecture that events like these may have had a substantial influence on the development of their accent identity. It seems that the phenomenon needs to be much more fully investigated in order to assess its implications for the teaching of ELF accents.

Teaching ELF accents

All the participants were asked at some point whether they would be interested in teaching ELF pronunciation (i.e. a model based on their local L2 accent with adjustments for international intelligibility). Most agreed that they would, but added that for themselves, they sought an NS accent. For example, H commented 'I should support EIL view as a teacher, but as a person maybe I'm aiming at native-like'. And despite their claims to believe in the legitimacy of ELF accents, most of the participants continually referred to any deviations from NS accents as errors rather than ELF variants. It seemed that, like Grau's (2005) subjects, they accepted ELF in theory, but had difficulties when it came to practice. To some extent, this may have been due to the current lack of ELF reference materials, which almost all participants mentioned, and which recalls the point made by Hüttner and Kidd (2000: above, 7).

As far as their colleagues were concerned, most believed they would not be favourably disposed to the idea of teaching ELF pronunciation. One participant (B) thought her colleagues would consider it 'wrongly pronounced', another (G) that they would consider NS accents to be better 'because that's where English was born', and several attributed any resistance to teaching ELF pronunciation to a lack of confidence about their own accents. On the positive side, some argued that their colleagues might teach ELF pronunciation both if appropriate materials became available, and if they became aware of the need to teach English for international communication. The problem, to some extent, they felt, was their colleagues' lack of international travel, such that their main contact with English was via NSs, whether in person or through NS-biased teaching materials. Three participants (A, F and G) thought their colleagues may change their minds in future if they travel and communicate more with NNSs from other countries. Three (A, C and F) also thought acceptance of NNS accents may depend on the individual accent variety, as they believed there was a hierarchy of NNS accents, with some being considered 'better' than others.

Conclusion to interview study

It would be premature to draw too many inferences from this small sample, although these findings are already being corroborated by the results of the other studies within the larger research project. The similarities in attitude across the eight participants, despite their differences in L1 and teaching experience, lead me to conclude that we cannot assume the existence of a straightforward desire to express membership of an international (ELF) community or an L1 identity in their L2 English. Past experiences, along with factors in their present situation, and judgements about the effect of their accent on their future opportunities, seem to exert a strong influence on speakers' attitudes to their accents and, in turn, on their choice of accent identity. In all but one case there was a strong sense that on the one hand, they desired an NS English identity as signalled by a 'native-like' accent, while on the other hand, they retained an attachment to their mother tongue which they were reluctant to relinquish. It is this pull in opposite directions which, I believe, led to the ambivalence revealed in their contradictory statements.

Looking to L2 pronunciation and identity in the future

The indications from the language and identity literature, the study outlined in the previous section, and the gradual unfolding of the larger research project of which this study is part, are that identity plays a critical role in individuals' orientations towards their L2 English accent. The relationship between L2 accent and identity is also turning out to be highly complex. Norton (2000) argues that one aspect of identity in language learning is 'how the person understands possibilities for the future' (5). Several of the participants in my interview study and in later interviews perceived clear links between a native-like English accent and the chance of success in their careers, and said this was their reason for wanting an RP or GA accent. On the other hand, several (often the very same people), as we saw above, also claimed that they wanted to retain their own NNS accent. They noticed the contradiction themselves, one even referring to her 'linguistic schizophrenia', which she explained as follows: 'I know that I don't need to speak like a British person, but [...] when I hear let's say someone speaking British English like a nice RP pronunciation, I *like* it'. Several participants accounted for their admiration for NS accents on the grounds that they are more 'original', thus linking NS accents with the 'ownership of English' debate (see Norton 1997; Widdowson 1994). Echoing Derwing's (2003) findings, all spoke in one way or another of the discrimination they felt they and other NNSs suffer as a result of having an NNS accent.

Whether or not ELF accents will be taken up by NNSs, and particularly by NNS teachers (and thence passed on to their learners) depends, it seems, on the extent to which they believe these accents will enhance their success and 'ownership' of the language rather than discriminate against them. For as Nero (2005) observes, 'the motivation to maintain affiliation with our ascribed language group(s) is contingent upon the benefits derived therefrom' (195). In the case of NNSs of English from the Expanding Circle, if they see an ELF identity as being to their future social and economic benefit, then they may choose to promote that identity through an ELF accent. On the other hand, if they see such an accent as potentially harmful to their future success, they may choose to promote a more native-like identity through their accent. But if this is the case, then as Bhatt (2002) observes, 'aspects of language use, such as language "choice" become less questions of choice than of economic, political and social coercion' (99). In effect, as Canagarajah (2004) puts it, they will have taken on 'the unitary identities (shaped by notions of deficiency, inferiority, and disadvantage) conferred on them by the dominant discourses' (117). At the time of writing, the outcome is not at all clear.

Notes

1   This relates to Kachru's three-circle description of the spread of English. The Inner Circle refers to the mother tongue English countries (e.g. the US, the UK), where English is spoken as a native language, often also known as ENL countries; the Outer Circle refers to the countries where English spread as a result of colonization (e.g. India, Singapore), often also known as ESL (English as a Second Language) countries; the Expanding Circle refers to those countries where English is learnt and used but does not have institutionalized functions (e.g. China, Germany). These are still often called EFL (English as a Foreign Language) countries. However, as their members most frequently learn English for international communication, i.e. for communication with other NNSs of English rather than for communication with NSs of English (as is the case with traditional EFL), some scholars now prefer to call them English as a Lingua Franca (ELF) countries.

2   English as a Lingua Franca (ELF) is also frequently known as English as an International Language (EIL). However, the former is the preferred term for an increasing number of researchers into English used in lingua franca communication, because it emphasizes both its use as a contact language primarily (but not exclusively) among its NNSs, and the leading role of NNSs in its development. It also counteracts the misleading impression given

by the use of the abbreviated version of EIL, namely 'International English', that 'there is one clearly distinguishable, codified, and unitary variety called *International English*, which is certainly not the case' (Seidlhofer 2004: 210).

3 It should be noted, however, that intelligibility in NNS–NNS communication has not been widely researched up to now, because of a preoccupation with the intelligibility needs of NS listeners to NNSs.

4 International Association of Teachers of English as a Foreign Language.

5 See Jenkins (2005b) for a full report of this study.

6 Subsequent interview participants came from China, Taiwan and Ukraine.

7 In the interviews I used the term EIL (English as an International Language) rather than ELF because most of participants were more familiar with it, and some had not come across the term 'ELF' previously.

References

Ammon, U. (2003), 'Global English and the non-native speaker: overcoming disadvantage', in H. Tonkin and T. Reagan (eds), *Language in the Twenty-First Century*. Amsterdam/ Philadelphia: John Benjamins, pp. 23–34.

Andreasson, A-M. (1994), 'Norm as pedagogical paradigm', *World Englishes*, 13, 395–409

Benecke, J. (1991), 'Englisch als lingua franca oder als Medium interkultureller Kommunikation', in R. Grebing (ed.), *Grenzenloses Sprachenlernen. Festschrift für Richard Freudenstein*. Berlin: Cornelsen, pp. 54–66.

Bhatt, R. M. (2002), 'Experts, dialects, and discourse', *International Journal of Applied Linguistics*, 12, 74–109.

Bonfiglio, T. (2002), *Race and the Rise of Standard American*. Berlin and New York: Mouton de Gruyter.

Bourdieu, P. (1977), 'The economics of linguistic exchanges', *Social Science Information*, 16, 645–68.

Canagarajah, S. (2004), 'Subversive identities, pedagogical safe houses, and critical learning', in B. Norton and K. Toohey (eds), *Critical pedagogies and language learning*. Cambridge: Cambridge University Press, pp. 116–37.

Crystal, D. (2003), *English as a global language* (2nd edn). Cambridge: Cambridge University Press.

Dalton-Puffer, C., Kaltenboeck, G. and Smit, U. (1997), 'Learner attitudes and L2 pronunciation in Austria', *World Englishes*, 16, 115–28.

Decke-Cornill, H. (2003), '"We would have to invent the language we are supposed to teach": The issue of English as a Lingua Franca in language education in Germany', in M. Byram and P. Grundy (eds), *Context and Culture in Language Teaching and Learning*. Clevedon: Multilingual Matters, pp. 59–71.

Derwing, T. (2003), 'What do ESL students say about their accents?', *The Canadian Modern Language Review*, 59, 547–66.

Graddol, D. (1997), *The Future of English?* London: The British Council.

— (1999), 'The decline of the native speaker', in D. Graddol and U. H. Meinhof (eds), *English in a changing world*. Milton Keynes, United Kingdom: AILA.

Grau, M. (2005), 'English as a global language – what do future teachers have to say?', in C. Gnutzmann and F. Intemann (eds), *The Globalisation of English and the English Language Classroom*. Tübingen. Gunter Narr, pp. 261–74.

Holliday, A. (2005), *The Struggle to Teach English as an International Language*. Oxford: Oxford University Press.

Hüttner, J. and Kidd, S. (2000), 'Reconstructing or Demolishing the "Sprechpraktikum" – A Reply to: Daniel Spichtinger From anglocentrism to TEIL: reflections on our English programme', *Vienna English Working Papers*, 9, 75–8.

Jenkins, J. (2000), *The Phonology of English as an International Language*. Oxford: Oxford University Press.

— (2002), 'A sociolinguistically based, empirically researched pronunciation syllabus for English as an international language', *Applied Linguistics*, 23, 83–103.

— (2005a), 'Teaching pronunciation for English as a lingua franca: A sociopolitical perspective', in C. Gnutzmann and F. Intemann (eds), *The Globalisation of English and the English Language Classroom*. Tübingen. Gunter Narr, pp. 145–58.

— (2005b), 'Implementing an international approach to English pronunciation: The role of teacher attitudes and identity', *TESOL Quarterly*, 39.

— (2005c), 'Misinterpretation, bias, and resistance to change: The case of the Lingua Franca Core', in K. Dziubalska-Kolaczyk and J. Przedlacka (eds), *English pronunciation models: A changing scene*. Frankfurt am Main: Peter Lang.

— (forthcoming), *English as a lingua franca: Attitudes and identity*. Oxford: Oxford University Press.

Joseph, J. (2004), *Language and Identity*. Houndmills, Basingstoke, UK and New York: Palgrave Macmillan.

Kachru, B. B. (1992), 'Teaching world Englishes', in B. B. Kachru (ed.) (pp. 355–65).

Kachru, B. B. (ed.) (1992), *The Other Tongue. English Across Cultures* (2nd edn). Urbana and Chicago: University of Illinois Press.

Kelly, G. (1991), *The Psychology of Personal Constructs*. London: Routledge.

Lippi-Green, R. (1997), *English with an Accent*. London and New York: Routledge.

Mauranen, A. (2003), 'The Corpus of English as Lingua Franca in Academic Settings', *TESOL Quarterly*, 37, 513–27.

McKay, S. (2002), *Teaching English as an International Language. Rethinking Goals and Approaches*. Oxford: Oxford University Press.

McLeod, J. (1994), *Doing Counselling Research*. London: Sage.

Miller, J. (2004), 'Identity and Language Use: The Politics of Speaking ESL in Schools', in A. Pavlenko and A. Blackledge (eds), *Negotiation of Identities in Multilingual Contexts*. Clevedon: Multilingual Matters.

Mufwene, S. (2001), *The Ecology of Language Evolution*. Cambridge: Cambridge University Press.

Nero, S. (2005), 'Language, identities, and ESL pedagogy', *Language and Education*, 19, 194–207.

Niedzielski, N. A. and Preston, D. R. (2003), *Folk Linguistics*. Berlin and New York: Mouton de Gruyter.

Norton, B. (1997), 'Language, identity, and the ownership of English', *TESOL Quarterly*, 31, 409–29.

— (2000), *Identity and Language Learning*. London: Longman.

Phillipson, R. (2003), *English-Only Europe?* London: Routledge.

Seidlhofer, B. (2004), 'Research perspectives on teaching English as a lingua franca', *Annual Review of Applied Linguistics*, 24, 209–39.

Smith, L. E. (1992), 'Spread of English and issues of intelligibility', in B. B. Kachru (ed.), *The Other Tongue. English Across Cultures* (2nd edn). Urbana and Chicago: University of Illinois Press, pp. 75–90.

Smith, L. E. and Bisazza, J. A. (1982), 'The comprehensibility of three varieties of English for college students in seven countries', *Language Learning*, 32, 259–70.

Smith, L. E. and Nelson, C. (1985), 'International intelligibility of English: directions and resources', *World Englishes*, 4, 333–42.

Smith, L. E. and Rafiqzad, K. (1979), 'English for cross-cultural communication: the question of intelligibility', *TESOL Quarterly*, 13, 371–80.

Sobkowiak, W. (2003), 'Why not LFC?', *Zeszyty Naukwe Panstwowej Wyzszej Szkoly Zawodowej w Koninie* [Scientific Journal of the Public Vocational School in Konin], 1, 114–24.

Szpyra-Kozlowska, J. (2003), 'The Lingua Franca Core and the Polish Learner', *Neofilologia*, V, 193–210.

Timmis, I. (2002), 'Native speaker norms and International English', *ELT Journal*, 56, 240–9.

Vaughan-Rees, M. (2001), 'Open Forum: Jennifer Jenkins responding to questions about her book', *Speak Out! Newsletter of the IATEFL Pronunciation Special Interest Group*, 28, 10–15.

Widdowson, H. G. (1994), 'The Ownership of English', *TESOL Quarterly*, 28, 377–89.

6 Shifting identities and orientations in a border town

Carmen Llamas

Introduction

A brief look through recent publications in sociolinguistics will reveal the central position that the notion of identity has assumed in the field:

> the study of meaning in sociolinguistic variation is a study of the relation between variation and identity (Eckert 2000: 42)

> Social identity is, more than any other aspect of social theory, sociolinguistics' home ground (Coupland 2001: 18)

> The underlying cause of sociolinguistic differences, largely beneath consciousness, is the human instinct to establish and maintain social identity (Chambers 2003: 274)

If we agree that the establishment and maintenance of social identities underlie sociolinguistic differences, as Chambers claims, then attempts to provide explanations for such differences should begin with efforts to deconstruct the social identities and orientations of speakers. This chapter presents findings from a broadly variationist study of the Northern English town of Middlesbrough. Although essentially quantitative in design, the study contains a strong qualitative element, and through macrolinguistic commentary, considers practices of categorization, self-making and 'othering' in the identity constructions of the speakers. Insight gained through these data coupled with knowledge of the social context in which the study is set inform the analysis of the phonological variation uncovered.

On a local level, Middlesbrough has something of a border town status and, as such, is a locality in which identity construction is particularly fluid and complex. It therefore offers an ideal test-site for a study on the language/identity nexus. In an article in a British national newspaper Middlesbrough was described thus:

> It is pretty much a place between places. It's not on the way to anywhere, it's not quite in Yorkshire, and in fact a lot of people don't know where it is. It is a forgotten part of Britain with no identity.

> (*The Sunday Times*, 5 March 2000)

In a more favourable light, the *Middlesbrough Official Guide* (Public Relations Department 1997: 16) describes the urban centre as a 'gateway to two regions'. Situated some 38 miles (61 km) South of Newcastle, the dominant urban centre of the North-East of England and around 50 miles (80 km) North of York in Yorkshire, Middlesbrough lies in a transition area between the extreme South of the North-East and the extreme North of Yorkshire in the North of England. This transitional nature has meant that the urban centre is not wholly in one region or the other; its identity is therefore not deep rooted and firmly felt by either inhabitants or outsiders. Whether this transitional nature has an effect on the claimed identities, orientations and linguistic behaviour of the inhabitants is central to the investigation.

On a national level, the study is situated in the context of rapid vernacular changes in current British English (henceforth BrE) which are argued to be leading to homogenization on a broad scale (Trudgill 1999; Foulkes and Docherty 2001). The increase in the extent of geographical and social mobility experienced by the population in recent years is frequently cited as a contributory factor in this large-scale homogenization. Furthermore, many spreading forms, particularly several widespread consonantal changes, are believed to be diffusing from a South-Eastern epicentre and are believed to have an historical association with London (Wells 1982; Tollfree 1999; Foulkes and Docherty 2001), the working class accent of which is considered 'today the most influential source of phonological innovation in England and perhaps in the whole English-speaking world' (Wells 1982: 301). Consequently, changes are argued to affect varieties closer to London more than those further removed from the South-East of England (Foulkes and Docherty 2001). Whether the urban variety of Middlesbrough, situated some 236 miles (378 km) North of London, has been affected by consonantal changes in BrE, and whether adoption of spreading forms is concurrent with a loss of localized forms or compromises the speaker's sense of regional/social identity are also questions of interest.

This chapter focuses on the distribution of two phonological features: glottalized /p/ which is a salient form in the North-East of England, and TH-fronting which comprises one of the current vernacular changes in BrE. The linguistic variation revealed over apparent time in the study is considered in light of the identity constructions, shifting orientations and local affiliations of the speakers. The chapter begins with consideration of the theoretical and contextual background which situates the study. Analysis of language use is then presented followed by analysis of speaker comment. Speakers' perceptions and comments on language and social categorization are then used to gain insight into the motivation for the linguistic variation uncovered.

Contextual and theoretical background

Germane to an investigation of the interdependence of language and identity is how speakers view language, and how speakers view themselves, particularly in opposition to others. In this section consideration is first given to language ideology, which offers a framework for understanding speakers' attitudes towards language. We then turn to the subject of social and community identity and consider how this can be constructed, particularly in relation to language use.

Language ideology

The concept of language ideology covers a vast area (see further Woolard 1992), but pertinent to the present discussion is the neutral value of the term and Silverstein's definition, 'sets of beliefs about language articulated by users as a rationalization or justification of perceived language structure and use' (1979: 193).

Irvine and Gal (2000: 37) argue that the ideological aspects of linguistic differentiation emerge as a consequence of attempts by individuals to formulate understandings of linguistic variation which can be mapped onto significant people, events and activities. Importantly, as Milroy (2000: 9) notes, people, events and activities viewed as significant will vary between communities. Furthermore, they may vary within communities as changes in reactions to saliences of locations can alter and attitudes towards salient social groups can shift, as is the case in the locality under investigation.

Silverstein (1992, 2003) views ideology as a system for making sense of the indexicality inherent in language: in other words, how language forms index speakers' social identities. This indexicality can be ranked into different orders of generality. First order indexicality involves an association or correlation, often assumed in much sociolinguistic work, of a linguistic form with some socially meaningful category. Second order indexicality involves overt or covert awareness and discussion of basic first order indexicality. Hence ideology can be identified through metalinguistic discourse, and can become visible in style shifting in careful speech, hypercorrections and hyperdialectisms (Milroy 2001). Language ideologies thus entail the selective association of a linguistic form with some meaningful social group. Such groups are socially positioned and emerge from specific local and social circumstance (Milroy 2003).

Within a language ideology framework, speakers' comments about language and other social phenomena are used as a means of interpreting and understanding linguistic variation, thus allowing insight into social psychological motivations for linguistic variation which may be otherwise inaccessible to the analyst. Such comments are not treated as irrelevant or unreliable, as is traditional in much variationist work.[1]

Additionally, a language ideology approach can allow insight into locally constructed categories which may differ from the global categories of gender, social class or ethnicity, for example, and which are often to be discovered, not assumed:

> an ideological analysis treats social categories as locally created by social actors and discoverable by analysis, rather than as a given. Consequently, an ideologically oriented account of language variation and change treats members of speech communities as agents, rather than as automatons caught up ineluctably in an abstract sociolinguistic system.
>
> (Milroy 2004: 167)

From this perspective, then, it can be argued that the speech community itself is one such locally created social category which can be examined and not simply imposed onto a sample of speakers.

Social and community identity

Social identity is a concept that pervades disciplines investigating human behaviour, both individual and collective. The body of ideas that became known as 'social identity theory' (coined by Turner and Brown 1978) has its roots in Tajfel's early work on categorization and social perception, and has as its essence the idea that an individual is motivated to maintain a distinct and positive social identity. Social identity is seen as 'a person's definition of self in terms of some social group membership with the associated value connotations and emotional significance' (Turner 1999: 8). In intergroup contexts people strive for positive distinctiveness for the group. The evaluation of in-group membership entails the requirement that relevant in-groups compare favourably with relevant out-groups:

> social comparisons between groups which are relevant to an evaluation of one's social identity produce pressures for intergroup differentiation to achieve a positive self-evaluation in terms of that identity.
>
> (Turner 1999: 8)

Other people are conceptually categorized or grouped according to perceived similarities between group members and perceived differences from members of other putative groups along one or more relevant dimension. Language, it can be argued, is one such dimension. This approach, in a way, is reflected in Le Page and Tabouret-Keller's (1985: 181) view of linguistic behaviour as 'a series of acts of identity' during which:

> the individual creates for himself the patterns of his linguistic behaviour so as to resemble those of the group or groups with which from time to time he wishes to be identified, or so as to be unlike those from whom he wishes to be distinguished.

Investigation of the accent or dialect groups to which speakers perceive themselves to belong and those to which they compare themselves may allow insight into speakers' self-categorization in terms of language and social or community identity, or, what we might term, the locally constructed speech community.

Furthermore, this locally constructed community identity is not necessarily fixed in time or space as the psychological reality of place can shift. How people orient to place, particularly in terms of region, is central to an understanding of the community identity they perceive:

> Regions have come to be seen as meaningful places, which individuals construct, as well as select, as reference points. Identification with a region is identification with one kind of 'imagined community'.
>
> (Johnstone 2004: 69)

Although community is to an extent 'imagined', as Anderson (1991) argues, or 'symbolically constructed', as Cohen (1985) describes, whether speakers from the same locality would identify the same 'imagined community' (or indeed recognize one imposed on them by the analyst) are key questions to be considered.

Despite this locally constructed or 'imagined' aspect of communities, there remain social realities, such as political borders, which contribute significantly to where psychological boundaries are drawn. We turn next to a consideration of the local, social situation which impacts on the identities, orientations and meaningful social groups perceived by the speakers in the study.

Local background

As noted, Middlesbrough is a location in which identity construction is complex and fluid and not deep rooted or firmly felt. A large part of the fluid identity construction can be traced to the repeated redrawing of local administrative boundaries in the region (see Figure 6.1). Traditionally, the River Tees divided the conurbation, with urban centres North of the river being situated in County Durham and those on the South bank, including Middlesbrough, forming part of the North Riding of Yorkshire. The conurbation was brought together in 1968 and given a political identity of its own in terms of local government with the formation of Teesside. This political identity was then changed when the region was expanded in 1974 with the formation of County Cleveland. It was changed again when the conurbation was once more divided in 1996 with the

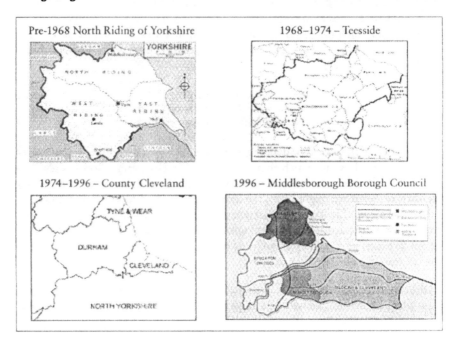

Figure 6.1: Changing local administrative boundaries

formation of four separate local authorities, each authority being regarded as a county in its own right. However, 'for cultural and ceremonial purposes' the old boundary running along the River Tees has been reinstated (Moorsom 1996: 22). Within a period of approximately 30 years, then, in terms of local government, Middlesbrough has been assigned four separate political identities.

Added to this, over approximately the same timescale, a shift in orientation can be discerned in terms of popular culture as the conurbation both North and South of the river has become increasingly associated with the North-East of England and increasingly dissociated from Yorkshire. Since independent regional television groupings were formed in 1959, Middlesbrough has been included in the Tyne Tees Television group and not in Yorkshire Television. Similarly, regional newspapers cover Middlesbrough and Tyneside. Additionally, local sports derby matches are now considered to be those played against teams from localities further North, and not with teams from Yorkshire.

From a linguistic point of view, the situation is much the same. In terms of traditional dialectology, the River Tees is often considered a boundary. Indeed, Orton, when working on the *Linguistic Atlas of England* (Orton *et al.* 1978), reportedly insisted that an isogloss following the River Tees be drawn (the Tees being the only river to have an isogloss follow it) because he knew it to be a boundary between Durham and Yorkshire (Clive Upton, *personal communication*). However, in modern dialect groupings, both Trudgill (1990) and Wells (1982) group Teesside with Tyneside in the 'north-east' or 'far north', respectively, with Trudgill (1990: 77) claiming that:

> no one from Middlesbrough would mistake a Tynesider for someone from Middlesbrough
> – but the accents are sufficiently similar to be grouped together, and sufficiently different
> from those of other areas. Londoners, for instance, might mistakenly think that
> Middlesbrough speakers were from Newcastle, but they would be much less likely to think
> that they were from, say, Sheffield.

Although, impressionistically the Middlesbrough accent is arguably closer to those of Tyneside than those of Yorkshire, as Trudgill implies, Middlesbrough lies between two regional accent types of BrE which are relatively easily identified by the lay person: that of Geordie, which is the accent of Newcastle and Tyneside, and that of Yorkshire. Such a position also adds to the transitional character of the town and often makes precise identification of the accent by an outsider difficult.

The transitional character of Middlesbrough, both geographically and dialectally, combined with its geographical distance from London, make the sense of identity construction and the local orientations of the speakers complex. Whether linguistic trends uncovered in the data correspond to the claimed identities and the shifting orientations of the speakers is, therefore, the focus of the study.

Design of the study

Fieldwork sample

The data presented are taken from a sample of 32 speakers from Middlesbrough who form a socio-economically homogeneous group. Speakers' self-assessment of their class was taken as an indicator of what socio-economic group they belong to (all speakers are what they term 'working class'). This self-assessment was supplemented with information on occupation, housing and level of educational attainment. Additionally, information was sought on speakers' experience of geographical mobility in terms of extent and duration. The young adult males were found to be the speakers who had experienced the most recent geographical mobility, with most members of the group having spent over 12 months outside the town since finishing their compulsory education.

Age was taken as a variable in the study, with four age groups identified (see Table 6.1). Young adults and adolescents, being almost contiguous, can be taken as a combined group of 16 young speakers. Gender was also taken as a variable.

Table 6.1 Design of Middlesbrough fieldwork sample

Old (60–80)		Middle (32–45)		Young (16–22)			
				Young adult (19–22)		Adolescent (16–17)	
Male	Female	Male	Female	Male	Female	Male	Female
4	4	4	4	4	4	4	4

Data elicitation

The Middlesbrough study is the first to employ a method of data elicitation designed for use in a large-scale study of variation in BrE, the Survey of Regional English (SuRE)[2] (for full discussion of the method of data elicitation see Llamas 1999, 2001, 2006). As the only consistently collected nationwide survey of dialectal variation in England remains the Survey of English Dialects (SED) (1962–71), the basic intention of the SuRE project is to create a computer-held database of systematically sampled material from a planned network of localities throughout Britain. Such an undertaking as SuRE must incorporate the collection of data which are analysable on three levels of potential variability: phonological, grammatical and lexical. The focus of the present study is on findings at the level of phonological variation, as noted.

Part of the interview involved an Identification Questionnaire (IdQ) which elicits data on informants' attitudes towards their language and their area, that is, it seeks to obtain instantiations of second order indexicality and categorizations of ingroups and relevant outgroups. Figure 6.2 presents questions from the IdQ of interest to this paper, the responses to which are discussed after consideration of linguistic data.

> **Your Language**
>
> - What accent would you say you had, and do you like it?
> - What would you think if your accent was referred to as Geordie or Yorkshire?
>
> **Your Area**
>
> - Do you remember when the county of Teesside was formed and Middlesbrough was no longer in Yorkshire? Do you think this change made a difference?
> - Would you consider Teesside to be in a larger 'north-eastern' part of the country or a larger 'Yorkshire' part of the country? Why?

Figure 6.2 Example questions from Identification Questionnaire

Additionally, an Affiliation Score Index (ASI) has been devised for use in the Middlesbrough study. This is an adapted and extended version of the 'Index of Texan Identification' used by Underwood (1988) which was an attempt to use Le Page and Tabouret-Keller's (1985) theory of acts of identity to account for linguistic variation in Texas. Underwood scored responses to three questions designed to test speakers' levels of local affiliation, which were patterned closely after those used in Reed's (1983) study of Southern identification in the USA.

The ASI used in the present study includes direct questions designed to test in-group preference. Each answer to the seven multiple choice questions included on the ASI carries a score of 1, 2 or 3, with a score of 3 indicating the strongest feeling of local affiliation (see Appendix 6.1 for example questions). Scores are calculated and categorized as points along a cline from negative to positive. Broadly, scores are grouped into two categories: negative to neutral and neutral to positive. Linguistic and social variables can then be correlated with results.

The data elicitation method thus allows for the elicitation of samples of conversational speech from which a quantitative analysis of linguistic variables can be undertaken, whilst simultaneously allowing for a qualitative and quantitative analysis of attitudinal data.

Linguistic findings

(p)

As with the other voiceless plosives, (t) and (k), (p) can be realized with a glottalled, a glottalized or a fully released variant.

Glottalization (also referred to as glottal reinforcement) in which the oral closure is reinforced by a glottal closure (see further Gimson 1989; Giegerich 1992) is usually transcribed as a double articulation, [ʔ͡p] or [p͡ʔ]. The realization of (p) as [p͡ʔ] is a salient feature of Newcastle and Tyneside English (Wells 1982; Milroy *et al.* 1994; Docherty *et al.* 1997; Watt and Milroy 1999; Watt and Allan 2003). It is also found in Durham[3] English (Kerswill 1987). It is therefore taken as a localized feature of the North-East of England. Whether its use is as prevalent in Middlesbrough as it is in the dominant urban centre of the North-East, Newcastle, will be of interest, particularly as it is suggested that glottalization of intervocalic (p) may be recessive in Newcastle and characteristic of Tyneside male speech (Docherty *et al.* 1997: 306).

In the conversational Middlesbrough data, 30 tokens per speaker for word-medial intervocalic (p) were sought and subjected to auditory analysis and one-tailed t-tests. Findings were compared with those from the recent study of Tyneside English undertaken by Docherty *et al.* (1997). Figure 6.3 below presents findings from the four age groups broken down by gender.[4]

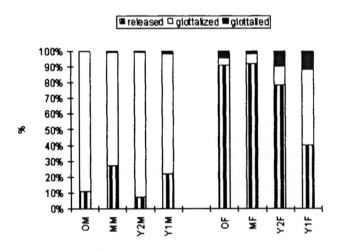

Figure 6.3 Distribution of variants of (p) by age and gender

[p͡ʔ] is revealed to be the preferred variant of male speakers, with all male groups' use being over 70 per cent. Young adult males reveal the highest use of [p͡ʔ], which, at 91.7 per cent, is effectively categorical in sociolinguistic terms. [p] is relatively low and [ʔ] is rejected virtually entirely by the males. Overall, the male speakers reveal relatively little variation over age, with use of the preferred male variant, [p͡ʔ], being comparable to the Tyneside male score of 87 per cent.

Not only is a significant gender difference in the distribution of variants of (p) apparent, but also a much higher degree of variation across age in the female data compared with the male data. The old and middle female speakers show similar patterns of usage with almost categorical use of [p] and marginal use of the other two variants. The younger females, however, demonstrate a considerable increase in use of [p͡ʔ]. Furthermore, a significant increase in use of [p͡ʔ] is observed in the adolescents' speech compared with the young adults' (p≤0.014). Although the female adolescent use of [p͡ʔ] is significantly lower than their male counterparts (p≤0.002), their usage stands in stark contrast with the other female usage. Young females in the sample also show a substantially higher use of [ʔ] for (p), which rises to its highest point amongst the female adolescents (11.6 per cent).

(th) and (dh)

Described by Wells (1982: 96) as 'persistent infantilism', the realization of interdental fricatives as labiodental fricatives is a spreading feature of BrE which has been particularly overtly stigmatized. Use of the fronted variants is generally associated with the speech of London or 'broad Cockney' (Wells 1982: 328; Cruttenden 1994: 168; Hughes *et al*. 2005: 74). Indeed, such is the association that it is used to dramatic effect in the title of Barltrop and Wolveridge's 1980 work on Cockney life and language, *The Muvver Tongue*.

Considering more northerly English locations, fronting of (th) and (dh) was evident in the speech of the young, particularly working-class speakers in the recent study of Derby, in the Midlands (Milroy 1996). In a recent study of Hull in East Yorkshire, use of the fronted variants was shown to be near categorical in the working-class, male group of adolescent speakers and used to a considerable extent amongst their female counterparts (Williams and Kerswill 1999). Furthermore, fronted forms are found amongst young working-class speakers in Glasgow (Stuart-Smith and Tweedie 2000), and also in Newcastle, although there they are still 'relatively scarce' (Watt and Milroy 1999: 30).

In the Middlesbrough data 30 tokens per speaker were sought and subjected to auditory anaylsis for (th) in word initial, medial and final positions and for (dh) in word medial and final positions as, according to Wells (1982: 328) and Milroy (1996: 215), fronting does not occur in word-initial tokens of (dh). No instances of the fronted variants are recorded from the 16 members of the old and middle groups, which emphasizes the suddenness of the emergence of the spreading feature in MbE. The fronted forms are in evidence in all young speaker groups, to some extent. However, a revealing pattern of use is revealed in Figure 6.4, as one group of young speakers, the young adult male group, appears to be almost wholly responsible for the appearance of these innovatory forms in the dataset.

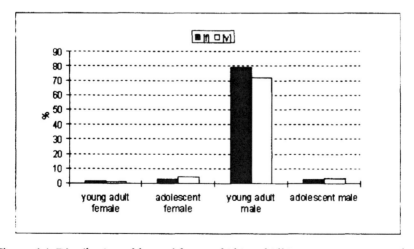

Figure 6.4 Distribution of fronted forms of (th) and (dh) amongst young speakers

Summary of linguistic findings and initial discussion

In terms of the use of the localized form of interest, [p̂ʔ], the speaker group showing the highest use of the form is the young adult male group. However, among the male speakers, (p) appears to be stable, with [p̂ʔ] the preferred form for all male speaker groups. In the speech of the females we see data which suggest change in progress. Although glottalized variants are not new to MbE, they are in a sense new to the female speakers in the environment under investigation: the older female speakers of the sample reject [p̂ʔ] virtually categorically. The adoption of the forms by the young females, coupled with the slight increase in use by the young adult males, suggest a degree of convergence of MbE with speech of further North where use of the glottalized forms is found to be higher. The fact that [p̂ʔ] is the preferred variant of the adolescent females suggests that the young females are at the vanguard of this convergent trend.

The decreasing use of the released variant of (p) indicates a degree of divergence which can be seen not only as divergence from the standard BrE unmarked variant, but also divergence from realizations found further South in Yorkshire wherein glottalized forms are not a salient form.

The shifting of Middlesbrough from an orientation towards Yorkshire to one towards the North-East, as discussed earlier, correlates neatly with this convergent linguistic trend suggested by the higher level of use of [p̂ʔ]. At this point, we may hypothesize that speakers, particularly the speakers of the sample at the vanguard of the linguistic trend, identify positively with varieties found further North, most particularly those of the dominant urban centre, Newcastle, and that such positive identification is a motivating factor in the increased use of [p̂ʔ].

In terms of the use of innovatory forms, the young adult male speakers are found to be almost wholly responsible for the use of [f] for /θ/ and [v] for /ð/ in the data. Given that these are the only speakers of the sample to have adopted ostensibly Southern innovatory forms wholeheartedly and that these are also the speakers to have experienced the most recent geographical mobility, we may assume that these speakers are more outward-looking and have a less locally-centred orientation than other speakers.

However, without accessing local knowledge that speakers operate with when constructing their sociolinguistic identities and assessing the strength of their local orientation and affiliation, the validity of such claims remains unclear. In order to gain further insight, we turn to examination of attitudinal information elicited through informants' responses to questions in the Identification Questionnaire (IdQ) and to the Affiliation Score Index (ASI) of the interview.

Attitudinal findings

Identities

Self and other - definition and delimitation

The first example question from the IdQ, 'What accent would you say you had, and do you like it?', seeks to establish contrastive self-definition in terms of what identity informants claim, or what in-group informants perceive themselves to be part of in terms of accent. This seemingly straightforward question proved revealing. All groups of speakers showed variation in the responses to this question. However, the majority response of each age group tallied exactly with the shifting identity of Middlesbrough.

Table 6.2 Definition of accent across age

	Total	Yorkshire n.	Teesside n.	Middlesbrough n.	North/NE n.
O	8	4	1	3	0
M	8	0	4	3	1
Y	16	0	3	11	2

Amongst older speakers, the most frequently given response is 'Yorkshire'. Most older speakers who defined their accent as Yorkshire qualified their response by stressing that it was not a 'broad Yorkshire' accent. This, combined with responses such as 'I would call it Yorkshire because I was born in Yorkshire', suggest that accent can be defined by geographical place regardless of whether it conforms to the speaker's perception of the accent in question. The most frequently given response of the middle-aged speakers is 'Teesside' further emphasizing the importance of geographical place in terms of definition of accent. Amongst the combined young speakers the most frequently given response is 'Middlesbrough', it being produced by 11 of the 16 young speakers. This suggests that speakers react to changing political boundaries of the area in which they live. If the political boundaries of the area change, so may how inhabitants perceive themselves which may result in changes to the in-groups they perceive and the saliences of relevant out-groups to which they may compare themselves.

In-groups and out-groups

Lying between two relatively easily identified accents of BrE, the Middlesbrough accent is not one that is readily identifiable by an outsider, as noted earlier. Therefore, as well as eliciting information on speakers' definitions of their own accent, informants were asked their reactions to perceived misidentifications of their accent as Geordie or Yorkshire. In all cohorts the most frequently given response was that a perceived misidentification as Geordie would cause greater offence, with only 5 of the 32 claiming otherwise. Interestingly, reasons for the aversion to a Geordie label appeared to vary across age.

Seven of the eight old speakers claimed to find being referred to as Geordie objectionable. However, as the majority of older speakers claimed an in-group status as Yorkshire, many expressed incomprehension at the frequent reference to Geordie with responses like:

I'm from Yorkshire not Geordieland – they might as well call you a Frenchman instead of an Englishman.

It is clear from such an example that an identification as Yorkshire is not, in fact, a perceived misidentification, but is an identity the speaker would claim.

The middle group had the highest number of informants stating that they would prefer a Geordie identification to one of Yorkshire. Positive feelings towards Yorkshire were still in evidence among some speakers from the middle group, however:

> if I went to Scarborough[5] and people said you were a Geordie you'd feel that you'd want to put them right – whereas if you went to Newcastle and they called you Yorkshire you'd just let it pass probably.

The large majority of speakers from the combined young group (13 of 16) claimed to find a Geordie identification objectionable, with many professing a strong aversion to the Geordie accent. Some young speakers expressed miscomprehension at the idea of being perceived as Yorkshire, it seeming not to be a realistic possibility.

Thus we see out-group derogation in the varying reactions to the perceived misidentification of the speakers. This is mostly directed at the perceived out-group of 'Geordie'. Such derogation is thought to be instrumental in promoting a positive self-image (Branscombe et al. 1999).

We also see evidence for the changing saliences of relevant out-groups to which the in-group is favourably compared. Responses to the question concerning the formation of Teesside and the removal of Middlesbrough from North Yorkshire are illuminating in this respect. By far the majority of the older speakers expressed regret at no longer being part of the Ridings of Yorkshire, with responses such as:

> we still think of ourselves as Yorkshire – we didn't want to be Teesside

A small majority of speakers from the middle group expressed the opinion that the conurbation North and South of the Tees should be united and not divided by the river. However, considerable expression of a lack of identity in Middlesbrough was in evidence amongst the middle group, with opinions such as:

> We're not Geordie. We're not Yorkshire. We're nothing really;

> We're no-man's land, aren't we? We don't know what we are;

> I remember people saying things like Geordies won't have you and Yorkshire won't have you and all that, as if we were almost sort of nothing really.

In the combined young group a much greater majority of speakers believed that the conurbation should not be divided (13 of 16). Two young speakers expressed the opinion that Middlesbrough should have city status. Only one young speaker expressed a desire to be in Yorkshire, whilst some were unaware of any historical association with Yorkshire and so appeared confused by the line of discussion.

Responses, then, correspond to the fact that speakers from the old group have spent the majority of their lives in Middlesbrough, Yorkshire; the middle groups' lifetime has seen constant changes of identity; and the young speakers have no memory, or in some cases no knowledge, of the Yorkshire political identity. Such life experiences appear to have an impact on the in-groups speakers perceive themselves to be part of and the relevant out-groups to which these in-groups are compared.

Interestingly, in light of the responses to the previous question, the last example question from the IdQ, that of whether informants would consider Middlesbrough to be in a larger 'North-Eastern' part of the country or a larger 'Yorkshire' part of the country, prompted all informants to answer 'North-Eastern'. Even older speakers who considered Yorkshire to be part of their identity gave responses such as:

you're right at the top of Yorkshire, so to get it across you'd have to say North-East.

Some informants had never considered the proximity of Yorkshire, so the suggestion of classing Middlesbrough with Yorkshire in a geographical sense appeared strange, with responses such as the following making manifest the irrelevance of Yorkshire to the speakers' sense of identity construction:

it's weird, even though you're the same distance, how much you don't class yourself with them [Yorkshire]

it's weird when you only go two minutes down the road and you're in like North Yorkshire. No I don't consider it at all. No I would definitely not say it. [that Middlesbrough was in Yorkshire]

Orientations

In order to gain awareness of speakers' feelings of local allegiance and to reveal whether differing levels correlate with speaker age and gender, two sources of information are utilized: an overall assessment of informants' responses in the IdQ, and results from responses to the Affiliation Score Index (ASI).

Although responses to all questions posed in the IdQ are borne in mind, particular attention is paid to those concerning whether informants have a positive attitude toward their accent and whether they would give a positive, negative or neutral image of Middlesbrough to an outsider. Reactions to the questions are categorized as points along a cline from negative to positive, with five points identified: negative, negative to neutral, neutral, neutral to positive and positive. The results for the four individual speakers of each speaker cohort are presented in Table 6.3.

Findings reveal that males demonstrate considerably higher levels of local allegiance than females of the sample. Of the 16 male speakers, 11 are located on the most positive point of the cline. Female speakers, on the other hand, are much more evenly distributed. Of the individual speaker groups, the most positive is the young adult male group, with all four speakers revealing a strong sense of local allegiance and local orientation. The least positive responses

Table 6.3 Levels of local allegiance for individual speakers

	Negative		Neutral		Positive
	← ── →				
Y1M	√		√		√√
Y2M					√√√
MM			√	√	√√
OM				√	√√
Y1F		√√		√	√
Y2F	√	√	√√		
MF	√√	√		√	
OF				√	√√

appear to be amongst the young adult and middle females, where five of the eight speakers revealed negative responses.

Results from the ASI, which tests the strength of the informant's local affiliation through, for example, in-group preference, provide an additional element to the rating of levels of local allegiance. The mean scores of the eight speaker groups are presented Table 6.4. Scores, again, can be seen to represent points on a cline, where the lower the score the more negative the response and the less strong the informant's feeling of local affiliation, and the higher the score the stronger the feeling of local affiliation and emotional identification with the in-group. Broadly, a score of 7–14 indicates a negative to neutral response, and a score of 15–21 indicates a neutral to positive response.

Table 6.4 Mean group scores for Affiliation Score Index

Speaker group	Mean score
Y1M	14.75
Y2M	18.25
MM	16.75
OM	15.00
Y1F	15.75
Y2F	12.25
MF	16.00
OF	17.00

Results from the ASI correspond to the reactions to the IdQ in that the speaker cohort with the highest score, and therefore the strongest feeling of local affiliation and emotional identification with the in-group, is the young adult male cohort (the group from which all members demonstrated a positive reaction to the IdQ). The group with the lowest score is the young adult female group (the group from which no members responded positively to the IdQ).

Summary of attitudinal findings and revised discussion

The attitudinal data presented reveal clear generational differences in linguistic orientation in Middlesbrough, as speakers' self-images, in terms of what accent they perceive themselves to have, differ across age. The way speakers overtly define and delimit their accents is central to the locally constructed community identity, and can reflect shared orientations. The attitudinal data presented reveal the realignment of orientations across age groups, as Middlesbrough is a different place for the different generations in the sample. The increased use of [p͡ʔ] can thus be seen as being ideologically motivated, as it appears to be contingent on local images of salient social categories that have shifted over time. Additionally, perceived space appears crucial in identifying these salient local groups. The significance of the North-East, and the irrelevance of Yorkshire to the younger speakers, despite its Euclidean distance from Middlesbrough, is clear in the data; it appears neither as part of the in-group they perceive themselves to belong to, nor as a relevant out-group to which they compare themselves favourably.

With insights from the attitudinal data, what initially seemed like a plausible interpretation of the motivation for the convergent linguistic trend, a conscious identification or 'act of identity' with Newcastle and Tyneside English, appears less convincing. An ardent sense of rivalry and even hostility towards the Geordie accent and what it is perceived to stand for is demonstrated in the responses of the informants. This hostility is expressed by all four adolescent females of the sample (the adolescent females being the speakers at the vanguard of the convergent trend). The hostility is expressed largely as a dislike of the accent and as a resentment towards the perceived dominance of Newcastle in the North-East. This would suggest that, on a conscious level, the young speakers from Middlesbrough do not identify openly and positively with the Geordie accent or with Tyneside as an in-group. Instead, the higher level of use of [p͡ʔ] is concurrent with an increased confidence expressed by young speakers in the status of Middlesbrough both in terms of its accent and as a 'place' in its own right. Young speakers can be said to be using a strategy of localism to construct their community identity, and the identity of Middlesbrough is simply Middlesbrough. Although linguistic convergence appears superficially to indicate speakers' high regard for and identification with the possible donor variety, speakers are able to reallocate forms to index locally relevant identities. This may occur when the groups are in tension, as Woolard and Schieffelin (1994: 62) argue:

> [c]ommunities not only evaluate but may appropriate some part of the linguistic resources of groups with whom they are in contact and in tension, refiguring and incorporating linguistic structures in ways that reveal linguistic and social ideologies.

As in Dyer's (2000) study of Corby, in the Midlands, in which historically Scottish features were argued to have been reallocated to function as indicators of local rather than Scottish identity, we find in MbE the recycling of a traditional feature found to be recessive in Newcastle (Docherty *et al.* 1997). The feature would appear to have strong symbolic value, hence its increased use. However, it appears not to symbolize contemporary Newcastle to the speakers of Middlesbrough, but rather to symbolize something which is more locally relevant.

As regards the innovatory forms in the data, the young adult males' use of [f], [v] for (th), (dh) is combined with the fact that they have experienced an amount of recent geographical mobility, as noted. Initially this was interpreted as implying that young adult males demonstrate low levels of local allegiance and local orientation, and appear outward-looking and open to the adoption of features associated with other geographical localities. However, conversely, we find that the young adult males are the speakers of the sample who exhibit the highest level of local allegiance and emotional identification with the in-group, whilst the young females demonstrate the lowest level of local allegiance and local orientation, despite their increase in use of [p͡ʔ].

The adoption of innovatory forms then may have little to do with positive identification with a geographical locality with which the feature is argued to be associated. Use of a feature which is thought to be associated with the South of England does not appear to compromise the speaker's self-identity as Northern or North-Eastern. Likewise, increased use of what is argued to be a localized variant appears not to equate with a heightened sense of local allegiance and an increased local orientation necessarily. What the innovatory form symbolizes to the speakers who adopt it may not be related to positive identification with a perceived donor variety in a geographical sense. Rather, speakers are able to adopt innovatory forms which symbolize something of value to them without compromising their local orientation.

Additionally, short-term geographical mobility appears not to compromise local orientation. On the contrary, a heightened sense of local affiliation and emotional identification with the in-group may be effected by increased geographical mobility. It can be argued that the significance of the individual's regional identity is intensified when it becomes counter-norm, that is, when the individual relocates. The increased significance of regional identity to the speakers who have experienced recent geographical mobility could surface linguistically as an increased or exaggerated use of localized forms (recall that the young adult males demonstrated the highest levels of use of [p͡ʔ] in the sample). Rather than increased mobility leading to homogenization, it could lead to increasing heterogeneity as speakers adopt forms which carry symbolic value to them, yet simultaneously increase localized forms as their regional identity becomes more salient and significant to their identity construction.

Conclusions

This chapter has presented results from a study of phonological variation in an urban variety of BrE, Middlesbrough. The urban centre lies on a regional border in the North of England and has been subject to repeated redrawing of local administrative boundaries, and shifting orientations in terms of popular culture. In terms of use of the localized phonological form, the shifting of Middlesbrough from an orientation towards Yorkshire to one towards the North-East was found to correlate neatly with the convergent linguistic trend suggested by the higher level of use of glottalized /p/, a salient form in the North-East of England. However, contrary to what may be assumed without access to attitudinal information, data on claimed and imposed identities and levels of local affiliation reveal that speakers at the vanguard of the linguistic trend do not identify with the dominant urban centre of the North-East of England, nor do they reveal high levels of local orientation.

Furthermore, in terms of use of the innovatory forms in the data, a tension was predicted between constructing and retaining a local identity, and appearing outward-looking through use of variants which form part of the current consonantal changes identified in BrE, which are argued to be spreading from a South-Eastern epicentre. However, we find that the speakers who have adopted the ostensibly Southern forms, the young adult males, are also the speakers who reveal the highest levels of local orientation and the highest levels of use of the localized form under consideration.

This chapter then has demonstrated how attempts to explain motivating factors in linguistic variation and change are enhanced considerably by insights gained from attitudinal information on identity construction, orientations and affiliations. Indeed, without such knowledge, initial interpretations of linguistic behaviour may prove to be ill-founded.

Notes

1   See Anderson and Milroy (1999) and Dyer (2000, 2002) for recent variationist research which uses a language ideology framework expressly to interpret findings and motivations for linguistic change.
2   The method of data collection has also been used by the BBC Voices project through which an extensive survey of linguistic variation in Britain has been undertaken (see further www. bbc.co.uk/voices/).
3   Durham is a city with a population of 87,000 lying some 39 miles (63 km) South of Newcastle and 20 miles (32 km) North of Middlesbrough.
4   Along the abscissa of all bar charts, the 8 speaker groups are represented thus: old male (OM), middle male (MM), young adult male (Y2M), adolescent male (Y1M), old female (OF), middle female (MF), young adult female (Y2F), adolescent female (Y1F).
5   Scarborough is a seaside resort located on the North Yorkshire coast.

References

Anderson, B. (1991), *Imagined Communities: Reflections on the Origin and Spread of Nationalism* (revised edn). London: Verso.
Anderson, B. and Milroy, L. (1999), Southern changes and the Detroit AAVE vowel system. Paper presented at *NWAV-28*, Toronto.
Barltrop, R. and Wolveridge, J. (1980), *The Muvver Tongue*. London: Journeyman Press.
Branscombe, N. R., Ellemers, N., Spears, R. and Doosje, B. (1999), 'The context and content

of social identity threat', in N. Ellemers, R. Spears and B. Doosje (eds), *Social Identity: Context, Commitment, Content*. Oxford: Blackwell, pp. 35–58.

Chambers, J. K. (2003), *Sociolinguistic Theory: Linguistic Variation and its Social Significance*. Oxford: Blackwell.

Cohen, A. P. (1985), *The Symbolic Construction of Community*. Chichester: Ellis Horwood.

Coupland, N. (2001), 'Introduction: Sociolinguistic theory and social theory', in N. Coupland, S. Sarangi and C. N. Candlin (eds) *Sociolinguistics and Social Theory*. Harlow: Pearson Education Limited, pp. 1–26.

Cruttenden, A. (1994), *Gimson's Pronunciation of English* (5th edn). London: Arnold.

Docherty, G. J. Foulkes, P., Milroy, J., Milroy, L. and Walshaw, D. (1997), 'Descriptive adequacy in phonology: a variationist perspective', *Journal of Linguistics* 33, 275–310.

Dyer, J. A. (2000), 'Language and identity in a Scottish-English community: a phonological and discoursal analysis'. Unpublished doctoral dissertation, University of Michigan.

— (2002). '"We all speak the same round here." Dialect levelling in a Scottish English community', *Journal of Sociolinguistics* 6 (2), 99–116.

Eckert, P. (2000), *Linguistic Variation as Social Practice: The Linguistic Construction of Identity in Belten High*. Oxford: Blackwell.

Foulkes, P. and Docherty, G. J. (2001), 'Variation and change in British English /r/', in H. Van de Velde and R. van Hout (eds), *'r-atics: Sociolinguistic, Phonetic and Phonological Characteristics of /r/*. Brussels: IVLP/ULB, pp. 27–44.

Giegerich, H. J. (1992), *English Phonology: An Introduction*. Cambridge: Cambridge University Press.

Gimson, A. C. (1989), *An Introduction to the Pronunciation of English* (4th edn). London: Arnold.

Hughes, A., Trudgill, P. and Watt, D. (2005), *English Accents and Dialects: An Introduction to Social and Regional Varieties of English in the British Isles* (4th edn). London: Hodder.

Irvine, J. T. and Gal, S. (2000), 'Language ideology and linguistic differentiation', in P. Kroskrity (ed.), *Regimes of Language*. Santa Fe: School of American Research Press, pp. 35–83.

Johnstone, B. (2004), 'Place, globalization, and linguistic variation', in C. Fought (ed.), *Critical Reflections on Sociolinguistic Variation*. Oxford: Oxford University Press, pp. 65–83.

Kerswill, P. (1987), 'Levels of linguistic variation in Durham', *Journal of Linguistics*, 23, 25–49.

Le Page, R. B. and Tabouret-Keller, A. (1985), *Acts of Identity: Creole-based Approaches to Language and Ethnicity*. Cambridge: Cambridge University Press.

Llamas, C. (1999), 'A new methodology: data elicitation for social and regional language variation studies', *Leeds Working Papers in Linguistics and Phonetics*, 7, 95–118.

— (2001), 'Language variation and innovation in Teesside English'. Unpublished doctoral dissertation, University of Leeds.

— (2006), 'Field Methods', in C. Llamas, L. Mullany and P. Stockwell (eds), *The Routledge Companion to Sociolinguistics*. London: Routledge, pp. 12–18.

Milroy, J. (1996), 'A current change in British English: variation in (th) in Derby', *Newcastle and Durham Working Papers in Linguistics*, 4, 213–22.

— (2000), 'Two nations divided by the same language (and different language ideologies)', *Journal of Linguistic Anthropology*, 9, (1), 1–34.

— (2001), 'Internally and externally motivated language change: Assessing the effects of "nature" and "nurture"'. Keynote address delivered at the *Third UK Language Variation and Change Conference*, University of York, July 2001.

— (2003), 'Social and linguistic dimensions of phonological change: fitting the pieces of the puzzle together', in D. Britain and J. Cheshire (eds), *Sociolinguistic Dialectology*. Amsterdam: Benjamins, pp. 155–71.

— (2004), 'Language ideologies and linguistic change', in C. Fought (ed.), *Critical Reflections on Sociolinguistic Variation*. Oxford: Oxford University Press, pp. 161–77.

Milroy, J., Milroy, L. and Hartley, S. (1994), 'Local and supra-local change in British English: The case of glottalisation', *English World Wide*, 15, (1), 1–33.

Moorsom, N. (1996), *Middlesbrough Re-Born: The Evolution of a Local Authority*. Middlesbrough: Moorsom.

Orton, H. and Dieth, E. (1962–71), *Survey of English Dialects. Introduction and 4 vols.* Leeds: E. J. Arnold.

Orton, H., Sanderson, S. and Widdowson, J. D. A. (1978), *The Linguistic Atlas of England*. London: Croom Helm.

Public Relations Department Middlesbrough Borough Council (1997), *Middlesbrough Official Guide*.

Reed, J. S. (1983), *Southerners: The Social Psychology of Sectionalism*. Chapel Hill: University of North Carolina Press.

Silverstein, M. (1979), 'Language structure and linguistic ideology', in P. R. Clyne, F. H. William and C. L. Hofbauer (eds), *The Elements: A parasession on linguistic units and levels*. Chicago: Chicago Linguistic Society, pp. 193–247.

— (1992), 'The uses and utility of ideology: some reflections', *Pragmatics*, 2, (3), 311–23.

— (2003), 'Indexical order and the dialectics of social life', *Language and Communication*, 23, 193–229.

Stuart-Smith, J. and Tweedie, C. (2000), *Accent change in Glasgow: A sociophonetic investigation*. Final report to the Leverhulme Trust.

The Sunday Times, 5 March 2000.

Tollfree, L. (1999), 'South East London English: discrete *versus* continuous modelling of consonantal reduction', in P. Foulkes and G. J. Docherty (eds), *Urban Voices: Accent Studies in the British Isles*. London: Arnold, pp. 163–84.

Trudgill, P. (1990), *The Dialects of England*. Oxford: Blackwell.

— (1999), 'Norwich: endogenous and exogenous linguistic change', in P. Foulkes and G. J. Docherty (eds), *Urban Voices: Accent Studies in the British Isles*. London: Arnold, pp. 124–40.

Turner, J. C. (1999), 'Some current issues in research on social identity and self-categorization theories', in N. Ellemers, R. Spears and B. Doosje (eds), *Social Identity: Context, Commitment, Content*. Oxford: Blackwell, pp. 6–34

Turner, J. C. and Brown, R. (1978), 'Social status, cognitive alternatives, and intergroup relations', in H. Tajfel (ed.), *Differentiation between Social Groups*. London: Academic Press, pp. 201–34.

Underwood, G. N. (1988), 'Accent and Identity', in A. R. Thomas (ed.), *Methods in Dialectology*. Clevedon: Multilingual Matters, pp. 406–27.

Watt, D. and Allen, W. (2003), 'Tyneside English', *Journal of the International Phonetic Association*, 33, (2), 267–71.

Watt, D. and Milroy, L. (1999), 'Patterns of variation and change in three Tyneside vowels: Is this dialect levelling?', in P. Foulkes and G. J. Docherty (eds), *Urban Voices: Accent Studies in the British Isles*. London: Arnold, pp. 25–46.

Wells, J. C. (1982), *Accents of English (3 vols)*. Cambridge: Cambridge University Press.

Williams, A and Kerswill, P. (1999), 'Dialect levelling: continuity vs. change in Milton Keynes, Reading and Hull', in P. Foulkes and G. J. Docherty (eds), *Urban Voices: Accent Studies in the British Isles*. London: Arnold, pp. 141–62.

Woolard, K. A. (1992), 'Language ideology: Issues and approaches'. *Pragmatics*, 2, (3), 235–49.

Woolard, K. A. and Schieffelin, B. (1994), 'Language Ideology', *Annual Review of Anthropology*, 23, 55–82.

Appendix 6.1

Example questions from Affiliation Score Index

1. Would you say you feel close to and feel you have something in common with people from your home town in general (that is people you don't know personally), or would you say you do not feel any closer to them than to people from somewhere else?
   a) feel closer to people from home town (3)
   b) don't feel any closer to people from home town than to other people (1)
   c) don't know, can't say (2)

2. If you were the manager of a company which was recruiting people and two equally qualified and experienced people applied for the position, but one had been born and educated in your home town and the other had been born and educated somewhere else, would you choose:
   a) the person from your home town (3)
   b) the person from somewhere else (1)
   c) don't know, wouldn't matter (2)

3. If you were voting in a local election, would the fact that a candidate was a local person persuade you to vote for them?
   a) yes it would (3)
   b) no it wouldn't (1)
   c) don't know (2)

7 Regional variation and identity in Sunderland

Lourdes Burbano-Elizondo

Introduction

The City of Sunderland is situated about 15 miles to the South of Newcastle-upon-Tyne in North-East England. This metropolitan district includes not only Sunderland but also Washington, Houghton-le-Spring and Hetton-le-Hole, all of which were until 1974 part of County Durham. In this year, as a consequence of the reorganization of county boundaries this metropolitan district of Sunderland was created and realigned together with North and South Tyneside, Newcastle-upon-Tyne and Gateshead to form the metropolitan county of Tyne and Wear. This new county spread around the estuaries of the rivers Tyne – traditionally the border between the counties of Durham and Northumberland – and Wear.

The North-East owes its growth and development to its prosperous industrial past based on coal, iron and steel, shipbuilding and heavy engineering. All this industry led to the development of three main compact and densely-populated urban centres (Tyneside, Wearside and Teesside) and of mining settlements and small towns. However, due to the economic depression in the 1930s the region went from being one of the richest regions in the country to being one of the poorest. The decline of the industrial sector led to a dramatic increase in male redundancy, early retirement and unemployment. In order to create employment in the region new branches of industry were brought to the region – e.g. the textile industry and a Japanese car manufacturer (Nissan) in Sunderland – and the service sector was developed (Bradley 1995).

It is believed, however, that the economic and social problems that resulted from the industrial decline in the region together with a sense of regional isolation and resentment towards the South have favoured the development of a strong regional identity in the North-East (Beal 1993). In fact a survey conducted by the BBC in 2000 revealed that '[t]he greatest sense of regionality is revealed to be in the North-East, where two in every five have a strong local identity'.[1]

Despite this compactness of the North-Eastern community, within its boundaries we can identify various strong and distinct local identities that distinguish the inhabitants of different North-Eastern localities. Sunderland people in particular often complain that their city is regarded as Newcastle's poor relation. Like other North-Eastern localities, Sunderland has generally remained in the shadow of Newcastle, the capital of the region, with which they are generally associated. There is a generalized tendency amongst those from outside the North-East to class all North-Easterners as 'Geordies'[2] on the grounds that when they speak they all sound very much the same, but for many non-Geordie North-Easterners this can be rather offensive because Geordies are only those who come from Newcastle. However, as many in the region point out, for outsiders there does not seem to be anything else in the North-East apart from Newcastle and Geordies. This is a matter of concern and often a source of annoyance for Sunderland people, who would like Sunderland to be acknowledged as a city with its own character, voice and identity distinct from Newcastle. As a result Wearsiders, as Sunderland people are often referred to, have developed a strong local identity which tends to embody the rivalry that they have with their Geordie neighbours. It is through symbols such as their football team, their city and their dialect that they seem to construct meaning and express their attachment and sense of belonging to the community.

The Sunderland dialect in particular is locally regarded as a marker of the Sunderland community, and its speakers – regardless of how strong their affiliation to the local community may be – hold that despite their proximity to Newcastle it is possible to tell Sunderland and Newcastle people apart by the way they speak. Given the evident relation between language and identity and the importance of the local dialect as a symbol of identity, in order to provide a meaningful account of language variation in Sunderland and understand its social function, identity and local attitudes needed to occupy a focal place. The local dialect needs to be explained within the social and ideological context in which it is being used.

In the last few years a number of sociolinguists have emphasized the need to incorporate speakers' language ideologies in the study of language variation and change (Milroy 2000 and 2004; Llamas 2001; Dyer and Wassink 2001). For this they have applied an ideological framework based on Silverstein's mode (1992) which identifies two orders of indexicality in language. *First-order indexicality* refers to the links speakers establish between particular linguistic forms and some specific social category. However, this first-order indexicality may be perceived and discussed differently by different communities. This is what Silverstein defines as *second-order indexicality*: how speakers may rationalize and justify the link between the linguistic form and a particular social category/meaning. It is in these second-order indexical processes that we see how speakers evaluate linguistic indices, by means of ideologies. Therefore since different communities will have different ideologies to interpret the link between language varieties or language features and social groups, and will therefore have different justifications for their language behaviour, we can expect as a result that different social groups and meanings will be foregrounded in different communities. Consequently, the same language or language feature may be rationalized differently by different communities (cf. Silverstein 1992 for a more detailed account).

In the light of this, speakers generally are able to not only identify the explicit referential meanings coded in linguistic utterances but also to identify other meanings implicit in linguistic utterances. They are able to draw associations between linguistic forms and particular social groups or social meanings and to justify and rationalize these links. Ultimately, therefore, it is this knowledge of language ideologies that allows them to shape their language so that it reflects their place in society.

This is the framework within which the local Sunderland dialect and identity are being studied. Nevertheless, by assuming that speakers are able to justify and rationalize their language behaviour, this ideological model also assumes that speakers are to some extent aware of the way they speak. The Sunderland study aims to ascertain whether those linguistic features which Sunderland people believe to characterize their local variety and distinguish them from Geordies are actually used by the speakers. To do this, the linguistic data collected in the city will be analysed (Burbano-Elizondo, forthcoming). This chapter, however, concentrates only on determining how Sunderland people perceive and define the boundaries of their community (section 2), examining actual attitudinal data collected in Sunderland and identify some of the local ideologies that surround the Sunderland dialect and turn it into such an important symbol of local identity (section 3). Having provided some insight into how the Sunderland community positions itself within North-Eastern society, section 4 will provide an account of the dialect differences that Sunderland people claim to exist between Newcastle and Sunderland English, and will look into how the local ideologies which help in the construction of the local identity and draw the boundary between the Sunderland and the Newcastle communities may be used to describe, justify and rationalize the local dialect.

All the linguistic and attitudinal data recorded for the Sunderland study was collected using the Survey of Regional English methodology originally designed by Llamas (1999) (see also Asprey *et al.* 2006). This flexible and structured methodology was adapted to meet the aims of the present research by adding a language questionnaire, an identity questionnaire (henceforth IdQ) and an Identification Index Score. This ensured the collection of lexical, grammatical and phonological data as well as qualitative and quantitative data on identity. This chapter, however, discusses only qualitative attitudinal data recorded in the IdQ and the interview.

Sunderland: A community in North-East England

Cohen refers to the concept of *community* as an entity that 'seems to imply simultaneously both similarity and difference' (1985: 12), meaning that whereas the members of a community share features with one another, these same features distinguish them from other communities. These similarities and differences make it possible to say where a community begins and where it ends – that is, they allow its boundaries to be established. Thus a community boundary may be understood as an entity which:

> encapsulates the identity of the community and, like the identity of an individual, is called into being by the exigencies of social interaction. Boundaries are marked because communities interact in some way or other with entities from which they are, or wish to be,

distinguished. [...] But not all boundaries, and not *all* the components of *any* boundary, are so objectively apparent. They may be thought of, rather, as existing in the minds of their beholders. This being so, the boundary may be perceived in rather different terms, not only by people on opposite sides of it, but also by people in the same side.

(Cohen 1985: 12)

Community boundaries, therefore, apart from being established on the basis of relative similarities and differences that delimit communities, seem to be defined quite subjectively. Rather than being a matter of 'objective' assessment, it is a matter of feeling and belonging: It resides in the minds of the members themselves. Community members attach meanings to the boundary. Within its limits, people share a series of symbols – e.g. values, beliefs, ways of talking – that distinguish them from other communities. These symbols are mental constructs which provide people with the tools to make meaning and express their sense of belonging to the community (Cohen 1985: 12–21).

The scope of the Sunderland study was delimited by establishing some arbitrary boundaries that would help to define the sociolinguistic sample to be explored. Only informants born and bred within the current official limits of the City of Sunderland would be recruited[3] (see section 1). However, given that in 1974 Washington, Houghton and Hetton were relocated as part of the City of Sunderland and then together with Sunderland itself separated from County Durham and realigned in the metropolitan county of Tyne and Wear alongside Tyneside, the Sunderland informants were asked to define the limits of their community in order to ascertain whether the political boundaries of the City of Sunderland coincided with the boundaries of the Sunderland community as perceived by its members. In other words, do the political boundaries reflect the ideological boundaries of the community? Do Sunderland people identify with the political boundaries?

The Sunderland community shares a series of symbols and ideologies through which they distinguish themselves from their Geordie neighbours. Probably one of the most salient factors that help to define the Sunderland community as an ideologically coherent social unit is the fact that they refuse to be classed as 'Geordies'. Many outsiders to the North-Eastern community, unaware of the ideological issues and symbols surrounding the Sunderland and Tyneside communities, are generally unfamiliar with the salience of these subjective boundaries and often are even completely unaware of the existence of this ideological divide, which explains why many refer to all North-Easterners as 'Geordies'.

In the IdQ, the Sunderland participants were asked to draw a line around the area where the 'Mackem' or Sunderland community[4] lives and in the subsequent interview they were asked to justify this boundary. Delimiting the Sunderland community was not as straightforward as expected. Most of the controversy centred around Washington. Despite the fact that most of the participants located Washington within the Mackem territory, there was a general awareness that although *officially* Washington is part of the City of Sunderland, it is a town that to some extent fails to identify with the Sunderland community. Identity-wise its population is divided and thus regarded as a mixture of Geordies and Mackems.

Some explained that Washington suffers from an 'identity crisis' and others referred to its inhabitants as 'Geordie rejects' due to the fact that they do not like to think of themselves as being from Sunderland but from Newcastle. They may belong to Sunderland but many do not adhere to the local culture or to the local symbols. Proof of this is the fact that many Washington people support Newcastle United, which seems to be evidence of their 'Geordieness'. Also their dialect seems to be perceived as different: closer to Tyneside English than Sunderland English. Football allegiances and dialect were the two main factors that seemed to determine Washington people's membership to the Sunderland community. However, there seemed to be yet another factor coming into play here: self-perception. Many of the informants commented on the fact that many Washington people refuse to class themselves as living in Sunderland. So belonging to the community depended not just on being perceived as part of it but also on wanting to belong to it. Consequently, although due to the high influence of the political boundaries Washington was acknowledged as part of the City of Sunderland, this membership was then subject to the acceptance of certain local symbols.

This provided an idea of what symbols and values are locally important when it comes to signal membership, and although language is definitely one of them, it is no more than one of the socio-cultural factors that contribute to construction of the local identity. As such, it needs to be regarded as closely related to, and influenced by, other locally meaningful social values, norms and stances. As Eckert states:

> [t]he designation of *speech community* confers on an aggregate of people the judgement that they constitute a sufficiently mutual sense-making unit that important aspects of linguistic organization are embedded in their social practice [...] The definition of a particular speech community is, above all, a way of defining both the limitations and the broader implications of the study, for in carefully articulating what this unit accounts for in the lives of the speakers it delineates, one can also articulate what it does not account for. It is not enough to describe a speech community as an isolated unit, for no community is isolable; the description of a speech community is most importantly an account of that community's linguistic place in the wider society. An account of a speech community, then, will optimally account for the articulation between the internal dynamics of the speech community and its relation to other localities.
>
> (Eckert 2000: 33–4)

Therefore, the Sunderland speech community ultimately needs to be described not as an isolated unit but in relation to the wider social and linguistic North-Eastern continuum. The following section analyses some of the attitudes and responses elicited in the IdQ and the interview so as to provide a global picture of how Sunderland people explain their community and their relation towards, and perception of Sunderland.

Making sense of the Mackem identity

Although Sunderland was part of County Durham until 1974, with the re-organization of county boundaries in 1974 it became part of the metropolitan county of Tyne and Wear together with Newcastle-upon-Tyne, which up to then had been part of Northumberland. Being the most developed city in the region, Newcastle is regarded as the capital of North-East England. The closest big city to the North of Newcastle is Edinburgh and the closest one to the South is Leeds. Thus it does not come as a surprise that the proximity of this urban centre has in some ways overshadowed the city of Sunderland, which is only about 15 miles to the South of Newcastle. Sunderland was granted city status in 1992 and this largely boosted their pride in their city (Beal 2000: 369). Nonetheless, Sunderland people often feel that their city is the less favoured one: there is a feeling that more money is invested in Newcastle and that therefore it always gets all the latest improvements. This was reflected in an article published in *The Guardian* in September 1979, in which the author stated that:

> [t]he problem was it [Sunderland] always suffered from Newcastle. [...] Why, they'll tell you, Newcastle has even pinched the design of their wonderful bridge – a beautiful orange and white iron bow, once reckoned the biggest in the world. The feeling that somehow they always deserved better than they got is still strong in Sunderland today, and who can say it is wrong?

On the same grounds, a few years later Mark Jensen, editor of Newcastle United fanzine the *Mag*, spoke about Sunderland people's resentment towards Newcastle in *The Independent* with these words:

> The Mackems have always had a chip on their shoulder because Tyneside – at least in local terms – has the superior facilities, such as the Metro underground railway and huge shopping centres (*The Independent*, 19 August 1992: p. 26).

These extracts provide an insight into why Sunderland people may feel such a hostility towards Newcastle and more particularly towards Geordies. The Sunderland informants widely admitted that the city has changed, developed and improved a lot in the last few years, hence some of the statements taken from newspaper articles may have become slightly outdated nowadays. Probably the most important development has been the extension of the Metro system from Newcastle to Sunderland, which is bound to have had an impact in the local community favouring contact with Newcastle. Also the city has been largely improved and provided with better shopping and sports facilities and entertainment, which have turned Sunderland into a more self-sufficient and independent city.

In spite of these developments, most still regarded Newcastle as the more favoured city and attribute this to the fact that Newcastle is a bigger and more important city, has more history and is regarded as the capital of the North-East. The following comments clearly reflected these feelings:

> Newcastle is more cosmopolitan and seems to get more business opportunities than Sunderland. Sunderland is clearly the poorer relative. (MM14 – IdQ: question 12)

> [Newcastle] historically is more important than Sunderland. It has a bigger and better city centre. It [is] seen as the capital of the north. Newcastle is more fashionable than Sunderland, we seem to be the second best on everything including football. (OM07 – IdQ: question 12)

<MM28> Newcastle, they are known as 'Magpies' because they steal stuff.[5]
<LBE> [laughter] OK.
<MM28> They have, they have stolen lots of things from Sunderland.
<LBE> Uh-huh
<MM28> Right? That's one of the reasons I hate them.

(Interview 15 – 72:03ff)

<MM28> But unfortunately the majority of people outside of the North-East, particularly in the south, they don't think there's anything more in the North-East than Newcastle.
<MM29> Yeah, yeah that's right.
<LBE> Mm-hm. That true.
<MM28> And that's down to f- that's probably down to the fact that Newcastle manages to get everything from the south,
<LBE> Uh-huh
<MM28> like, government allocated money to Newcastle.
<MM29> Yeah.
<LBE> Yeah.
<MM28> Which is another reason for hating them.

(Interview 15, part 2 (15:42 – 16:01))

These quotations reveal evident feelings of resentment: feelings that help to mould a local identity that often strongly opposes Geordies and their city. Moreover, an underlying feeling of inferiority also seems to pervade these assertions. Sunderland is not only the 'poorer relative' but also 'the second best' when set alongside Newcastle.

Interestingly, when questioned about their opinion towards their city, the Sunderland informants elicited mixed feelings. Whilst some clearly demonstrated feelings of pride towards their city and viewed the process of development and improvement the city has undergone in the last few years in a positive light (see comments (i) and (ii) below); others, in spite of this development, provided negative views of Sunderland and a lack of pride towards it which may well provide evidence of an inferiority complex (see comments (iii), (iv), (v) and (vi), below):

(i)   Very proud of it, love it, it is the biggest and most important city in North-East. (MM28)
(ii)   It is the most progressive city in the North-East at the moment.
(iii) Uninspiring, small minded. (MF40– IdQ question 11)
(iv)   No expectations. That way, we'll never be disappointed. Characterizes Sunderland folks, I think. Generally shows a lack of civil vision backed by inferior planning. (OM25– IdQ question 11)
(v)   Characterless. (MF39 – IdQ question 11)
(vi)   An industrial town. There have been a lot of recent changes. I don't think it will ever be a beautiful city. Sadly, what I really feel denigrates Sunderland is a bad attitude amongst some areas of the population. There does at times seem to be a great lack of pride and vision. I hope I'm wrong, but I feel this is holding us behind. (OM12– IdQ question 11)

In the interview, the informant who produced statement (vi) admitted that this lack of pride to which he was referring could indeed be attributed to an inferiority complex.

Thus, in spite of Sunderland's development in the last few years, some people do seem to look at their city with shame. These tended to be those who were not concerned about the Geordie–Mackem rivalry and would often even condemn it. By contrast, others demonstrated a very strong sense of identity and attachment to Sunderland and held negative views against everything related to Newcastle. These generally were very proud of Sunderland and of the fact that lately it has improved quite a lot. Nevertheless, although they could not deny that Newcastle is a more important city and has better public facilities, they often hold this as a factor that to some extent fuels the rivalry between the two communities. This, however, does not seem to be the main reason that stirs up the rivalry nowadays. Other factors throughout the history of the region seem to have promoted it. Some explained that the feeling has always been there and pointed to the industrial past of the two cities, and a desire by their respective populations to be better than the other ones, as the reason that fostered that rivalry in the past. Yet the general consensus was that football is the main reason that feeds the rivalry nowadays. This is reflected in some of the answers to the question 'what are the main reasons for the Geordie–Mackem rivalry?' in my IdQ:

> Brought into focus by football rivalry. Some industrial apartheid. Civil war rivalry, possibly started with rivalry over the coal trade in the Middle Ages. (OM25– IdQ question 15)

> Traditionally competing industry (shipyards, coal miner, port activity), and much more recently, football. (MM14 – IdQ question 15)

Whilst most of the Sunderland participants seemed to be indifferent to this hostility that exists between the two neighbouring communities, most did make it clear that they would not stand being classed as 'Geordies' and would actually correct anyone who made such an assertion. However, it was at this point when they were asked to explain how they would define themselves if they were not Geordies that some controversy emerged since not everyone accepted the label 'Mackem'. Many explained that they preferred to say they were Wearsiders or merely *from* Sunderland. Not everyone in Sunderland seemed to accept this label to define their identity partly due to a widespread belief that the term 'Mackem' is a derogatory term used by Geordie football fans to refer to Sunderland people. This would explain why some Sunderland people do not like this label: 7 out of 30 people interviewed even found this label offensive. The rest of the sample did not find the term particularly offensive. However, some did point out that this depended on *how* the term was used and, most importantly, *who* used it. It was also suggested that the term, whatever its origin and despite of its originally derogatory connotations, may have filtered through the Sunderland community little by little and as a result it could have become accepted at least by some as a label for their identity. Nevertheless, the etymology of this term continues to be rather uncertain. What is certain is that 'Mackem' derives from the traditional Durham/Sunderland pronunciation of the words *make* and *take*, which is [mak] and [tak] respectively (Beal 1999: 45). However, whilst some believe that the term was created by Geordie football fans to insult Sunderland football fans as a result of the rivalry, another popular story holds that the term arose in times of the shipyards in Wearside when Sunderland workers would *mak* the ships and then others would *tak 'em* away – hence 'Mackems':

> One story states that during World War II shipyard workers from Wearside were asked to help out building ships on the Tyne (Newcastle), probably due to their vast experience in the shipbuilding trade. This was not well met by the local Geordies who viewed it as taking work away from local people, thus the Wearside workers were making the ships and taking away jobs from Tyneside folk – 'Mak'em and Tak'em'. Thus the term 'Mackem' was born and used to insult Wearside shipyard workers.
>
> (www.virtualtourist.com/m/2587d/4a601/)

One of middle-aged informants, whose father had worked in the shipyards in the 1960s, referred to the use of the term 'Mackem' as a derogatory term by Geordies as early as the 1960s:

<MM14> I wouldn't consider myself a Geordie.
<LBE> Uh-huh.
<MM14> But, eh, 'Mackem' seems as always like a pejorative term.
<LBE> Yeah.
<MM14> So, eh, imposed on us and
<LBE> Yeah.
<MM14> for some reason people are using it
<LBE> Do people use it? [—]
<MM14> Yeah, yeah. Well in the *Sunderland Echo* for example.
<LBE> Uh-huh.
<MM14> Eh, any reference to Sunderland F. C., 'Mackem this and Mackem that'. So
<LBE> Yeah.
<MM14> it's certainly been adopted and localized and nativized as a, as a term.
<LBE> But do you think it's offensive?
<MM14> I think originally it was offensive.
<LBE> Uh-huh.
<MM14> In the eh so like when my father was starting work in the mid-sixties and early seventies
<LBE> Yeah.
<MM14> and he had a lot of contact with Tyneside workers, they would refer to 'Mackems'.
<LBE> Uh-huh.
<MM14> And whenever they mentioned the word 'Mackem', that was never in a good light.
<LBE> Right.
<MM14> But by the time I was in working age or going to university, 'Mackem' was just a word that we would use.
<LBE> Uh-huh.
<MM14> But curiously, eh, for some other research I'm doing I went through all of the papers from 1982. I did four months worth of research in the early part of this year.
<LBE> Yeah.
<MM14> And in 1982 nowhere is the word 'Mackem' mentioned
<LBE> Right.
<MM14> in those papers. And in fact people are referring to themselves as 'Geordies' in the letters to the editor and stuff.

(Interview 7 (74:20 – 75:51))

So what is certain is that 'Mackem' is a term that originally was used by Geordies in order to cause offence to Wearsiders, and whilst some section of the Sunderland community still rejects it, to a large extent nowadays it seems to have become associated mainly – yet not exclusively – with supporters of Sunderland A. F. C. With time, the term would have become slightly more accepted in Sunderland as a label for their identity, a term that would constitute the antithesis of the term 'Geordie'.

There seems to be some truth though in what this speaker said about Sunderland people referring to themselves as 'Geordies' in the 1980s. Some people in the oldest age group still feel more attached to County Durham and do not really accept the new relocation of the City of Sunderland as part of Tyne and Wear. For instance, when I asked whether he considered himself a Mackem, a Geordie or neither of them, a 69-year-old ex-miner born in Houghton-le-Spring – which is now part of the City of Sunderland – defined himself as a Geordie. In answering the question 'do you find it offensive to be called "Mackem"? Why?' (IdQ question 16), he explained:

> I'm not bothered because in my opinion everyone born in the county of Durham is a Geordie. (OM27 – IdQ question 16)

Nevertheless, Sunderland people do not accept to be labelled as 'Geordies' today. Like people from other areas in the North-East, they often have to put up with being classified as Geordies by outsiders to the area on the grounds that when they speak they sound very much like them. Whether Sunderland people define themselves as *Mackems*, *Wearsiders* or merely as *being from Sunderland*, the vast majority agree in one thing: they are definitely not Geordies. It is at this point that they all come together as a community in order to shape and delimit their strong local identity, and construct meaning together. Amongst the strategies they use to distinguish themselves from Geordies, probably the main one is their local dialect. Sunderland English emerges as a symbol of local identity. The following section will focus upon this marker of identity as a device which, according to its speakers, differentiates them from Geordies.

Sunderland English as a symbol of local identity

As mentioned at the end of the previous section, the 'Geordie' label is not particularly welcome by Sunderland people given the strong sense of local identity and the rivalry that exists between the inhabitants of these two urban centres. For outsiders, however, most of the North-Eastern dialectal varieties sound basically the same: they are all 'Geordie' English and by extension, unfamiliar as they are with the regional rivalries and other issues of identity that exist within the North-East, all North-Easterners are Geordies. Yet, these perceptions are not completely unfounded. A general review of how modern dialectology has delimited the different dialect regions around England shows that the whole of the North-East, from Teesside to the Eastern side of the English–Scottish border, tends to be grouped together (Wells 1982; Trudgill 1990). The various local dialects within this area do share a significant number of features, which would explain why they have been grouped together and therefore, why they all tend to be perceived as 'Geordie'. However, they also have features that will distinguish one from another, which is why North-Easterners can generally identify whether someone comes from Sunderland, Tyneside, Durham or Middlesbrough merely by the way they speak. As Trudgill explains:

> [o]f course, there remain distinctive differences *within* all of these areas – no one from Middlesbrough would mistake a Tynesider for someone from Middlesbrough – but the accents are sufficiently similar to be grouped together, and sufficiently *different* from those of other areas. Londoners, for instance, might mistakenly think that Middlesbrough speakers were from Newcastle, but they would be much less likely to think that they were from, say, Sheffield.
>
> (Trudgill 1990: 77)

This, therefore, would to a certain extent excuse those who are not from the North-East for taking someone from Sunderland for a Geordie.

However, given that the two varieties sound so similar that outsiders are unable to tell them apart but so clearly different for Sunderland speakers, the Sunderland informants were asked to try and identify those features that in their view distinguish Sunderland and Tyneside English with the intention of ascertaining how aware they are of their language behaviour.

Answering the questions: 'Is your accent different from the accent of nearby cities such as Newcastle and Durham? Can you think of any specific ways in which it is different? For instance, are there any words which are pronounced differently?' (IdQ question 3) proved to be a difficult task for most of the participants, who usually struggled to identify specific differences. Many explained that the Sunderland accent does not sound as broad as the Geordie one but were unable to go into much more detail. This raised the question of whether or not in building their sociolinguistic identity Sunderland speakers are conscious of the repertoire of linguistic variants that are characteristic of their local dialect. Indeed, some differences between Sunderland and Tyneside English were identified. However, evidence needs to be found to determine whether these perceived differences have a real foundation or, on the contrary, are merely perceptions.

Perceived differences between Sunderland and Tyneside English

'Moun' vs 'moon'

One of the most commonly identified differences was the vowel quality in words like *moon* and *spoon*. According to some of my informants, whilst Geordies would pronounce them as [mu: n] and [spu: n] respectively, in Sunderland English they would be [mᵊun] and [spᵊun]. In the following extract, a 71-year-old male informant from Sunderland (OM10) explained that their Tynesider friends generally ask him to pronounce the words *moon* and *spoon* for them since he pronounces them differently to them. His wife (OF11), who was from Tyneside, was also aware of this aware of this dialect difference between her and her husband and commented on the fact that if she had to reflect this difference in writing she would probably spell these words as *'moun'* and *'spoun'* respectively to show the Sunderland pronunciation:

<OF11> All our friends are Tynesiders.
<OM10> They always say to me 'spoon' say 'spoon' [spᵊun] and 'moon' [mᵊun].
<LBE> Uh-huh.
<OM10> Because she says 'moon' [mu: n].
<OF11> You see, I couldn't write that down. I know when (¿I know?) about the differences in the dialect because how do you put that down? Otherwise, I'd say, eh or you spell it M-O-U-N. I think you would. I say 'moon' [mu: n], 'look at the moon', and he says 'look at the moon' [mᵊun], or something like that.

(Interview 7 – 72:23ff)

/h/-dropping

Another pronunciation feature that is generally perceived to distinguish Sunderland and Tyneside English is /h/-dropping. Beal (2000) refers to this feature as a North-Eastern shibboleth of Mackem speech that reinforces the Geordie feeling of superiority over Mackems:

[W]ithin the North-east h-dropping is a shibboleth of Makkem speech. In 1998, I took part in a phone-in of Radio Newcastle for which the main topic was local accents. One caller told me that, since moving from Tyneside to Washington, which is now within the City of Sunderland, she had noticed that her daughter was the only one who could speak 'correctly', as all the other children in her class dropped their aitches. Since h-dropping is perhaps the single most stigmatized feature of English regional accents [...], the fact that Makkems drop /h/ whilst Geordies retain it reinforces the Geordies' belief in their inherent superiority and in the status of their speech as a true dialect rather than 'bad English'.

(Beal 2000: 368)

According to Trudgill (1990: 27–8), the only remaining non-/h/-dropping areas in England were mostly peripheral regions: East Anglia and Northumberland and Durham. The dialects of these regions have certainly preserved /h/ despite the fact that the vast majority of the British dialects drop it. Nevertheless, the area in the North-East of England may need to be revised if it is true that Sunderland speakers tend to drop their aitches.

Some of the Sunderland informants did comment on this regional stereotype. One of the older males in particular related the following personal anecdote with one of his college teachers:

<OM07> Sunderland people tend not to produce, to pronounce aitch.
<LBE> Uh-huh. Would you say that is general in Sunderland?
<OF08> Yes, uh-huh, from schools, yeah.
<LBE> Yeah.
<OM07> They pick it up. I- I- When I was doing me teaching practice at South Shields,
<LBE> Yeah.
<OM07> I got some stick because of me Sunderland accent. One teacher had a like, was having a go at us all the time.
<LBE> Uh-huh.
<OM07> And eh your hands are tied you cannot say – you know if we had a confrontation when I couldn't, might have been, tossed, you know, tossed out,
<LBE> Yeah.

<OM07> excluded sort of thing, you know, and sent back to college. But uh, he uh, he got on about that,
<?> [—]
<LBE> Mm?
<OM07> about uh the aitches. We always leave our aitches off.
<LBE> Yeah.
<OM07> And that was, so that's only about six miles away.
<LBE> Yeah.
<OM07> and it was so distinctive to them that we didn't pronounce our aitches.

(Interview 4, part 1 (16:46 ff))

Preliminary results point towards a clear tendency in Sunderland English to retain /h/ more than it could have been expected from a dialect variety which is popularly characterized for its /h/-dropping.

'Ower' vs 'wor'

There also seem to be grammatical features that distinguish Sunderland and Tyneside English which are evident for Sunderland people. One of them is the form of the first person singular possessive pronoun *our*. Previous dialect studies on Tyneside and Northumberland English have attested the use of *wor* in these varieties (Beal 1993). In order to ascertain whether this feature is used in Sunderland, it was included in the Sunderland grammar questionnaire and the vast majority agreed that *wor* is definitely not a local feature. Furthermore, they generally identified it as a Geordie feature and clarified that in Sunderland they would say *ower* [awa] instead, as we can see in the following extract:

<MM28> And er, number six, 'wor'.
<MM29> [Laughter]
<MM28> That is like, that's an insult that.
<MM29> Yeah.
<LBE> [Laughter]
<MM28> 'Wor' is definitely Newcastle.
<MM29> Yeah.
<LBE> Right.
<MM29> Aye.
<MM28> We, we would have. They'll pronounce a single syllable 'wor [wɔː],
<LBE> Uh-huh.
<MM28> and we pronounce it 'ower' [awa]. Two syllable.
<LBE> Right. Uh-huh.
<MM28> It's a completely different word.
<MM29> Aye. I've written that down. '"Ower" would be used not wor', definite. Nobody have, not a tick in that box at all.
<LBE> Right.
<MM28> If you, if you used the word 'wor' in a pub in Sunderland,
<MM29> Aye.
<MM28> then, you you would like be noticed as being an outsider.
<MM29> I mean that that
<LBE> Yeah.
<MM29> that would be a big noticeable difference between Newcastle and Sunderland.
<LBE> Right.
<MM28> 'Wor' and 'ower', yeah. [—]

<MM29> You would say. If in Newcastle you'd say 'wor lass',
<LBE> Uh-huh.
<MM29> and here you'd say 'ower lass'.
<LBE> Alright, yeah, uh-huh.
<MM29> That'd be,
<MM28> That's one of them.
<MM29> It's big demarcation that one.
<LBE> Right.

(Interview 15, part 2: 01:05 – 01:46)

'Divvent' vs 'Dinnet'

The use of *div/divvent* for the present form of the auxiliary verb *do* is also a characteristic feature of Tyneside and Northumberland English (Beal 1993). Previous research in Sunderland (Burbano-Elizondo 2001) also attested the presence of an alternative form in this variety: *dinnet*. Both forms, *divvent* and *dinnet*, were included in the grammar questionnaire in order to find out what was the general response in Sunderland.

The sentences *I do all the work, dinnet I?* and *I dinnet like him* recorded a higher level of usage than *Ye divvent like him, div ye?* Just about 31.5 per cent of my informants reported that the latter construction would be heard in Sunderland against 60 per cent and 85.7 per cent respectively in the former two. In the interview, however, very few would identify these two different forms as dialect markers that distinguish Sunderland and Tyneside English.

Lexical differences

Lexical differences between these two urban varieties proved to be the hardest ones to identify for speakers. Some of the lexical items that seem to be typical of the Sunderland dialect are *kets* for 'sweets' (also recorded in Durham in the Survey of English Dialects (cf. Orton and Dieth 1962–1971) and *doll off*, an expression for 'playing truant' that is exclusive to Sunderland.

However, the discussion of some lexical items did prompt comments that reflected not only how difficult it is for speakers to identify differences but also how speakers may use their local ideologies to justify the use of certain language forms. One of the middle-aged males who demonstrated a very strong sense of identity argued that *stottie*, which is a round flat bread bun, in fact was a Sunderland word that had been stolen by Geordies:

<MM28> 'Stottie' is definitely a Sunderland word. Newcastle borrowed it.
<LBE> [Laughter]
<MM28> It's ower word not theirs.
<LBE> Alright!
[...]
<LBE> And why do you say it was stolen by...?
<MM28> Because it's our, it's our bread. They'll, they'll. Newcastle, they're know as 'Magpies' because they steal stuff.
<LBE> [laughter] OK.
<MM28> They have, they have stolen loads of things from Sunderland.
<LBE> Uh-huh.
<MM28> Right? That's one of the reasons I hate them.

(Interview 15: part 1 (71:00–71:06 and 71:56–72:13))

The way in which the Sunderland informants focused upon all these phonological, grammatical and lexical differences between their local dialect and Tyneside English very much demonstrates that the Sunderland community not only mark their opposition to the Tyneside community by means of ideologies but also by linguistic means. According to Sunderland people, there seem to be a number of linguistic forms which they believe distinguish the speech of the two communities and their discussion and justification of these features clearly reflects the local ideologies and willingness to be acknowledged as a community that is independent and different from the Geordie one.

Concluding remarks

An examination of instantiations of second-order indexicality (see section 2, above) in my Sunderland corpus has demonstrated how the speakers' language behaviour may index their social identity. Explaining language differentiation is not as simple as merely stating, for example, that females tend to use more prestige variants than males; it is necessary to look into the speakers' ideologies and see how these sets of beliefs are used to justify their own and others' linguistic behaviour. Only by identifying these ideologies can we ascertain whether any of them could be determining their use of language and ultimately account for linguistic differentiation in a meaningful way.

Having obtained some insight into what it is that turns the Sunderland community into a coherent meaning-making social unit, the question at this point is whether the local linguistic perceptions identified in the course of this research are actually characteristic of this North-Eastern variety. The next stage of the Sunderland study therefore will concentrate upon these metalinguistic observations and will aim to (a) confirm whether or not they are corroborated by the linguistic data recorded in Sunderland; and (b) explain them in the light of the local ideological framework.

Notes

1 www.bbc.co.uk/england/thinkofengland/survey.shtml
2 Strictly speaking 'Geordies' are only the people from Newcastle-upon-Tyne although the term is often used more loosely to refer to the citizens of the whole Tyneside conurbation – i.e. from Newcastle, North and South Tyneside and Gateshead.
3 The City of Sunderland includes the towns of Houghton-le-Spring, Hetton-le-Hole and Washington.
4 'Mackem' is the term used to refer to the citizens of the City of Sunderland.
5 Newcastle United players are popularly called 'Magpies' due to the fact that their black and white striped shirt reminds of the black and white thieving bird.

References

Asprey, E., Burbano-Elizondo, L. and Wallace, K. (2006), 'The survey of regional English and its methodology: conception, refinement and implementation'. In Honero, A. M., M.

J. Luzón and S. Murillo (eds), *Corpus Linguistics: Applications for the Study of English* (*Linguistic Insights. Studies in Language and Communication*, Volume 25) Bern: Peter Lang, pp. 431–49.

Beal, J. C. (1993), 'The grammar of Tyneside and Northumbrian English', in J. Milroy and L. Milroy (eds), *Real English: the Grammar of English Dialects in the British Isles*. London: Longman, 187–213.

— (1999), '"Geordie Nation" language and regional identity in the North-east of England', in *Lore and Language*, 17, 33–48.

— (2000), 'From Geordie Ridley to *Viz*: popular literature in Tyneside English', in *Language and Literature*, 2000, 9, (4), 359–75.

Bradley, H. (1995), 'Gender relations and changing patterns of employment in the North-east region', in M. Erickson and S. Williams (eds), *Social Change in Tyne and Wear*. Proceedings of the Jobs, Training and Society (JETS) Conference, held at the University of Sunderland Washington Campus, 13 May 1994.

Burbano-Elizondo, L. (2001), 'Lexical erosion and lexical innovation in Tyne and Wear'. Unpublished MLitt dissertation, Department of English Linguistic and Literary Studies, University of Newcastle-upon-Tyne.

— (forthcoming), 'Mackem: the urban dialect of Sunderland'. Unpublished doctoral thesis, University of Sheffield.

Cohen, A. P. (1985), *The Symbolic Construction of Community*. London and New York: Routledge.

Dyer J. and Wassink, A. B. (2001), 'Taakin braad and talking broad: Changing indexicality of phonetic variants in two contact situations', Texas Linguistic Forum, 4, (2), 288–301. Proceedings of the Ninth Annual Symposium about Language and Society – Austin, 20–22 April 2001. URL: www.utexas.edu/students/salsa/index.shtml.

Eckert, P. (2000), *Linguistic Variation as Social Practice*. Oxford: Blackwell Publishers.

Llamas, C. (1999), 'A new methodology: data elicitation for social and regional language variation studies', *Leeds Working Papers in Linguistics and Phonetics*, 7, 95–118.

— (2001), 'Language Variation and Innovation in Teesside English'. Unpublished doctoral thesis, University of Leeds.

Milroy, L. (2000), 'Two nations divided by the same language (and different language ideologies)', *Journal of Linguistic Anthropology*, 9, (1), 56–89.

— (2004), 'Language ideologies and linguistic change', in C. Fought (ed.), *Sociolinguistic Variation. Critical Reflections*. Oxford: Oxford University Press.

Orton, H. and Dieth, E. (1962–1971), *Survey of English Dialects*. Leeds: Arnold.

Silverstein, M. (1992), 'The uses and utility of ideology: some reflections', *Pragmatics*, 2, (3), 311–23.

Sunderland – Land of the Mackems (www.virtualtourist.com/m/2587d/4a601/)

Trudgill, P. (1990), *The Dialects of England*. Blackwell.

Wells, J. C. (1982), *Accents of English* (3 vols). Cambridge: Cambridge University Press.

Part III

Identity in Macro-sociolinguistics

8   Guernsey French, identity and language endangerment

Julia Sallabank

Introduction

This chapter examines the effects of identity on revitalization efforts in the context of a small and dwindling language community. It discusses the nature and inter-relationship of identity, ethnicity and culture, and their roles in language choice and attitudes, relating these to the ethnolinguistic vitality of the indigenous language in Guernsey.

It is often assumed that language plays a significant part in identity construction and identification, but this view is not necessarily consistent with the language shift taking place in many places around the world: Krauss (1992) estimates that 90 per cent of the world's languages will have disappeared by 2010. This chapter considers the extent to which each instance of language loss or language death entails the loss of part of group or individual identity, and the role of identity in language maintenance.

Background

The focus in this chapter is on language shift on Guernsey, the second largest of the Channel Islands, in the Gulf of St. Malo off the coast of Northern France (see the map in Figure 8.1). Despite its proximity to France, its political allegiance is to Great Britain.

The main industries at present are finance (Guernsey is a tax haven) and tourism, but before World War II the economy was based on agriculture and horticulture. The Channel Islands are not part of the UK and have their own parliaments which regulate local affairs, although they are dependent on the UK for foreign policy. The Islands are only associate members of the European Community, and are not subject to European laws and agreements such as the Charter for Regional and Minority Languages. Eight hundred years of political autonomy have not increased the status of the indigenous vernacular, nor has autonomy stopped it from declining – indeed, it might be argued that language is not a symbol of independence. Guernsey French[1] is now at around level 7 on Fishman's (1991) 8-point scale of language endangerment, i.e. most native

Figure 8.1 Geographical location of Guernsey. Image courtesy of
VisitGuernsey www.visitguernsey.com/

speakers are past child-bearing age. It has no official status and its existence is
largely ignored by the island government.

Guernsey French is a variety of Norman French, related to the varieties
spoken in other Channel Islands and in mainland Normandy, with which it
is to a large extent mutually comprehensible. Norman has been spoken in the
Channel Islands for at least a thousand years; English is a relatively recent
newcomer. In the eighteenth century Methodist missionaries found very few
people who understood English (Marquis 1997), and even in the first half of
the twentieth century Norman French was still being used for most day-to-day
purposes outside the main town. Linguistic and cultural shift accelerated in the
twentieth century and the islands are now almost completely anglicized.

The Channel Islands have been a bastion of the British Crown against France
since 1204, when they 'chose' to remain linked to the UK instead of mainland
Normandy, which had been conquered by the French king Philippe Auguste.[2]
The islands were heavily fortified and withstood numerous attempts at invasion
from France. This inevitably had an effect on the islanders' view of themselves
in terms of national identity, which may explain the rapid acceptance of English
once it gained a foothold, although standard French remained the High language
until the end of the nineteenth century.[3]

The history of immigration into the island is particularly relevant to the
development of its language and identity. In the Middle Ages, Norman was an
important international language and was spoken by all classes. However, from
the sixteenth century onwards, standard French was promoted by the French
monarchy. In the seventeenth century Protestant refugees fled to Guernsey from
religious persecution in France. At that time Guernsey was ruled by a strict
Puritan 'theocracy' which almost wiped out traditional songs and dances, and
which welcomed Calvinist preachers who were fluent in French. According to

De Garis (1973: 260 and personal communication), standard French speakers thus gained positions of influence and introduced negative attitudes towards the indigenous vernacular. A stable diglossic relationship developed, with standard French as the 'High' language and Guernsey French as the 'Low' vernacular. Although it was often despised, it is only since the introduction of English, in the late eighteenth century, that the survival of Guernsey French has actually been threatened.

Although sizeable contingents of British soldiers were stationed in the Channel Islands during the Napoleonic wars, it was not until the start of regular steamboat services in 1824 that large-scale immigration and tourism from the UK became feasible. Well-to-do immigrants came to enjoy the mild climate, and labourers came to work in the granite quarries and, to a certain extent, in horticulture. 'Polite society' disdained Guernsey French and hoped that their daughters would marry British officers (Inglis 1835), while English-speaking labourers envied and resented the landed, Guernsey French-speaking farming families (Crossan, personal communication). Nevertheless, intermarriage and mass media brought English into the domestic domain and broke up the stable diglossia under which Guernsey French was the language of the home and of primary identification.

Crossan (2005) documents the rise of English in the nineteenth century through historical records and observes that it was seen as a 'modernizing' force, whereas those who upheld the role of French were seen as trying to maintain social barriers. This view of English as modern continued into the twentieth century, especially after World War II. Half of the population, including most of the children, were evacuated to the UK just before the Germans invaded in 1940, which led to a break in intergenerational transmission. Returnees brought back less insular attitudes which viewed the old language and culture as backward.

There is no higher education in the Channel Islands, and there is a general skills shortage. The finance industry, with its high salaries, is the first choice of career for many islanders, while young people leave for higher education and training, many of whom are never to return. A considerable proportion of teachers and civil servants have to be imported, mostly from the UK.[4] There are, however, some native speakers of Guernsey French in the civil service, who use the language at work (unofficially of course). One told me how she had just finished a telephone conversation in Guernsey French when an English colleague came up to her and asked her what language she had been speaking. He had not even been aware that Guernsey had a language of its own. Thus, those who are responsible for policy decisions often have little knowledge of local culture. Many imported teachers are ignorant of local history and culture, which are given little space in the curriculum. Virtually the only local history taught is the German occupation from 1940 to 1945 and the evacuation of children to England beforehand. Eleven-year-olds interviewed in September 2001 did not even know the date of the Norman conquest of England. One language campaigner suspects that the lack of teaching of local language and culture in schools is deliberate, to prevent separatist sentiments from growing, and to encourage Anglicization and integration; but a more likely explanation is 'benign neglect' or apathy.

Guernsey is self-governing in internal matters such as education and finance, but since there is such a strong British influence in policy-making, it tends to follow a British (or, more specifically, English) model, although in education, for example, it could easily have followed a Welsh bilingual model (or any other, for that matter). Islanders are proud of the Norman legal tradition, but this aspect of Guernsey identity is also under threat. Interviewees note that property laws, one of the last extant areas of traditional Norman law, and which used to be replete with Norman terminology, are gradually being altered to follow an English model with English terminology.

Current sociolinguistic situation

According to the 2001 census, which was the first one ever to ask a language question, 14 per cent of the total population of nearly 60,000 (1 in 7) have some understanding of Guernsey French, but only 2 per cent speak it fluently. Most of these speakers are elderly, and there are relatively few second language learners due to the lack of official support and infrastructure for doing so, together with widespread negative attitudes towards the utility of Guernsey French.

The data in this chapter are taken from two surveys and interviews with informants. Forty residents of Guernsey (mostly native speakers of Guernsey French) were interviewed in 2001 and 2002, and a postal questionnaire was sent out to members of a local society which used to have a philology section (now defunct). This brought in 90 replies, just under half of which were from native Guernsey French speakers. It can be said that data from postal responses may be less reliable than face-to-face data, and admittedly they allow less negotiation and discussion, but postal distribution in fact reached a more representative sample, including more isolated speakers (see below). The interviewees tended to be 'primary contacts', recruited by the 'friend of a friend' method (Milroy 1987), many of whom are active in the language revitalization movement, so their views may not be typical of speakers of Guernsey French, and even less typical of the majority population. Informants recruited by the 'friend of a friend' method are also, by definition, part of a social network. Many speakers are elderly: the people they used to speak Guernsey French with have died, and they have few opportunities to speak it now. It might therefore be possible to get a skewed picture of the pattern of use if only socially integrated speakers were surveyed. The postal responses were followed up by more interviews in 2003. As most of these informants were from older generations, visits were made to four schools to talk to young people aged 11, 13, 15 and 17.

A second survey focused on the attitudes of the majority anglophone population towards language and identity. It was carried out in 2004, when celebrations of the 800th anniversary of independence had led to public discussion of issues of island identity, coupled with anecdotal reports of more positive attitudes towards Guernsey French. A questionnaire consisting of Likert scale attitude statements and open questions was circulated via the social and work networks of anglophone contacts. Although it is difficult to elicit responses from informants without a pre-existing interest in language issues to a survey on this topic, 200 replies were received and the profile of the respondents matched that of the general island population in terms of the proportion speaking Guernsey French fluently (2.26 per cent) and in that a third were born outside the island. Follow-up interviews were carried out in 2005.

The core of the first survey concerned the extent and contexts of the use of Guernsey French nowadays, in order to establish baseline data. The sampling differences between face-to-face and postal respondents revealed significant variations, as is shown in Tables 8.1 and 8.2.

Table 8.1 How often do you speak Guernsey French?

	Face-to-face interviewees	Postal respondents (speakers only)
Every day	58%	3%
More than once a week	16%	19%
Less than once a week	21%	48%
Never	5%	23%

Half of the speakers who responded by post reported that they spoke Guernsey French less than once a week (not including the non-speakers). By comparison, 58 per cent of the face-to-face interviewees said that they speak Guernsey French every day; nevertheless, a quarter speak it less than once a week. There is a community of retired people who still use Guernsey French for their entire social life, for example at 'Darby and Joan' clubs, whist and euchre drives and playing bowls; but this contrasts sharply with the isolation felt by other elderly speakers.

Isolation is an increasing problem for endangered language communities, as the average age profile of speakers is rising, and the friends and relatives they used to speak with are passing away:

(1) 'I've had nobody to speak it to since my mother died in 1995.'

In addition, they are increasingly infirm and immobile. Over two-thirds of the Guernsey French-speaking postal respondents reported having 20 or fewer Guernsey French interlocutors. In contrast, two-thirds of the face-to-face interviewees reported having 'at least 100', 'about 50' or 'many' (see Table 8.2). As well as being important for language maintenance, the loss of social networks in a particular language may also affect self-identification as a speaker of a particular language if it is no longer used on a regular basis, especially if attrition processes have set in, as was witnessed in a number of interviews.

Since the first survey, the questions 'who speaks what language when, and where' (Fishman 1965) have been expanded to include *why*. A major question, which relates communities of use to questions of identity, is why some people maintain their ancestral language and transmit it to their children, while others give it up.

Table 8.2 How many people do you speak Guernsey French with?

	Face-to- face interviewees	Postal respondents (speakers only)
At least 100	11%	0
About 50	28%	6%
'Many'/'several'	28%	24%
10 to 20	6%	12%
Under 10/ 'not many'	28%	41%
None	0	18%

Language and identity among majority language speakers

As mentioned above, anecdotal reports that the negative attitudes of the nineteenth and twentieth centuries might be changing instigated a survey of the attitudes of anglophones in Guernsey. On a scale of 1–5, 70 per cent of respondents reported 'agreeing strongly' with the statement 'Guernsey should maintain a unique identity of its own', with 25 per cent agreeing mildly (remembering that only 67 per cent of respondents were born in Guernsey). Only half a per cent disagreed strongly with this statement. However, respondents were more equivocal about the statement 'Speaking Guernsey Norman French is an important part of Guernsey identity', with 25 per cent agreeing strongly, 34 per cent agreeing mildly, and 25 per cent neutral; nevertheless, only 9 per cent disagreed strongly and 9 per cent mildly. On the other hand, 57 per cent agreed strongly and 27 per cent mildly that 'Guernsey Norman French is an important part of our heritage' (with only 2 per cent disagreeing strongly), and only 7 per cent agreed strongly that 'It doesn't matter if Guernsey Norman French dies out'. Comments in interviews and in answers to open questions indicated that island heritage, independence and the calmer pace of life are highly valued, and that there is increasing concern for a loss of Guernsey distinctiveness and at growing Anglicization:

(2) 'Unfortunately [the differences] are becoming less, but the main one would be a community spirit in Guernsey, and pride in our heritage.'

(3) 'We must maintain our independent culture and heritage.'

(4) 'Very sad to see Anglicization [of] many aspects of Guernsey life.'

A number of respondents stressed the importance of language in local identity:

(5) 'Guernsey French identifies the island even though I don't speak it ... necessary to keep it going to keep island identity.'

(6) 'When I was at school (1960s), it was the perception that Guernsey French was an inferior language, a language of peasants! One was looked down upon as being 'countrified' if one was associated with the language. There seemed to be no comprehension, or if there

was, no acceptance, that Norman French was the language of William the Conqueror; that it preceded French; that it is our heritage! As such, I feel strongly that it should not be allowed to disappear ... I believe there has to be a greater effort yet to promote the language at the political level, at this eleventh hour so as to try to ensure that our own heritage is preserved.'

However, some were more ambivalent:

(7) I would be pleased if my children were able to speak or at least understand Guernsey French but there are so few opportunities to actually make use of it, the question arises how practical it would be? I would think that learning Guernsey French would help children to have a better sense of identity and understanding of the past, but I can't be sure of this since I don't speak it myself, and Guernsey may be distinct enough without the language element to provide a sense of identity.'

This will be discussed further in later sections of this chapter.

Culture, ethnicity, identity and language

Culture

It is beyond the scope of the discussion in this chapter to examine cultural theory in detail, but for its purposes a working definition of culture is 'the material and social values of any group of people ... a patterned sphere of beliefs, values, symbols, and discourses' which is autonomous and 'cannot be explained away as a mere reflection of underlying economic forces, distributions of power, or social structural needs' (Smith 2001: 3–4). Culture has close links with identity, although the latter is 'seen as a signifier at play in cultural fields rather than as a biological or psychological quality of individuals' (*ibid.*: 242).

The traditional essentialist view of culture is exemplified by Hallowell (1969). According to this view, the concepts of identity and culture are interdependent: the one cannot exist without the other. Fishman (1999: 444) claims:

Languages do not just symbolize their associated cultures ... and they are not just indexically better suited to their related cultures than are any other languages ... what is most unique and basic about the link between language and culture is that in huge areas of real life the language is the culture and that neither law nor education nor religion not government nor politics nor social organization would be possible without it.

However, this claim does not stand up to a comparison with reality: in Guernsey, for example, most of these institutions have rarely, if ever, been conducted in the medium of the indigenous language, yet Guernsey people of all backgrounds staunchly defend their unique governmental and legal system. Atkinson (1999) calls this a 'received' view of culture, according to which cultures are seen 'in their most typical form as geographically (and quite often nationally) distinct entities, as relatively unchanging and homogeneous, and as all-encompassing systems of rules or norms that substantially determine personal behavior' (*ibid.*: 626). Atkinson advocates what he terms a 'middle ground' approach to culture which, while accepting that an individual's identity is influenced by his/her cultural roots, recognizes that individuals have choice or what he terms 'agency', the ability to make choices about which cultural norms they accept. A 'middle ground' approach to culture thus recognizes the complex relationship that exists between an individual and his/her cultural background.

Ethnicity

It is impossible to define ethnicity in terms of quantifiable physiological differences. Jenkins (1997: 170) defines it as follows: 'ethnicity and its allotropes are principles of collective identification and social organization in terms of culture and history, similarity and difference'. There is thus very little difference between 'ethnicity' and 'culture' as defined earlier. 'Identification' is included in this definition, indicating an intimate link between ethnicity and identity. However, as will be seen below, the interface is mostly one-way: although identity is a necessary part of ethnicity, ethnicity is not an essential feature of identity.

Gumperz and Cook-Gumperz (1982: 5) distinguish between an 'old' ethnicity based on common regional background and social networks which 'joined people through clusters of occupational, neighbourhood, familial, and political ties', and a 'new' ethnicity depending 'less upon geographic proximity and shared occupations and more upon the highlighting of key differences separating one group from another'. This latter is very similar to Tajfel's (1981: 225) definition of social identity: 'that part of an individual's self-concept which derives from his [sic.] knowledge of his membership in a social group (or groups) together with the value and emotional significance attached to that membership'. It could be said that language shift often accompanies a shift from the first type of ethnicity to the second, which is more typical of modern societies.

Identity

There are many views on identity. Some social constructivists argue against the possibility of even studying self and identity objectively, whereas many psychologists and sociologists implicitly assume that they can be studied objectively (Jussim et al. 2001: 5). This chapter takes the second view, and uses as a working definition that of Holland (1997: 162): 'a self-understanding or self-objectification to which one is emotionally attached'.

Many psychological texts on identity, such as Giddens (1991), Craib (1998) and Du Gay et al. (2000), scarcely mention language as a factor. Even Gumperz (1982) does not focus on a putative link between language loyalty and culture/ethnicity, but on the communicative production of identity through discourse (Gumperz and Cook-Gumperz 1982: 1).

Nevertheless, in sociolinguistic literature a link between language and identity is often simply assumed and is treated as a given, with little discussion of its nature, and with a tendency to appeal to emotional responses (e.g. Fishman 1989; Krauss 1992; Skutnabb-Kangas 1999). Recent theoretical work on identity in the fields of literary theory (Moya and Hames-García 2003) and feminism (Bucholtz *et al*. 1999, which includes a chapter on Irish language revitalization) proposes a 'realist' view of identity, recognizing as problematic the traditional essentialist view of identity as fixed: 'the tendency to posit one aspect of identity as the sole cause or determinant constituting the social meanings of an individual's experience' (Moya 2000: 3). However, Moya also claims that deconstructionist and postmodern views of identity as an epistemologically unreliable construct are inadequate, as 'cultural identities can be enabling, enlightening, and enriching structures of attachment and feeling ... significant modes by which people experience, understand, and know the world' (*ibid.*: 8). Mohanty (2000: 32) maintains that there is no necessary opposition between 'lived experience' and 'scientific thinking': 'theory-laden and socially constructed [interpretation of] experiences can lead to a knowledge that is accurate and reliable' (*ibid.*: 36). He goes on to define identities as theoretical constructions that enable us to read the world in specific ways; they are therefore valuable and their epistemic status should be taken seriously (*ibid.*: 43). A purely functional view of the world, which ignores emotional factors, can thus miss important information. Essentialist views of language and identity are still fairly common:

(8) One's identity I think is very tied back into one's traditions and background – they are what make you and the culture that you exist in different to any other, in my opinion. And as a result of that if you have a language which adds to and enrichens that then I think that it's very important that that be continued. ... my dearest wish is that before the language dies completely in Guernsey that it be – not resurrected but given rebirth really to some extent – people who still speak it can encourage the people who want to learn it – that's my feeling.

The emotional link between language and identity is illustrated by a number of my informants' responses, and will be discussed further on pp. 147–8.

Culture, identity and language loyalty

Language is often thought to be purely about communication, following Austin's (1975) speech act theory and Grice's (1989) Cooperative Principle and Maxims, which were taken up enthusiastically by the communicative language teaching movement (e.g. Widdowson 1978). We can communicate in any language; and from a purely functional viewpoint, the better known that language is, the easier communication is. This is a point of view often expressed in Guernsey by people who see the indigenous language as 'useless', both economically and functionally: it was 'holding people back'. Such views tend to be held by older people whose forebears shifted language for economic reasons, or whose ancestors were immigrants. When it is suggested that Guernsey French should be taught in schools, their reaction is often that it would be more useful to teach standard French:

(9) 'If children are going to learn another language at school they should learn proper French or German or Spanish or even an Eastern language – a language that's widely spoken.'

These informants have no interest in the ancestral language as a marker of island identity. On the other hand, very few of them would describe themselves as English. As Le Page and Tabouret-Keller (1985: 239–40) note, feelings of ethnic identity *can* survive total language loss. Dorian (1999: 31) comments, 'Because it is only one of an almost infinite variety of potential identity markers, [language] is easily replaced by others that are just as effective. In this respect the ancestral language is functionally expendable.' Atkinson (1999) observes that individuals have various social allegiances and assume multiple social roles, which are constantly open to change; this is echoed by Joseph (2004: 8) and several of the contributors to this volume (see Omoniyi in Chapter 2, for instance). Other possible identity markers include nationality, ethnicity, parental status, class, age, gender, job, religion, personality, political persuasion and interests. Some of these factors are individual, while others express social or group membership. They are not mutually exclusive, and different identities may, at times, be more salient (Fishman 1989).

Much of the discourse on endangered languages seems rather essentialist and deterministic. The strong version of the Sapir–Whorf hypothesis claims that our way of thinking, and thus our cultural identity, are determined by the lexicon and syntax of our language (Mandelbaum 1949; Carroll 1956). This is the argument followed by many endangered language campaigners when they claim that when a language dies out, a unique way of looking at the world also disappears (Nettle and Romaine 2000; Baker 2002). For example, Grimes (2001) claims that the disappearance of a language means the extinction of a unique creation of human beings that houses a treasure of information and preserves a people's identity. Yet Gumperz and Cook-Gumperz (1982) stress that grammar, semantics and language variation must be seen in the light of social and political contexts:

> We do not intend to claim that ideology shapes language and that since language shapes social reality there is no way out. Our main goal in this book is to show how ideology enters into face-to-face speaking practices to create an international space in which the subconscious and automatic sociolinguistic processes of interpretation and interference can generate a variety of outcomes and make interpretations subject to question (*op. cit.*: 3).

Fishman (1991) claims that one 'cannot be Xish through language Y'. However, in a survey of Jersey Norman French speakers, Skeet (2000) asked this very question and found that although most retained a strong affective attachment to and identification with Jersey Norman French, they saw in their daily lives numerous people who were adequately identified both by themselves and by others as fully Jersey without speaking the indigenous language, so were forced to conclude that speaking Jersey Norman French was not an essential indicator of 'Jerseyness'. To maintain that it both flies in the face of observed reality and also risks alienating the majority population. Myhill (1999) warns that the equating of language with individual identity can undermine efforts to preserve indigenous languages threatened by demographic swamping. This would seem to be particularly important at a time when majority attitudes towards the indigenous variety are softening, as confirmed by the results of the survey of anglophones in Guernsey reported on p. 136.

The development of efficient communications has brought more cultures into contact than ever before. The extent to which this entails cultural and linguistic change or shift depends on how confident speakers are in their local language and culture, which in turn is a reflection of their status in the society (see pp. 149–50). In Guernsey the effects of improved transport links to the UK and mass media (very little of which are in the indigenous language) have been accentuated by the recent economic dominance of the finance and tourism industries. As discussed above, feelings of distinctive identity are multifaceted and can outlive objective measures such as language and culture, so that a Guernsey person can still feel pride at being from Guernsey, although linguistically and culturally they may well be indistinguishable from one who is from England.

It is necessary to recognize that culture and ethnicity are by no means the only, or necessarily the overriding, factors in determining identity feelings. Mackie comments: 'spurious arguments suggest that it is "natural" to feel closest to people of one's own "culture", ignoring all the differences of class, gender, and personality that operate against any notion of cultural homogeneity' (Barker 1981, cited in Mackie 1996: 40). We must not be tempted by neat theories such as linguistic or cultural determinism to forget real life. As Craib (1998: 176) points out, 'Neither the self or identity are simple social products, rather in the end they are areas of individual and collective freedom which are constantly threatened by the structures and ideologies of the wider society'. Although we are influenced by social attitudes and language ideologies, these can be changed, as shown in quotes 28–29 from interviews in Guernsey. Mackie promotes a 'reflexive' view of self, similar to Atkinson's 'middle ground', in which 'people are still part of that cultural patterning, but they *see* their position within that patterning and how they are shaped according to it. Then they may be able to exercise choice between those aspects they wish to adopt and those they wish to overcome, jettison, or change in themselves' (*ibid.*: 42). As humans we thus have the individuality to accept or reject roles and cultures, and to add new dimensions to our ways of thinking by cross-cultural communication and language learning. This can be a way of asserting our individual identities in the face of social pressure to conform. Some of the language shift in Guernsey is as a result of individuals rejecting the old culture, which they perceive as rigid or repressive. It is also possible to reject a culture while retaining a strong affection for the language associated with it; some of my informants have done this (see pp. 136–7). Mohanty claims that even collective identity can be consciously forged through re-examination of accepted cultural meanings and values, and given definitions of personal and political interests (Mohanty 2000: 56). In the context of language shift such re-examination could, conceivably, challenge accepted concepts such as 'majority language = progress', as has happened in Wales.

The re-forging of Guernsey collective identity to omit Guernsey French in the nineteenth and twentieth centuries may not have been entirely voluntary. As Dorian (1994) notes, people are often faced with a lack of freedom in language choice and identity formation, resulting from economic necessity and internalized ideologies of language inferiority, which can lead to linguistic and cultural shift. This will be explored further in the next section.

Identity in Guernsey

Individual and group identity in relation to the wider world

This section examines to what extent feelings of ethnic group distinctiveness affect language loyalty and shift in Guernsey. Many Guernsey people, especially older ones, are adamant that they are not English. Some even claim that England belongs to Guernsey because as part of Normandy, Guernsey won the Battle of Hastings in 1066. Guernsey identity is therefore not necessarily in conflict with Britishness:

(10) 'We are not English but we are British.'

Many Guernsey people are staunchly in favour of the British royal family; the island's loyalty is directly to the Crown, not to the British Parliament. The traditional toast is 'La Royne, not' Duc' ('The Queen, our Duke'), referring to the dukedom of Normandy. The royal family is not seen as a threat to the Guernsey French language, and on the occasion of a royal visit in 2000 a welcoming speech was read in Guernsey French.

Informants often express regret at Anglicization, but very few express outright resentment, perhaps out of politeness (a highly regarded trait in Guernsey). The resentment in the next example is directed more at rich incomers buying up country properties. English speakers tend to be equated with people of English origin by older Guernsey French speakers, no doubt because originally English was brought in by immigrants. This informant first makes this assumption, but then checks himself, recognizing that anglophones can be Guernsey people (of a sort) too:

(11) 'J'travaillais dauve mon père – et tous les vaïsaoïns ch'était tout en guernesiais ... mais aucht'haeure i saoïent tous partis ain? Aucht'haeure – ya iocque d'angllais ou pus angllais saoïn doute – ou p'tête guernesiais saoïn doute.'
['I worked with my father – and all the neighbours it was all in Guernsey French ... but now they've all gone eh? Now – there's only English or more English no doubt – or perhaps Guernsey no doubt.']

Some Guernsey people claim Norman French identity, on the basis of shared cultural traits rather than political grounds:

(12) I get on well with Normandy French people – they're on the same wavelength. You never know where you are with the English.

This was reciprocated by a recent arrival from Normandy:

(13) Being from Normandy, I felt very at ease with the geographical aspect of the island ("paysage"), and all the French names (streets, family names) when I first came to the island.

Of course trading contacts have always been strong: even in times of conflict between France and Britain, when Guernsey was nominally in the front line, smuggling was widespread. There has also been considerable immigration from France in Guernsey's history, especially in times of religious persecution. However, in the twentieth century contact with France lapsed, and for several years there was not even a ferry service. For most purposes, Channel Islanders have turned their backs on France. Language, food, media and religion are now almost wholly English.

A link between language and national identity is often assumed in discourse on language and ethnicity, but just what the national identity is in Guernsey is not easy to ascertain. There is a strong sense of local pride, but the Channel Islands are not thought of as a nation or even as an entity. There are strong (if good-natured) rivalries between the islands,[5] and even within Guernsey there is rivalry between parishes (see examples 14 and 29). For administrative purposes Guernsey is divided into ten parishes, each with its own character and, formerly, its own distinct dialect of Guernsey French (see the map in Figure 8.3). Nowadays they also have websites. In Figure 8.2, the Castel parish presents its view of its own identity to the world. The lack of reference to Britain could be interpreted in several ways: as a statement of separate identity, as an attempt to avoid offence by being neutral and not identifying with any external nation at all, or as a snub to Britain – but as noted above, there is little overt resentment of Britain, although most Guernsey people would probably bridle at being described as English. It is notable that this website is entirely in English and that Guernsey French is not mentioned on it at all, although Castel has a relatively high level of Guernsey French ethnolinguistic vitality. Most Guernsey French speakers are elderly and are not Internet users (with some exceptions of course).

The Parish and Community of Castel
in the Island Bailiwick of Guernsey
Channel Islands - Europe

Welcome to
The Castel Parish Web Site

Figure 8.2 The Castel Parish website (www.castelparish.org.gg – accessed 22 April 2003). Reproduced with the permission of the webmaster.

This emphasis on local identity influences the view of language. Many of my informants are keen to differentiate Guernsey French from standard French, and point out differences, although Guernsey French is often referred to as *frènçais*

(French). Guernsey French speakers are often at pains to point out that Guernsey French is not monolithic, and that regional differences are significant:

(14)   a   I'm from St Saviour's and I'd say *ieau* /jo/ but he'd say *iaou* /jaʊ/ [water] and that's Torteval. Terry as well would say *iaou* you see they were St Peter's Torteval – and

      b   no just St Peter's and Torteval

      a   not the Forest I don't think?

      b   Forest was again different

      a   and I say *là-haut* /laho/ but he says *là-haout* /lahaʊ/

    JS   ah for up high

(15) 'That depends on where you come from [laugh] how you say it you see. Les Vâlais saoïent aen p'tit pus sus les angiais – éiouque les sians des hautes paraisses i saoïent pus sus l'frènçais qui fait qué nou-z oime à dire qué nou-z est aen p'tit dans l'mide les câtelandes (laugh)' ['The Vale people tend a bit towards the English – whereas those from the high parishes tend more towards French so we like to say that we're a bit in the middle the Castel people.'] (See Figures 8.2 and 8.3.)

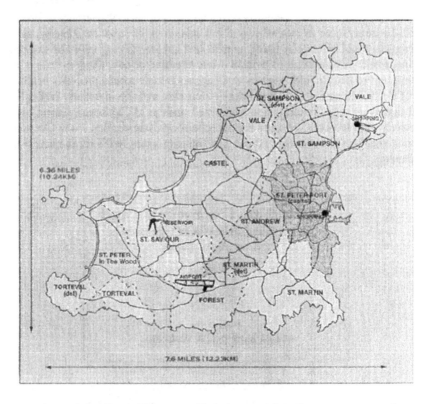

Figure 8.3   Map of Guernsey showing parishes. Image courtesy of VisitGuernsey www.visitguernsey.com/

The respondents to Pooley's (1998) survey in the Nord department of France expressed similar views, with more explanation:

> Chaque village a son propre parler picard; en apprenant le patois d'un autre village, on ne retrouvera pas ses racines. (Pooley 1998: 48)
> [Each village has its own variety of Picard; if you learn the dialect of another village, you won't find your roots.]

This concern is at the root of the emphasis on local differences: if a 'unified Guernsey French' were taught in schools, as is happening with other European minority languages such as Breton or Basque, it would not be the variety which would connect learners to their roots. There is also some debate about the 'best accent', as some view the accent of many younger speakers, and of those who were evacuated in World War II, as unacceptably Anglicized.

In addition, some older speakers recognize that some of the younger activists who are campaigning for Guernsey French in schools are in fact 'semi-speakers' in Dorian's (1977) terms, and they fear for the integrity of the language. They have quite a proprietary attitude towards Guernsey French, and would almost rather it died with them than survive in a garbled, or modernized, form.

> (16) 'No offence but I wouldn't say that you're good enough – that your Guernsey French is good enough to teach children – it's like the Ravigotteurs [a language revitalization organization] you see, they're going to change the language to teach it – it won't be the Guernsey French we know.'

Such an attitude could be seen as counter-productive by language campaigners, but the last fluent generation is also the repository of oral traditions which have not yet been recorded and are fast dying out; and if the language is to be documented and preserved, is important that it be in as expressive a form as possible.

Despite this strong sense of local distinctiveness, Anglicization continues. Although there are restrictions on house purchases by outsiders, English speakers continue to move in. In recent years rich anglophones have tended to buy properties in country areas which were previously bastions of Guernsey French. Thus, a language community (and old-type ethnicity in Gumperz and Cook-Gumperz' (1982) terms) is being eroded, and opportunities for isolated older people to speak Guernsey French decrease further.

At the other end of the social scale, there is also a shortage of workers willing to take on lower-paid jobs such as hotel, catering and care work. Hotel workers are recruited from Portugal (mainly Madeira) and Latvia, originally on a seasonal basis, but there has been some intermarriage and permanent settlement; there may now even be as many speakers of Portuguese as Guernsey French on the island, but the 2001 census, which asked about competence in Guernsey French, did not ask about other languages. As mentioned on pp. 131–2, the majority of speakers of Guernsey French are elderly, and are increasingly housed in care homes. Nursing and care workers are recruited from the UK, Portugal and the Philippines. I was told anecdotally about an old man in a home who was thought by the care staff to be mad because he was 'rambling incoherently'. It was only when someone visited who knew Guernsey French that it was realized he was speaking coherently, in Guernsey French. This case highlights the need for policies to cater for Guernsey French speakers, especially the elderly who may forget their second language due to stroke or stress. In Wales, ambulances carry a Welsh speaker for such an eventuality.

A major strand in the literature on language and ethnic identity is the view of language as an inter-group phenomenon (Giles 1977; Tajfel 1978 and 1981; Giles and Johnson 1981; Hogg and Abrams 1988, *inter alia*). However, in the Guernsey context it is not clear where ethnic or group boundaries can be drawn. Speakers and non-speakers are physically indistinguishable, and even native-speaking campaigners for Guernsey French admit to having problems telling from the accent in English who is a speaker of Guernsey French. Although Guernsey French speakers distinguish between people of native stock and those of English descent, there has been so much intermarriage that it would cause family rifts to identity English speakers as an 'out-group'. A large proportion of my native-speaker informants have monolingual English-speaking spouses; only one claims to have no immigrants in her family. As another said:

(17) 'Al est finie la laingue pasque ya aen amas qui saoïent mariaï ... coume mé – j'ai mariaï un angllais et i n'saï pas la laingue et i n'est intéressé'
['The language is finished because there are a lot [of people] who got married ... like me – I married an Englishman and he doesn't know the language and he's not interested']

It is likely that such peaceable inter-group coexistence contributes to language shift; but would conflict be preferable? When asked whether he made efforts to find opportunities to speak Guernsey French, one native-speaker informant commented:

(18) I don't make much effort to find them really apart from meeting people you know that know it – I don't go to any societies that specifically speak in Guernsey French – I didn't join l'Assembllaïe d'Guernesiais [a language preservation society] because my wife doesn't know it and I feel that it would be a division you know?

In the 2001 census, 36 per cent of the population reported being born outside the island. Of the remaining 64 per cent, a considerable proportion must have immigrant backgrounds: there has been a continuous and substantial influx of outsiders since the mid-eighteenth century (Crossan 2005). It can be generalized that descendants of immigrants are less likely to speak Guernsey French. However, non-Guernsey ancestry does not preclude an interest in the local language. I have several examples of more recent immigrants to Guernsey and Jersey, and also Ireland, attending, and even running, classes in the indigenous language, and also becoming leaders of the revitalization movement. Some immigrants from the UK have been influenced by official acceptance and promotion of indigenous languages such as Welsh and Cornish. One Cornishman who was working in Guernsey on licence was sympathetic because of this, and told me that his daughter (aged 9) was learning a Guernsey French poem for the Eisteddfod festival, and was very keen. A supply teacher overseeing the 15-year-old interviewees had not heard of Guernsey French previously, but expressed immediate interest and asked for a translation of her house name.

Language and the emotions

Much language use is not purely functional; language is not only for communication but also about establishing and maintaining relationships and expressing identity, i.e. the phatic function (Jakobson 1960). Goffman (cited in Schiffrin 1996: 309) argued that the way people choose to speak plays a crucial role in 'creating and maintaining the roles we fill, the statuses we occupy (our social identities), and the personalities we feel ourselves and others to have (our personal identities)'.

I have found evidence of profound affective attachment for the indigenous language, even among informants who do not speak it in their homes:

(19) 'Guernsey French is wonderful … people's eyes dance when they speak it.'

(20) 'plloin /pjɔĩ)/ – it's a nice word'

(21) 'If I was kidnapped like Terry Waite or on a desert island, although I'm a Christian and I should say I'd like the Bible, what would mean the most to me would be a recording of someone speaking Guernsey French.'

Several informants have told me that when relatives were dying, they reverted to their first language. For many older Guernsey French speakers the language is connected with memories of loved ones who have now passed away – perhaps bittersweet memories make for ambivalent attitudes:

(22) 'With my brothers when we were having a fun evening we used to tell each other a lot of stories – which were really funny and I always meant for us to record it – when we were having one of those sessions – but it never actually happened – and it's lost now.'

This informant also noted that self-expression is easier in the first language:

(23) Aen caoup dans l's États je dis que si ch'était en guernesiais je pourrais mé – m'expressaï bian mus [laugh] – i riyaient' ['Once in the States[6] I said that if it were in Guernsey French I would be able to express myself much better – they laughed.']

Some of my informants have 'come back to their roots' after a number of years when they rejected traditional language and culture. They may be criticized by others because they did not speak Guernsey French when they were younger, but at least some are now trying to make up for lost time in their enthusiasm for the language. Unfortunately however, this 'conversion' often takes place too late to raise children speaking the ancestral language (see Fishman's Graded Intergenerational Disruption Scale 1991). The time of life when people are able to transmit a language to their children is also the period when they may be rejecting the old culture, or busy perfecting their proficiency in the dominant language for economic or educational reasons.

For older non-speakers, discussion of language issues, far from arousing pleasant emotions or nostalgia, can invoke anger and resentment. This might perhaps reflect the historical negative attitudes among non-speaking immigrants, but another possible explanation is guilt and resentment at having had to switch language for economic reasons. However, the survey of anglophones showed that attitudes among non-speakers are becoming less negative; reasons for this will be examined in the next section.

Identity, attitudes and language maintenance

As stated above, many older speakers express an emotional attachment to Guernsey French. But it must also be remembered that it is their generation who caused its demise by not transmitting it to their children. Emotional attachment does not necessarily inspire speakers to act to save their language from dying out. Bankston and Henry (1998) agree that a strong identification with a minority language may not always correlate positively with language maintenance, in particular when it comes to transmitting a low-status variety to children.

Negative attitudes towards minority languages are well documented. It is not uncommon for such attitudes to be internalized by the speakers themselves: Labov (1966: 489) claimed that 'the term "linguistic self-hatred" may not be too extreme'. Classification of one's own language as a 'non-language' or as 'deformed French' (as opposed to 'good French', as Guernsey French and standard French are still sometimes known respectively), is indicative of a lack of confidence in traditional identity, and leads to acquiescence in language shift.

It may therefore be a mistake for language campaigners to stress the link between language and traditional culture too strongly. For many islanders, especially those whose families shifted to English, the old language and culture are associated with poverty and backwardness. For example, Guernsey French has no word for 'bathroom', because its development stopped with World War II and many pre-war Guernsey houses had no bathroom (Harry Tomlinson, personal communication). In this respect, Denison's (1977) charge of 'language suicide', and Ladefoged's (1992) assertion that many minority language speakers consciously trade their traditional language for economic gain, are quite likely to have more than a grain of truth in the Guernsey context.

But, as noted earlier, it would be ingenuous to claim that those 'choosing' language shift have free choice. Bourdieu (1991) interprets this as due to the 'cultural capital' attributed to different languages in an unequal sociolinguistic relationship which parallels their economic relationship in a 'linguistic market'. More powerful languages exert 'symbolic power' and intimidation, which individuals may not be aware of and to which they vary in susceptibility. These predispositions are acquired through a 'gradual process of inculcation in which early childhood influences are particularly important' (ibid.: 12). Walker (1993) supplies another explanation, using the analogy of Maslow's (1954) Hierarchy of Needs, according to which basic needs such as food and security have to be satisfied before 'higher' concerns such as esteem and self-actualization. Thus, people whose main concern is food and shelter are motivated to learn a language which they perceive as more likely to fulfil those needs – indeed, in many cases the dominant language is the only route to education and jobs. Once their descendents are economically secure, they have the leisure to regret what they have lost. This 'attitude shift' is increasingly found among younger generations in minority groups (Dorian 1993; Crystal 2000: 106), and tallies with the findings of the second Guernsey survey. The following quote is from a woman in her 20s:

> (24) 'Guernsey French should definitely be taught in schools, I wish I had learnt it. ...
> Everyone I meet in the UK asks if I speak French/Guernsey French and sadly I speak French,
> not fluently though, and can't speak Guernsey French much at all.'

But, as Crystal points out, 'by then, without any preservation measures, it is too late' (*ibid.*: 106).

The Guernsey French speakers I have interviewed are largely from former farming families. In the past, Guernsey French was seen as a low-status peasant dialect. Several speakers report being called 'country bumpkins': a common insult is 'oh you come from the country you'. However, this has changed in recent years, as 'identity' and language revitalization come to be seen as middle-class concerns, which tallies with Walker's analysis in some respects. This can also backfire:

> (25) 'The only people who want to save the language are intellectuals.'

> (26) 'I don't agree with trying to revitalize something just for the kudos.'

The young people interviewed displayed a somewhat different view of language and identity to older informants. When asked about how they identified themselves, as many of the 11-year-olds said they felt English as Guernsey; one felt French and one Thai. The majority of all the school students wanted to leave Guernsey when they were older; this may just be due to general teenage disaffection and lack of local opportunities, but it also reflects feelings towards traditional language and culture, especially insularity.

Although over half of the 11-year-olds had an English parent, nearly half had heard Guernsey French, and a third had relatives who spoke it. Some said they would like to speak it with their grandparents. Most of the 11-year-olds thought it would be a good idea to learn Guernsey French in schools, but with 13- to 17-year-olds the proportion dropped to a small minority. Nevertheless, the following comment was heard independently from several young people, and may offer a way to 'sell' traditional language and culture to them, as they place little value on it otherwise:

> (27)   'A secret language of our own – cool.'

This also calls into doubt language revitalizers' current strategy of focusing on festivals of traditional culture.

Linguistic pride regained?

As mentioned earlier, negative attitudes are a major factor in loss of confidence in local identity and in promoting language shift, but a sense of pride is gradually regaining ground, with the language being reclaimed as a positive identity marker:

(28) 'I think that was the thing – that's how we started to lose it after the war er it wasn't the in thing – to speak Guernsey French and that is right that in certain company you didn't speak it – because it made you feel a bit inferior but now it's the other way round – you don't feel at all inferior if you know it, it's completely the opposite you know?'

(29) 'I was put down at school for being from the country and didn't admit to speaking Guernsey French. ... J'oïmerais bian que tout ma fomille [pâle] pasque quënd j'étais p'tite j'étais embarrassaï dé lé pâlaï mais ... aucht'haeure je sis aen amas fière que je peux le pâlaï.' ['... I'd like all my family [to speak] because when I was little I was embarrassed to speak it but ... now I'm very happy that I can speak it']

(30) 'Nou joue à bowls et nou se d'vise, nou veit des gens là qu'nou se counnit en guernesiais – et l'onnaïe passaï y'a aen haoume qui dit – huh, that foreign language! You come from the country – et je li dis yes, and all our rubbish goes down the Vale!' ['We play bowls and we speak to each other, we see people there we know in Guernsey French – and last year there was a man who said huh, that foreign language! You come from the country – and I told him yes, and all our rubbish goes down the Vale!'[7]]

There has also been a shift in how Guernsey identity is presented to the outside world. In the 1960s and 1970s, the message to the banking industry and tourists (and even printed on postcards) was that there was 'no language problem'. Now the tourist board website stresses 'heritage', and boasts the only official sign in Guernsey French (see Figure 8.4).

Figure 8.4 Sign outside tourist board offices (photo: J. Sallabank)

Identity or vitality?

There is a worrying trend for campaigners to focus their attention on language as a symbol of identity, rather than on the social and economic factors which caused language shift, or on revitalization of the living language through inter-generational transmission. Fishman (1987), cited in Crystal (2000: 83), calls this trend the 'folklorization' of language: the use of an indigenous language only in irrelevant or unimportant domains. In a similar vein, Bankston and Henry (2000) describe the 'commodification of ethnic culture' amongst Cajuns in Louisiana, which involves an increased emphasis on Acadian heritage despite increasing acculturation, including a continued importance placed on the French language despite its decreasing use (Bankston and Henry 1999). Cultural festivals are a relatively uncontroversial language activity, and the only type which attracts official funding in Guernsey (from the Tourist Board rather than the Heritage Committee, which concerns itself only with buildings and monuments). Although cultural festivals are an important expression of linguistic pride and identity, and provide an opportunity for the audience to meet fellow speakers and speak the language during the event, the focus is on linguistic identity as display rather than on language as a living part of everyday life. As more non-speakers enter who have learnt set pieces without much other knowledge of the language, judges 'help' them by commenting in English, so the Guernsey French environment is further diluted. A similar process has happened in an association originally set up to preserve the language through speaking it at social events: as more non-speaking members have joined, albeit with good intentions to support the language, the medium of meetings has switched to English. So the opportunities to speak the language dwindle and even people who win prizes for their Guernsey French in cultural festivals cannot always hold a conversation in it.

Around the world, language revitalization movements are still at early stages in their development. Many ideas have been tried, some of which seem more successful than others. There are some common strands which can be identified, for example the tendency to abdicate responsibility noted, for example, by King (2001) and Dauenhauer and Dauenhauer (1998). Language communities and campaigners find it easier to focus on getting the language introduced into the school curriculum than on changing their own and their neighbours' behaviour, although intergenerational transmission in the home is the only real gauge of a language's vitality (Fishman 1991). It may be that campaigns all have to go through this stage in order to gain acceptance and maturity. Getting the minority language accepted into the school curriculum is also an important part of status planning and thus in countering negative attitudes.

In some places language revitalization has progressed considerably further than in Guernsey, and further stages of awareness have been reached. This is particularly the case where official support has been attained, as in Wales or New Zealand. I have recently heard about a scheme to teach prospective parents their minority language some years before they have a child, focusing on childcare and child-raising language. But this was only after the community had realized for itself that school-based language teaching, even full immersion, was not delivering long-term revitalization: children had not accepted it as a language of primary identification, were not using it after they left school, and did not know vital domestic expressions.

The main reason given by language campaigners for not using Guernsey French in their own homes is lack of confidence. It can sometimes be difficult to tell the difference between lack of confidence in language proficiency, and lack of confidence in the validity and usefulness of a low-status variety. This may help to explain the discrepancy in figures between those who reported themselves as fluent in Guernsey French in the census (2 per cent) and those who claim to be able to understand some (14 per cent). 'Understanders' (or 'latent speakers', in the terms of Basham and Fathman 2003) clearly have a good knowledge of structure and lexis, but lack the confidence to speak. I have witnessed conversations where one interlocutor speaks in Guernsey French and the other in English; this was apparently common between parents and children a generation ago.

One possible way to improve both kinds of confidence might be a scheme along the lines of the Master-Apprentice programme developed by Native American language campaigners in California (Hinton 1997), where older fluent speakers are paired with learners or latent speakers. This would also serve a useful social purpose in providing interlocutors for isolated older speakers or those in care homes.

Conclusion

Language revitalization in Guernsey still has a long way to go before it can claim the success of Welsh or Maori, and it is likely that the current older generation will be the last fluent native speakers. People are coming to recognize what is being lost, with the anglophone majority also seeing Guernsey French as an important part of heritage and distinctiveness, as well as a way of forging links to this heritage for incomers:

> (31) 'I think it could be a positive way of creating an 'inclusive' Guernsey identity if a limited amount of Guernsey French was taught at school as part of a course on local culture and traditions. I am English but from a Guernsey family on my mother's side. Her mother's first language was Guernsey French but she did not teach her children and so none has been handed on to me – apart from a word or two.'

This informant is advocating 'symbolic ethnicity', as discussed at the beginning of this section. Although it raises the prestige and linguistic capital of Guernsey French, this does not necessarily promote ethnolinguistic vitality or intergenerational transmission; and identification with a language, and strong emotional bonds to it, do not guarantee its maintenance either. But it is hard to see how a minority language can be preserved without a focus on identity: it is difficult to rationalize on functional grounds alone. A major justification for minority language revitalization must therefore be to maintain links with a community's roots and identity.

Acknowledgements

This paper originated at a mini-symposium on Language and Identity at the University of Reading in February 2003, organized by Paul Kerswill, to whom I am grateful for ideas and suggestions. I would also like to thank Alison Sealey for comments which considerably improved the paper, and Sandra Lee McKay for tips on bibliographical references.

I am grateful to the Economic and Social Research Council and to Reading University Research Endowment Trust Fund for financial support for this study.

Notes

1 The name 'Guernsey French' is used in this paper as it is in common use in the island. Strictly speaking, however, it refers more accurately to a form of standard French previously used in the island's parliament and for other High functions (see note 6). The term 'Guernsey Norman French' describes the variety's linguistic genus and was used in the 2001 Census for this reason to avoid any confusion, but it is not in general use. The variety has no official name and is often called 'the *patois*', French for 'dialect', but some language campaigners object to this. The majority of native speakers I have questioned prefer to call it 'Guernesiais'.

2 In return, they gained the political and tax privileges which form the basis of the economy today.

3 This in itself might be seen as remarkable given the constant political links with England (Marr 2001), but it must be remembered that French remained the court language in England until the fifteenth century, and was still used in British law until the early eighteenth century (Paradis 2005).

4 These incomers are nowadays only given fixed-term licences rather than full residence rights, and cannot buy property on the local market (i.e. at local prices), although some settle and marry local people.

5 On the radio I recently heard a weather saying recounted by a Jersey resident: 'Red sky in the morning, sailor's warning; red sky at night: Guernsey's on fire.' In both islands it is said that if you can see the other it is going to rain.

6 This informant was a member of the island parliament (the States of Deliberation) at the time. It is only since 1948 that government business has been conducted entirely in English, although English has been allowed since 1898. Before then the official language was standard French, although an American philologist who sat in on some debates (Lewis 1895) commented that the French used was in fact often not very standard. Unlike in the modern devolved Welsh, Scottish and Northern Irish assemblies, the indigenous vernacular is not used in parliamentary debates, and there is no provision for translation.

7 The granite quarries which drew immigrant labourers in the nineteenth century, especially to Northern Guernsey, are now used as rubbish tips.

References

Atkinson, D. (1999), 'TESOL and culture', *TESOL Quarterly*, 33, 625–54.
Austin, J. L. (1975), *How to do Things with Words*, 2nd edn. Oxford: Clarendon Press.
Baker, P. (webmaster) (2002), *Foundation for Endangered Languages Manifesto*. www. ogmios.org/manifesto.htm. Accessed 19 February 2003.
Bankston, C. L. III and Henry, J. (1998), 'The silence of the gators: Cajun ethnicity and intergenerational transmission of Louisiana French', *Journal of Multilingual and Multicultural Development*, 19, 1–23.

— (1999), 'Louisiana Cajun ethnicity: Symbolic or structural?' *Sociological Spectrum*, 19, 223–48.

— (2000), 'Spectacles of ethnicity: Festivals and the commodification of ethnic culture among Louisiana Cajuns.' *Sociological Spectrum*, 20, 377–407.

Basham, C. and Fathman, A. (2003), 'Developing language skills of latent speakers', Paper given at American Association for Applied Linguistics annual conference, Arlington, Virginia, 24 March 2003.

Bourdieu, P. (1991), *Language and Symbolic Power*, edited by J. B. Thompson and translated by G. Raymond and M. Adamson. Cambridge: Polity.

Bucholtz, M., Liang, A. C. and Sutton, L. A. (eds) (1999), *Reinventing Identities: The Gendered Self in Discourse*. Oxford: Oxford University Press.

Carroll, J. B. (1956), *Language, Thought and Reality: Selected Writings of Benjamin Lee Whorf*. MIT Press.

Craib, I. (1998), *Experiencing Identity*. London: Sage.

Crossan, R. (2005), 'Guernsey, 1814–1914: Migration in a Modernising Society'. Unpublished doctoral thesis, University of Leicester.

Crystal, D. (2000), *Language Death*. Cambridge: Cambridge University Press.

Dauenhauer, N. M. and Dauenhauer, R. (1998), 'Technical, emotional, and ideological issues in reversing language shift: examples from Southeast Alaska', in L. A. Grenoble and L. J. Whaley (eds), *Endangered Languages: Language Loss and Community Response*. Cambridge: Cambridge University Press, pp. 57–98.

De Garis, M. (1973), 'Philological Report', *Transactions of La Société Guernesiaise*, XIX, 260–1.

Denison, N. (1977), 'Language death or language suicide?', *International Journal of the Sociology of Language*, 12, 13–22.

Dorian, N. C. (1977), 'The problem of the semi-speaker in language death', *Linguistics*, 191, 23–32.

— (1993), 'A response to Ladefoged's other view of endangered languages', *Language*, 69, 575–9.

— (1994), 'Choices and values in language shift and its study', *International Journal of the Sociology of Language*, 113–24.

— (1999), 'Linguistic and ethnographic fieldwork', in Fishman (ed.), 25–41.

Du Gay, P., Evans, J. and Redman, P. (eds) (2000), *Identity: A Reader*. London: Sage/Open University.

Fishman, J. A. (1965), 'Who speaks what language to whom and when', *La Linguistique*, 2, 67–88.

Fishman, J. A. (1987), 'Language spread and language policy for endangered languages', in *Proceedings of the Georgetown University Round Table on Languages and Linguistics*. Washington: Georgetown University Press, pp. 1–15.

— (1989), *Language and Ethnicity in Minority Sociolinguistic Perspective*. Clevedon: Multilingual Matters.

— (1991), *Reversing Language Shift: Theoretical and Empirical Foundations of Assistance to Threatened Languages*. Clevedon: Multilingual Matters.

— (ed.) (1999), *Handbook of Language and Ethnic Identity*. Oxford: Oxford University Press.

Giddens, A. (1991), *Modernity and Self-identity*. Oxford: Blackwell.

Giles, H. (ed.) (1977), *Language, Ethnicity and Intergroup Relations*. New York: Academic Press.

Giles, H. and Johnson, P. (1981), 'The role of language in inter-group relations', in J. Turner and H. Giles (eds), *Intergroup Relations*. Oxford: Blackwell.

Grice, H. P. (1989), *Studies in the Way of Words*. Cambridge, MA: Harvard University Press.

Grimes, B. (2001), 'Global language viability: causes, symptoms and cures for endangered languages', *Notes on Linguistics* 4, 205–23.

Gumperz, J. J. (ed.) (1982), *Language and Social Identity*. Cambridge: Cambridge University Press.

Gumperz, J. J. and Cook-Gumperz, J. (1982), 'Introduction: language and the communication of social identity', in J. J. Gumperz (ed.), *Language and Social Identity*. Cambridge: Cambridge University Press.

Hallowell, A. I. (1969), *Culture and Experience*. New York: Schocken.

Hinton, L. (1997), 'Survival of endangered languages: the Californian Master-Apprentice program', *International Journal of the Sociology of Language*, 123, 177–91.

Hogg, M. A. and Abrams, D. (1988), *Social Identifications: A Social Psychology of Intergroup Relations and Processes*. London: Routledge.

Inglis, H. D. (1835) (revised edn), *The Channel Islands*. London: Whittaker.

Jakobson, R. (1960), 'Concluding statement: linguistics and poetics', in T. Sebeok (ed.), *Style in Language*. Cambridge: Technology Press.

Jenkins, R. (1997), *Rethinking Identity*. London: Sage.

Joseph, J. E. (2004), *Language and Identity: National, Ethnic, Religious*. Basingstoke: Palgrave.

Jussim L., Ashmore, R. D. and Wilder, D. (2001), 'Introduction: Social identity and intergroup conflict', in R. D. Ashmore, L. Jussim and D. Wilder (eds), *Socail Identity, Intergroup Conflict, and Conflict reduction*. Oxford: Oxford University Press, pp. 3–14.

King, K. A. (2001), *Language Revitalization Processes and Prospects: Quichua in the Ecuadorian Andes*. Clevedon: Multilingual Matters.

Krauss, M. (1992), 'The world's languages in crisis', *Language*, 68, 4–10.

Labov, W. (1966), 'The effect of social mobility on linguistic behavior', *Social Inquiry*, 36, 186–203.

Ladefoged, P. (1992), 'Another view of endangered languages', *Language*, 68, 809–11.

Le Page, R. and Tabouret-Keller, A. (1985), *Acts of Identity*. Cambridge: Cambridge University Press.

Lewis, E. S. (1895), *Guernsey: its People and Dialect*. Baltimore: Modern Language Association of America.

Mackie, F. (1996), 'The ethnic self', in A. Kellehear (ed.), *Social Self, Global Culture*. Oxford: Oxford University Press, pp. 34–44.

Mandelbaum, D. G. (ed.) (1949), *Selected Writings of Edward Sapir*. University of California Press.

Marquis, J. (1997), 'La situâtiaon d'la langue en Guernesi depis la Réformâtiaon au jour d'ogniet', *Le Viquet*, 117, 6–16.

Marr, J. (2001), *The History of Guernsey: The Bailiwick's Story*. Guernsey: The Guernsey Press.

Maslow, A. (1954), *Motivation and Personality*. New York: Harper and Row.

Mohanty, S. P. (2000), 'The epistemic status of cultural identity', in P. M. L. Moya and M. R. Hames-Garcia (eds), *Reclaiming Identity: Realist Theory and the Predicament of Postmodernism*. Berkeley: University of California Press, pp. 2–26.

Moya, P. M. L. (2000), 'Introduction: reclaiming identity', in P. M. L. Moya and M. R. Hames-Garcia (eds), *Reclaiming Identity: Realist Theory and the Predicament of Postmodernism*. Berkeley: University of California Press, pp. 2–26.

Moya, P. M. L. and Hames-Garcia, M. R. (2003), *Reclaiming Identity: Realist Theory and the Predicament of Postmodernism*. Berkeley: University of California Press.

Myhill, J. (1999), 'Identity, territoriality and minority language survival', *Journal of Multilingual and Multicultural Development*, 20, 34–50.

Nettle, D. and Romaine, S. (2000), *Vanishing Voices: The Extinction of the World's Languages*. Oxford: Oxford University Press.

Paradis, M. (2005), 'Not in Latine or French or any other language than English...'. Paper presented at LingO: Postgraduate Linguistics Conference at Oxford University, 23–24 September 2005.

Pooley, T. (1998), 'Picard and regional French as symbols of identity in the Nord', in D. Marley, M-A. Hintze and G. Parker: *Linguistic Identities and Policies in France and the French-*

speaking World. London: Centre for Information on Language Teaching and Research, pp. 43–55.

Schiffrin, D. (1996), 'Interactional sociolinguistics', in S. L. McKay and N. H. Hornberger (eds), *Sociolinguistics and Language Teaching*. Cambridge: Cambridge University Press, pp. 307–28.

Skeet, R. M. (2000), 'Remarks on Language Revival and Survival: A Case Study of Jersey Norman French'. Unpublished master's dissertation, University of Newcastle-upon-Tyne.

Skutnabb-Kangas, T. (1999), *Linguistic Genocide in Education—Or Worldwide Diversity and Human Rights?* Mahwah, NJ: Lawrence Erlbaum.

Smith, P. (2001), *Cultural Theory: An Introduction*. Oxford: Blackwell.

Tajfel, H. (1978), *Differentiation Between Social Groups*. London: Academic Press.

Tajfel, H. (1981), *Human Groups and Social Categories*. Cambridge: Cambridge University Press.

Walker, R. (1993), 'Language shift in Europe and Irian Jaya, Indonesia: toward the heart of the matter', in K. De Bot (ed.), *AILA Review 10: Case Studies in Minority Languages*. Bradford: Association Internationale de Linguistique Appliquée.

Widdowson, H. G. (1978), *Teaching Language as Communication*. Oxford: Oxford University Press.

9 Narrative constructions of gender and professional identities

Louise Mullany

Introduction

Conducting narrative analysis within sociolinguistic research is a long-standing tradition, following the seminal investigations of narratives of personal experience by Labov and Waletzky (1967) and Labov (1972). These works focused on analysing narratives in terms of their structural properties, assigning the categories of Labov's now-classic 'diamond'-shaped framework to narratives elicited during sociolinguistic interviews. Narratives of personal experience have long-dominated sociolinguistic research (Schiffrin 1996), and the immense value of continuing to investigate personal narratives is explored in this chapter. As investigations in this area of sociolinguistic research have grown, analysts have expanded their focus to consider the functions that narratives fulfil (Johnstone 2001; Thornborrow and Coates 2005a).

Researchers from a variety of disciplines have argued that a key reason for investigating the functions of personal narrative is due to the fundamental role it plays in helping us make sense of the world (Gee 1991; Giddens 1991; Coates 1996, 2003; Musson 1998; Johnstone 2001). Johnstone (2001) points out that, as humans, we all tell personal narratives in order to engage in the process of sense-making, both as individuals and as members of particular groups. Quoting Linde (1993: 3), Johnstone (2001: 640) elaborates on this viewpoint by arguing that 'a coherent, acceptable and constantly revised life story' is needed in order for individuals to have 'a comfortable sense of being a good, socially proper, and stable person'.

Narratives which focus on gender and professional identity are part of creating an acceptable life story and of making sense of our place and role in society. This chapter will explore how social identities are constructed and enacted within professional organizations, examining the narratives produced by business managers within the context of sociolinguistic interviews. The study focuses in particular on the performance of gender and professional identities within these interviews conducted as part of a larger ethnographic case study of gender, discourse and management within a manufacturing company in the UK. The analysis of gender identity has a strong tradition in sociolinguistic narrative research (Johnstone 1990; Coates 1996, 2003; Meinhof 1997; Sawin

1999; Capps 1999; Page 2002). Thornborrow and Coates (2005b: 8) point out that, in many of the chapters in their collection, narrative plays 'a key role in the construction of gender' with gender being 'a key part of the identity work going on'. Investigating narratives that take place within a professional workplace context is still a rather under-investigated area of sociolinguistic research. Holmes and Marra (2005) analyse how narratives work to construct professional identities in the workplace, and my chapter can be seen to build upon this work. However, their focus is on narratives that occur in meeting interactions, whereas this chapter examines narratives elicited during sociolinguistic interviews, in the Labovian methodological tradition. It adopts Labov's (1997: 398) definition of narratives of personal experience, conceptualizing such narratives as 'a report of a sequence of events that have entered into the biography of the speaker by a sequence of clauses that correspond to the original order of events'. The terms narrative and story are used as synonyms, following Thornborrow and Coates (2005b).

Narrative: self, identity and culture

The link between narrative as a form through which self, identity and culture can be expressed is well founded in sociolinguistic investigations, and this chapter is very much influenced by previous researchers who have made these connections clear. In her examination of women's stories, Coates (1996) makes the relationship between narratives and identity explicit, pointing out that, through story-telling, 'we create and re-create our identities and experiment with possible selves' (1996: 115). Holmes and Marra (2005: 201) argue that 'it is precisely in narratives that people's individuality is most clearly expressed'. Drawing on Giddens (1991) Cameron (2003: 459) posits that, in order to have a sense of identity in late modernity, individuals need to be able to 'order the various fragments of their life-experience into a coherent, on-going autobiographical narrative'. Schiffrin (1996) presents the appealing notion of narratives as 'self-portraits' which enable sociolinguistic constructions of identity to be observed. She argues that personal narratives are, at a global level, 'socially and culturally situated', with the teller drawing on 'cultural knowledge and expectations' (1996: 168). Additionally, personal narratives are also situated at a more local level, with the teller making them relevant to the specific setting in which the telling takes place. According to Schiffrin, in the process of telling a story, the self is evaluated in light of cultural 'meanings, beliefs and normative practices', and it is from these practices that 'our identities as social beings emerge as we construct our own individual experiences as a way to position ourselves in relation to social and cultural expectations' (1996: 170). Schiffrin's work neatly emphasizes the influences that social and cultural expectations place on the teller, and her distinction of global and local levels is a useful one.

This chapter can also be viewed in light of the current importance being placed on self, identity and culture in narrative sociolinguistic studies, as highlighted in Thornborrow and Coates' (2005a) collection. They argue firstly that 'the growing confluence of social scientific ideas of social identity with social psychological ideas of the "self" mean that identity is currently centre stage in sociolinguistics' (2005b: 14), a view that could be said to be exemplified by publications such as the essays in this volume. Thornborrow and Coates (2005b) make the point that it is not surprising that sociolinguists have fully embraced narrative study, as it is an excellent method of exploring identity and culture. Quoting Brockmeier and Carbaugh (2001: 16), they reiterate the crucial point that investigations of narrative involve 'not only examining the cultural construction of personal identity, but also the construction of one's social culture' (2005b: 15). This is based, in part, on a tendency in sociolinguistic research to pay attention to context, and in particular, to examine communities of practice (Lave and Wenger 1991; Wenger 1998), whereby the sense of an individual self is questioned in light of the view that individual selves can only be seen to develop in practices with others. They describe a 'healthy tension' between individual and more community-based perspectives, which is thought to be beneficial in terms of enhancing the field (2005b: 15). The communities of practice framework (henceforth CofP) has been very influential in recent language and gender studies (Eckert and McConnell-Ginet 1992, 1999) and its influence can be seen in this chapter, with the portraiture of narrative selves and identities as emerging through the narrators' telling stories of engagement in social practice with others who belong to the same CofP.

Performing identity

In addition to the CofP approach, this chapter also explores the notion of performativity (Butler 1990), which has also been influential in recent socio-linguistic language and gender studies (Cameron 1996, 1997; Bergvall *et al.* 1996; Coates 1999; Mills 2003). Thornborrow and Coates (2005b) highlight the importance of Butler's influence on narrative study as part of their focus on the importance of identity and culture within current sociolinguistic work. They assert that 'performance is central to any discussion of narrative discourse' (2005b: 9).[1] Butler (1990) argues that gender should be viewed as a *performative* social construct, as it is 'always a doing' and there is 'no gender identity behind the expressions of gender ... identity is performatively constituted by the very "expressions" that are said to be its results'. Therefore, Butler believes that masculinity and femininity are effects we perform by the activities in which we partake, not predetermined traits we possess.

Despite my adoption of Butler's conceptualization of performativity, it is important to note that I am not advocating that individuals are free to perform whatever gender identity they choose, a criticism that has been made of the performative approach (Kotthoff and Wodak 1997; Walsh 2001). Butler herself does acknowledge that acts of identity performance take place within a 'rigid regulatory frame' (1990: 33). Larger societal forces are therefore not necessarily neglected by adopting the performativity approach. As Cameron (1997: 49) points out, Butler 'insists that gender is regulated and policed by social norms'. By adopting the view that self and identity develop through practices with others, following a CofP-influenced approach, I'm arguing that individuals are not just simply selecting the type of identity they want to perform and then going ahead with this. Identity performance is influenced by a range of local and global factors. The identity that is performed can be seen as a complex process of negotiation between the self and others who engage in the same practices, taking place within CofPs and within a broader societal context that has rigid regulatory norms. If social norms are broken, then negative evaluation can occur.

Cameron (1996, 1997) was one of the first feminist linguists to put forward the argument that Butler's socially constructed notion of performativity may provide a theoretical framework to advance language and gender research. Cameron (1996) attacks sociolinguistics for failing to provide feminist linguistics with the theoretical apparatus necessary to interrogate the relationship between gender and language. She urges sociolinguists to look outside of the discipline, advocating a more multi-disciplinary approach by arguing that the more sophisticated theories of gender developed in critical social theory should be integrated with detailed linguistic analyses. Cameron summarizes her position by arguing that language and gender researchers should be prepared to 'challenge our co-optation by those within our discipline who would set narrower agendas for "sociolinguistics proper"'. Cameron's calls accord with the views of Eckert and McConnell Ginet (1992), that in order to succeed in bringing about social change, language and gender researchers need to form an interdisciplinary scholarly community of practice. Indeed, since the influence of social constructionist approaches has really taken off in language and gender sociolinguistic research, interdisciplinary publications have begun to emerge (Bucholtz et al. 1999). This chapter, influenced by the work of researchers from within the disciplines of social theory, sociology, psychology and organization studies, can be seen as part of this movement towards interdisciplinary language and gender research. Indeed, as has already been highlighted, narrative itself is a topic investigated in a variety of disciplines, and it lends itself well to study from an interdisciplinary perspective (Mishler 1997).

Gendered discourses

Language and gender researchers have also embraced an investigation of *gendered discourses*, following the oft-cited Foucaultian (1972: 49) view of discourse as 'practices that systematically form the objects of which they speak'. In this chapter, the notion of gendered discourses will be utilized in conjunction with the performativity and CofP approach (see Mullany forthcoming). Drawing on Foucault's definition, Mills (1997) highlights how gendered discourses can be identified:

> A discursive structure can be detected because of the systematicity of the ideas, opinions, concepts, ways of thinking and behaving which are formed within a particular context ... women and men behave within a certain range of parameters when defining themselves as gendered subjects. These discursive frameworks demarcate the boundaries within which we can negotiate what it means to be gendered.
>
> Mills (1997: 17–18)

Coates (1997: 291) makes the crucial link between Foucaultian discourses and performativity when she states that we all have 'access to a range of discourses, and it is these different discourses which give us access to, or enable us to perform, different "selves"'. Litosseliti (2006: 61) also makes the link between gender identities and gendered discourses clear when she argues that 'we produce or construct our multiple gendered selves through the choices we make from the different discourses available'. Based on a hegemonic view of power, Coates (1997) defines *dominant* discourses, which legitimize male superiority, as well as *resistant* and *subversive* discourses, such as feminist discourses. These discourses compete and can co-occur within the same stretch of talk.

Coates (1996, 2003) highlights dominant discourses of femininity and masculinity that can be observed within women's and men's narratives, reflecting the rigid social and cultural boundaries of acceptable gendered behaviour. Additionally, she also found resistant and subversive discourses, with stories being used as arenas to explore different selves, or being used to critique cultural expectations. Coates (1997) argues that ideologies are imposed by dominant discourses. This is similar to a point Sunderland (2004) makes, that gendered discourses carry ideology, and these work to position women and men in different ways. A key dominant discourse which carries ideological assumptions about gender is the discourse of *gender difference*. Sunderland (2004) highlights that this discourse can be seen to overarch most other discourses about gender that are circulating at a global level in society. Within the discourse of gender difference, women and men are seen as inherently different, usually attributed to biological differences between them, thus naturalizing persistent notions of difference, resulting in the legitimization of discrimination. This study examines how gender identities and professional managerial identities are enacted through available gendered discourses in narratives of personal experience. Cultural knowledge, expectations and overall ideologies that exist about gender within the manufacturing company and within wider society can then be revealed.

Methodology

The narratives analysed in this chapter were collected as part of a multi-method ethnographic case study of the manufacturing company.[2] As mentioned earlier in this chapter, the manufacturing company is viewed from the perspective of a CofP. In previous work, the CofP concept has been utilized on a smaller scale (Mullany 2004, 2006), in that different departments within the manufacturing company have been identified as CofPs in their own right. The CofP concept can also apply at a broader level (Eckert and McConnell-Ginet 1999), so whilst the company can be seen to be made up of different, smaller CofPs, the organization as a whole can be viewed as constituting a broader CofP, with participants mutually engaging with one another in the company as a whole in a jointly negotiated enterprise, drawing on a shared set of negotiable resources (Wenger 1998).

In terms of eliciting narrative report within interviews, Mishler (1986: 69) argues that it is 'no more unusual for interviewees to respond to questions with narratives if they are given room to speak'. Indeed, the sociolinguistic interview studies mentioned previously in the chapter are all good examples of how narratives can occur in interviews if the interviewer adopts the appropriate techniques. The interviews I conducted were semi-structured, in that I had a list of questions which were divided into three sections: general managerial role, perceptions of gender in the workplace and the role of gender in business meetings. Whilst these questions gave the interview a somewhat formal structure, I adopted a flexible approach in order to increase the production of spontaneous narratives of personal experience. As Mishler points out, even when interviewers do have a list, they will inevitably drift from the exact wording of these as speakers are engaging in unplanned discourse.

Mishler (1997: 224) argues that, within some narrative studies, there is an assumption that stories are monologues that belong solely to the teller. In order to remedy this, he points out that this perspective ignores the 'dynamic process through which a story takes on its specific shape', as well as losing crucial meaning and interaction between speaker and hearer(s). Whilst sociolinguistics as a discipline does not tend to be guilty of this, it is essential that narratives are perceived as speech events where discourse is jointly produced. In order to make this explicit, all interaction within the interview is transcribed, not just the monologic report of the narrative itself. The interviews are encounters between myself and the interviewee(s). Labov (1997: 397) argues that, within a sociolinguistic interview, the interviewer should be 'an ideal audience: attentive, interested and responsive', a principle which I aimed to follow. All forms of verbal interaction that occur within the interviews, including the verbal encouragement given in bringing about and supporting narrative production, are included in the transcripts. This consideration of the discourse of joint production corresponds with Schiffrin's identification of the importance of examining the local context in which narratives are produced.

In this chapter, the narratives that are analysed have been produced in interaction within dyadic interview encounters with me, with the exception of one interview where two women managers were present (see extract 2).[3] As an ethnographic fieldworker, I was known to all interviewees beforehand, and I had observed all of these interviewees taking part in business meetings. Whilst I had integrated into the company somewhat, my position was very much as a *peripheral* CofP member, with all participants aware that I was never going to become a *core* member (see Mullany 2006). Participants knew that the interviews were being conducted by someone who was located outside of the company hierarchy and the company culture. Informants were told that I was conducting a study on 'gender and workplace communication'. In total, 13 interviews were conducted, 11 with women and 2 with men, despite attempts to get more men involved (see Mullany forthcoming). In this chapter I focus on three narratives elicited during three different interviews. The first is from a woman manager who has broken through the glass ceiling, the second is produced during the only non-dyadic interview with two women managers at a middle-management level, and the third is taken from an interview with one of the male interviewees at the same management level and part of the same departmental CofP as the women middle-managers. These narratives therefore enable identity performance at both a senior (director) level and a middle-management level to be examined. They were also selected as they focus specifically on the interviewees' performance of their gender and professional identities in terms of how they perceive these to directly intersect and affect one another. All interviews were audio recorded and conducted in a small meeting room at the company's premises.

Analysis

The first narrative to be analysed was elicited during an interview with Carrie,[4] one of only two female managing directors in the company out of a board of ten. We have been talking about whether she thinks her gender affects how seriously her opinions are taken:

Extract 1

```
 1  Carrie:  I've kind of noticed that coming back off maternity leave I'm a lot
 2           bigger (.) than before //(.)// and err you know I think there's quite a
 3  Louise:  //mm//
 4  Carrie:  change in attitude towards me because of that (-)
 5  Louise:  Really?
 6  Carrie:  Yeah so I'm on a diet now (-)
 7  Louise:  More of a maternal figure do you think?
 8  Carrie:  Yeah yeah in in for people underneath //(.) yes// much more switched
 9  Louise:  //mm//
10  Carrie:  on to me //(.)// erm for erm people above or whatever are much more
11  Louise:  //yeah//
12  Carrie:  (.) don't take you so seriously when you're fatter definitely definitely
13           I'm sure about that //(.) // so we'll see when I've been on a diet
14  Louise:  //mhm//
15  Carrie:  //((laughs))// and I'm not getting younger either
16  Louise:  //((laughs))//
```

There were lengthy pauses at lines 4 and 6 so I issued interrogatives (lines 5 and 7) in order to attempt to get as much narrative production as possible. When Carrie introduces the view that her opinions are not taken as seriously since she has become fatter, she repeats 'definitely' twice to strengthen her viewpoint, adding additional emphasis to her argument. She laughs after saying that she has been on a diet (line 15), and I join in simultaneously, showing my support for what I interpreted to be Carrie's use of self-deprecating humour. Carrie's enactment of her gender and professional identities can be perceived through the dominant discourse of femininity. She draws attention to the existence of an ideal feminine image of the young, slim and thus stereotypically sexually attractive woman that exists in this workplace. Whilst she used to fall into this category, she no longer does as she is getting older and has put on weight due to giving birth. In the identity performance she has given in this interview, Carrie's narrative rather disturbingly suggests that, in order for women managers' opinions to be taken seriously in this business, they need to be sexually attractive, i.e. young and slim. Carrie therefore presents her professional identity as being constrained and negatively affected by the gendered identity that others have imposed on her. It is notable that the performance Carrie gives in this narrative is that it is others' perceptions of her identity that have changed; she does not present herself as someone who has chosen to perform her gender and professional identities differently. This can therefore be seen as an example of attribution of identity from others that has affected the manner in which Carrie perceives her own identity. Overall, she can be seen to be constricted and disadvantaged by the dominant discourse of femininity that maintains the idealized image of the youthful, slender female body as the one that is required in order to be taken seriously as a woman manager in this CofP.

In contrast, the first part of Carrie's narrative tells of how her subordinates are 'much more switched on to me' since her period of maternity leave. This observation of a change in her professional identity which Carrie presents is again attributed by others, rather than her presenting herself as someone who has changed the way she manages since becoming a mother. It can be analysed in light of the identity category of the 'mother role' (Tannen 1994; Wodak 1997; Stubbe et al. 2000). The 'mother role' is defined as when women enact power and control by adopting a nurturing, mothering identity which serves as a valid means through which women in positions of authority can exercise power (see Mullany 2006). The mother role identity can be perceived as part of the overarching gender differences discourse, whereby Carrie is being perceived as a more maternal manager by her subordinates, thus drawing a gender-based difference in Carrie's managerial style. Furthermore, Carrie's narrative representation of herself through her subordinates' opinions of her implies that, before she had a child, she was not perceived to be as effective as a manager, as it is the maternal association that has now enabled her subordinates to be more 'switched on' to her.

The next narrative is taken from an interview with middle-managers Kate and Becky. I asked them whether they think their gender will affect their career progression and we have been discussing the topic of children. Kate embarks on a narrative concerning a recent social event:

Extract 2

1	Kate:	I remember going out for a meal it was the first meal for the Services
2		Committee //and// the {job title} director was there and there
3	Louise:	//mm //
4	Kate:	was a few people there and I remember her saying "you you don't
5		want kids you'll be a career woman" and I said "no actually I do
6		want kids" and it was quite ((puts on a mocking voice)) "no no you
7		can't" //((laughs)) no I CAN'T have them//
8	Louise:	//((laughs))//
9	Becky:	//((laughs))// yeah I remember that it is though something that
10		you probably don't mention //like we// might talk to each other about
11	Louise:	//no//
12	Becky:	it but it wouldn't be a thing which we'd tell our boss about like what
13		we plan to do

The director referred to in this extract was Janette, the only other woman director apart from Carrie in this company. Prior to the narrative, Kate and Becky had said that they would really like children but it is something that they never mention at work. This accords with Halford and Leonard's (2001) observation that women hide their personal lives at work in order to protect their professional reputations. Kate uses the technique of direct speech as a narrative device in order to directly report the 'exact' conversation she had with Janette for additional emphasis. Kate quotes Janette's viewpoint that there is only one legitimate identity that a woman can adopt if she wants to succeed in business: the 'career woman'. By adopting a mocking voice (line 6), Kate performs her disquiet with the director's opinion, and makes clear her own position, again through direct speech, that she does want to have children herself. Kate's use of humour through mocking, and her use of laughter questions the director's perspective, and both Becky and I join in to support Kate by laughing simultaneously (lines 8 and 9). Kate's position can be seen as a form of resistant discourse, whereby she is resisting the dominant gender ideology that women cannot progress in their careers and be mothers at the same time. When Janette was interviewed, she openly stated that she thought she had been able to break through the glass ceiling because she did not have children. It is notable that Carrie had become a director before she decided to have children, and in her interview she talked extensively about work–home balance problems she was experiencing since giving birth. The narrative representation of Janette's opinion can be seen in light of a gendered discourse of discrimination. She appears to be aligning herself with the view that mothers cannot make good managers, in contrast to Kate, who presents herself as someone that wishes to adopt both identities in the future. Kate's narrative reporting of Janette's opinion indicates that the 'mother role' is not regarded as a legitimate identity by all, and it is a prime example of a sexist view held by a woman in this CofP who is Carrie's only other female colleague. Furthermore, the overarching discourse of gender difference can also be seen in Kate's narrative with her reporting of Janette's distinct identity category of 'career woman'. Sunderland (2004) argues that the discourse of gender difference can reflect the perspective of 'male as norm'. The marked gendered term of 'career woman', as opposed to the semantically non-equivalent term 'career man', strongly implies differences between women's and men's career paths, with women's careers being marked.

The next narrative was elicited during my interview with David, who occupied the same middle-management level as Kate and Becky, and who was also part of the same departmental CofP as them. We have been talking about whether David thinks his gender has affected his career progression:

Extract 3

1   David: In recent history erm erm I felt until three years ago I'd got on (.)
2   very well in this business //(.)// through my own abilities
3   Louise: //mm//
4   David: erm (-) and err more recently (.) erm (.) a new person came in who
5   you will know but who's no longer with us Sharon Jones //(.)//
6   Louise: //mhm//

```
 7  David:   who was bought in by one of the exec (.) directors (.) erm (.)
 8           and who was a previous colleague of that person ///(.)// so they
 9  Louise:  //mhm//
10  David:   brought 'em in er and I (-) I have no (.) doubt in my mind that
11           she used her sexual ///(-)// erm wiles if that's the right
12  Louise:  //mm//
13  David:   word ///((laughs))// er you know (-) to get what she wanted in the
14  Louise:  ///((laughs))//
15  David:   business and that probably to some degree (.) er had a negative
16           //effect// on me (.) so I I found myself (.) less able to exert (.) my
17  Louise:  //mm //
18  David:   influence based on skill ///(.)// er in the light of others er ability to
19  Louise:  //right//
20  David:   (.) apply their sexual influences if you like
```

In this story, David draws a dichotomy between his own masculine identity as a successful manager based on 'skill' (line 18), contrasted with Sharon's managerial identity based on 'sexual wiles' (line 11) and 'sexual influences' (line 20). When David introduces the expression 'sexual wiles' at line 11 he pauses, hesitates using 'erm' as a filler and then questions his own lexical choice of 'wiles', using metalanguage and the conditional, 'if that's the right word'. He then laughs and uses 'you know' as a hedge (line 13). As the hearer, David's hedging and laughter signalled to me potential embarrassment on his behalf, perhaps because he was expressing a personal, potentially unfavourable opinion to a woman interviewer. I laughed supportively and simultaneously at line 14 as a tactic to support David's narrative to its conclusion.

David's comments can be interpreted in light of the overarching discourse of gender difference. Men will be effective managers and gain career progression based on their skill and ability to do the job, whereas women will manage and gain career progression by being sexually manipulative. David's narrative can also be seen as an example of the 'battle of the sexes' discourse (Sunderland 2004: 42). He directly draws attention to the competition for achievement between himself and his female colleague based on the manipulative manner in which he perceives her to perform her gender identity. Furthermore, Sunderland (2004: 43) also coined a 'poor boys' discourse which can equally be applied to men when they are portrayed as being in need of understanding and pity. David's narrative can thus be seen in light of a 'poor man's' discourse, as he is performing the role of the victim due to his career being hampered by his allegedly sexually manipulative female colleague. It is notable that, at lines 18 and 20, the sexual manipulators become plural, with David referring to 'others' who apply *their* sexual influences'. This plurality indicates that he thinks other women in the company also use their 'sexual wiles' to advance their career. Indeed, later in the interview he cites Carrie, Kate and Becky as women colleagues who have done this, and, to quote David, it's 'causing resentment from other males'.

Discussion

A range of gender and professional identities have been performed in the narratives of personal experience, and these have been analysed through the gendered discourses that are in existence both in this company CofP and in wider society. Following Schiffrin, analysis of narratives has enabled cultural meanings, beliefs, normative practices and overall ideologies to be observed, with gender and professional identities emerging through narrative report. The overarching discourse of gender difference is clearly prevalent, adding weight to Sunderland's (2004) theory that it guides a great deal of discourse which takes place in today's society. The majority of gendered discourses in these narratives have been dominant, with women managers being constrained by dominant discourses of femininity in terms of their appearance and the mother role, as well as being presented as sexual manipulators. Evidence of these dominant gendered discourses reflect the limited set of legitimate, acceptable identities that women managers can adopt in the workplace (Alvesson and Billing 1997). These gendered identities reflect the rigid cultural expectations based on gender and professional identities that women managers have available to them. The dominant discourses of femininity are incompatible with the social and cultural expectations that make up the identity of a successful manager in the professional workplace. Even when a legitimate identity is allegedly found, conflicting opinions of this are observed, with Kate's report of Janette's view of the career woman being incompatible with being a mother. This contrasts with the more positive views which Carrie gives in terms of her subordinates being more 'switched on' to her, but this must also must be viewed in light of the negative reactions that Carrie reports from her superiors.

These conflicting opinions of legitimate identities expressed through narrative report neatly emphasize the levels of complexity which women managers can face when searching for legitimate social identities as managerial professionals. Some progress has been made in this company, as two directors have reached the higher echelons of power, but this is at some social cost, seen through Carrie's report of negative evaluations of her, and the strict identity boundaries that Janette lays out to herself and fellow staff, observed through Kate's narrative. The fact that Janette draws on the discourse of discrimination illustrates that women, including those that have broken through the glass ceiling, can be just as responsible as men for uttering sexist opinions. Kate's narrative also clearly illustrates heterogeneity within women's perceptions of legitimate social identities within this CofP, as well as demonstrating how resistant discourses can be used to critique and challenge a mainstream, culturally acceptable viewpoint within narrative report.

As well as the dominant discourse of femininity constraining women in terms of their appearance, the narrative analysis has also brought out another facet of this identity in terms of the sexually attractive woman using this to her advantage. During general interview talk, David commented that 'it is nice to have attractive women around the office'. However, in his narrative, it became clear that if women are perceived to be gaining kudos due to sexual attractiveness, they become a threat, and are thus subjected to negative evaluation, perceived as managing and gaining career progression by using their bodies, not their skills or abilities.

David's performance of his gender identity as a victim at the hands of sexually manipulative women managers demonstrates that, when women have made career progression, they can be subject to negative evaluation. The 'battle of the sexes' and 'poor man's' discourses identified in David's narrative can be interpreted in light of the view of masculinity being 'in crisis' (Johnson 1997; Swann 2002), a term which has been frequently used to describe an apparent crisis within masculinity that has taken place particularly as a result of the impact of feminism (Johnson 1997). Johnson points out that advocates of such a position urge men to 'reassert innate and essential differences from women' (1997: 17), based on the perception that real masculinity is 'rooted in natural or biological states' (1997: 19). Men are thus being urged to draw upon the discourse of gender difference in order to attempt to reverse social change. David's identity perfomance can be viewed in light of this as he draws a clear gender difference between the manner in which female managers sexually manipulate versus male managers' use of skill.

By adopting a CofP approach, it has been observed that the identities presented through narrative report in this chapter have not been produced in isolation. Individual selves and performed identities can be seen as developing in practices with members of the CofP. The manner in which identities emerge by individuals positioning themselves in relation to other members of the CofP has been illustrated. This includes examining the manner in which the identities of others within the company are portrayed in order to see how the narrator is positioning herself/himself in order to enact gender and professional, managerial identities.

Overall, the findings in this chapter accord with McConnell-Ginet's (2000) view:

> The disturbing documented sex differences in workplace achievement still found are differences in how people are judged and evaluated ... both women and men expect different things of women and of men, and these expectations lead them to respond to and evaluate women and men quite differently, often in professional contexts undervaluing women's talents and work and over-valuing men's.
>
> (McConnell-Ginet 2000: 269)

Although McConnell-Ginet does not mention it specifically, the discourse of gender difference is clearly evident here, and this quotation neatly illustrates how both women and men can be responsible for judging and evaluating women managers' identities as different from those of men – still perceived as the norm. It also highlights how women's talents are 'under-valued', for example, being perceived to be successful as a consequence of sexual manipulation instead of through skills and abilities.

Conclusion

This chapter has explored the manner in which individual selves and identities are performed through narratives of personal experience, and highlights the use of these narratives as lenses through which social and cultural knowledge, expectations and ideologies can be observed. It has also demonstrated the usefulness of integrating performativity with the CofP approach and the notion of gendered discourses. The analysis has shown how business managers' identity performances develop in practices that take place with others, as well as examining how these displays of self and identity are enacted through gendered discourses which operate within wider society. This integrated approach demonstrates the importance of a continued move towards interdisciplinary sociolinguistic studies within language and gender research (Mullany forthcoming).

Despite the increase of women entering managerial positions since the 1970s (Davidson and Burke 2000), the glass ceiling is still firmly in place in the UK (National Statistics Office 2004), and the narrative analysis here indicates that there are still deeply entrenched identity categories, based on gender ideologies and maintained by gendered discourses, as to the legitimate identities that women managers should perform. Socially acceptable managerial identities are very often at odds with dominant discourses of femininity, which continually emphasize gender difference and serve to place women at a disadvantage (cf. Brewis 2001). The evidence presented here, along with the continued existence of the glass ceiling demonstrates that, within professional workplaces such as this manufacturing company, social change needs to be brought about in order for women managers to avoid negative evaluation and reach the higher levels of power. Schiffrin (1996: 170) argues that 'when our social and cultural expectations change, so do our perceptions of identities'. Therefore, in order for perceptions of managerial identities to change, a change in social and cultural expectations needs to be brought about. Cameron (2003: 453) argues that 'if enough people can be induced to doubt that the status quo is natural or legitimate, a climate is created in which demands for change are much harder for their opponents to resist'. It is hoped that, by producing studies such as this, awareness can be raised of the dominant gendered discourses which regulate our social and cultural identities, with the overall aim of bringing about social change.

Notes

1 Thornborrow and Coates identify a second definition influenced by ethnography and social anthropology. In these fields, researchers have applied to narrative 'the everyday use of the word 'performance' in relation to plays and poems and songs being performed in public' (2005b: 10).
2 Other facets that make up the multi-method approach include audio recordings of meetings, shadowing, informal talk and analyses of written documents.
3 I had arranged to interview Becky but she had double-booked our interview slot for a meeting with Kate. I conducted an interview with both of them whilst they were completing a hands-on task.
4 All names are pseudonyms. The transcription conventions are as follows:
   (.) Indicates a pause of one second or less
   (-) Indicates a pause of two seconds or more
   // //
   // // Double slashed brackets indicate simultaneous speech
   { } Indicates material was deleted for confidentiality

(xxx) Indicates material was impossible to make out
((laughs)) Double brackets give additional information

References

Alvesson, M. and Billing, Y. (1997), *Gender, Work and Organization*. London: Sage.

Bergvall, V., Bing, J. and Freed A. (1996) (eds), *Rethinking Language and Gender Research: Theory and Practice*. New York: Longman.

Brewis, J. (2001), 'Telling it like it is? Gender, language and organizational theory', in R. Westwood and S. Linstead (eds), *The Language of Organization*. London: Sage, pp. 283–309.

Brockmeier, J. and Carbaugh, D. (2001), *Studies in Autobiography, Self and Culture*. Amsterdam: Benjamins.

Bucholtz, M., Liang, A. and Sutton L. (1999) (eds), *Reinventing Identities: The Gendered Self in Discourse*. Oxford: Oxford University Press.

Butler, J. (1990), *Gender Trouble: Feminism and the Subversion of Gender Identity*. New York: Routledge.

Cameron, D. (1996), 'The language-gender interface: challenging co-optation', in V. Bergvall, J. Bing and A. Freed (eds), *Rethinking Language and Gender Research: Theory and Practice*. New York: Longman, pp. 31–53.

— (1997), 'Performing gender identity: young men's talk and the construction of heterosexual masculinity', in S. Johnson and U. H. Meinhof (eds), *Language and Masculinity*. Oxford: Blackwell, pp. 47–64.

— (2003), 'Gender and language ideologies', in J. Holmes and M. Meyerhoff (eds), *The Handbook of Language and Gender*. Oxford: Blackwell, pp. 447–67.

Capps, L. (1999), 'Constructing the irrational woman: Narrative interaction and agoraphobic identity', in M. Bucholtz, A. Liang and L. Sutton (eds), *Reinventing Identities: The Gendered Self in Discourse*. Oxford: Oxford University Press, pp. 83–100.

Coates, J. (1996), *Women Talk*. Oxford: Blackwell.

— (1997), 'Competing discourses of femininity', in H. Kotthoff and R. Wodak (eds), *Communicating Gender in Context*. Amsterdam: Benjamins, pp. 285–313.

— (1999), 'Changing femininities: the talk of teenage girls', in M. Bucholtz, A. Liang and L. A. Sutton (eds), *Reinventing Identities: The Gendered Self in Discourse*. Oxford: Oxford University Press, pp. 123–44.

— (2003), *Men Talk*. Oxford: Blackwell.

Davidson, M. and Burke, R. (2000), *Women in Management: Current Research Issues*, Vol. II. London: Sage.

Eckert, P. and McConnell-Ginet, S. (1992), 'Think practically and look locally: language and gender as community-based practice', *Annual Review of Anthropology*, 21, 461–90.

— (1999), 'New generalizations and explanations in language and gender research', *Language in Society*, 28, (2), 185–201.

Foucault, M. (1972), *The Archaeology of Knowledge*. London: Routledge.

Gee, J. (1991), 'A linguistic approach to narrative', *Journal of Narrative and Life History*, 1, 15–39.

Giddens, A. (1991), *Modernity and Self-Identity: Self and Society in the Late Modern Age*. Cambridge: Polity Press.

Halford, S. and Leonard, P. (2001), *Gender, Power and Organisations: An Introduction*. Basingstoke: Palgrave.

Holmes, J. and Marra, M. (2005), 'Narrative and the construction of professional identity in the workplace', in J. Thornborrow and J. Coates (eds), *The Sociolinguistics of Narrative*. Amsterdam: Benjamins, pp. 193–213.

Johnson, S. (1997), 'Theorizing Language and Masculinity: A Feminist Perspective', in S. Johnson and U. H. Meinhof (eds), *Language and Masculinity*. Oxford: Blackwell, pp. 47–64.

Johnstone, B. (1990), *Stories, Communities and Space*. Bloomington: Indiana University Press.
— (2001), 'Narrative', in D. Schiffrin *et al.* (2001), *The Handbook of Discourse Analysis*. Oxford: Blackwell, pp. 635–49.
Kotthoff, H. and Wodak, R. (1997), 'Preface: gender in context', in R. Wodak and H. Kotthoff (eds), *Communicating Gender in Context*. Amsterdam: Benjamins, pp. vii–xxv.
Labov, W. and Waletzky, W. (1967), 'Narrative analysis: oral versions of personal experience', in J. Helms (ed.), *Essays on the Verbal and Visual Arts*. Seattle: University of Washington Press.
Labov, W. (1972), *Language in the Inner City*. Philadelphia: University of Pennsylvania Press.
— (1997), 'Some further steps in narrative analysis', *Journal of Narrative and Life History*, 7, (14), 395–415.
Lave, J. and Wenger, E. (1991), *Situated Learning: Legitimate Peripheral Participation*. Cambridge: Cambridge University Press.
Linde, C. (1993), *Life Stories: The Creation of Coherence*. New York: Oxford University Press.
Litosseliti, L. (2006), *Gender and Language: Theory and Practice*. London: Arnold.
McConnell-Ginet, S. (2000), 'Breaking through the glass ceiling: can linguistic awareness help?', in J. Holmes (ed.), *Gendered Speech in Social Context: Perspectives from Gown to Town*. Wellington: Victoria University Press, pp. 259–82.
Meinhof, U. H. (1997), '"The most important event of my life" A comparison of male and female written narratives', in S. Johnson and U. H. Meinhof (eds), *Language and Masculinity*. Oxford: Blackwell, pp. 208–28.
Mills, S. (1997), *Discourse*. London: Routledge.
— (2003), *Gender and Politeness*. Cambridge: Cambridge University Press.
Mishler, E. (1986), *Research Interviewing: Context and Narrative*. London: Harvard University Press.
— (1997), 'The interactional construction of narratives in medical and life-history interviews', in B. L. Gunnarsson *et al.* (eds), *The Construction of Professional Discourse*. Harlow: Longman, pp. 223–44.
Mullany, L. (2004), 'Gender, politeness and institutional power roles: humour as a tactic to gain compliance in workplace business meetings', *Multilingua*, 23, 13–37.
— (2006), '"Girls on tour": Politeness, small talk and gender identity in managerial business meetings', *Journal of Politeness Research: Language, Behaviour, Culture*, 2, (1), 55–77.
— (forthcoming), *Gendered Discourse in the Professional Workplace*. Basingstoke: Palgrave.
Musson, G. (1998), 'Life histories', in G. Symon and C. Cassell (eds), *Qualitative Methods and Analysis in Organisational Research: A Practical Guide*, pp. 10–27.
National Statistics Office (2004), *Working Lives*. www.statistics.gov.uk.
Page, R. (2002), 'Evaluations in childbirth narratives told by women and men', *Discourse & Society*, 4, (1), 99–116.
Sawin, P. (1999), 'Gender, context and the narrative construction of identity: Rethinking models of "women's narrative"', in M. Bucholtz, A. Liang and L. Sutton (eds), *Reinventing Identities: The Gendered Self in Discourse*. Oxford: Oxford University Press, pp. 241–58.
Schiffrin, D. (1996), 'Narrative as self-portrait: sociolinguistic constructions of identity', *Language in Society*, 25, 167–203.
Stubbe, M., Holmes, J., Vine, B. and Marra, M. (2000), 'Forget Mars and Venus: let's get back to earth!: Challenging gender stereotypes in the workplace', in J. Holmes (ed.), *Gendered Speech in Social Context: Perspectives from Gown to Town*. Wellington: Victoria University Press, pp. 231–58.
Sunderland, J. (2004), *Gendered Discourses*. Basingstoke: Palgrave.
Swann, J. (2002), 'Yes, but is it gender?', in L. Litosseliti and J. Sunderland (eds), *Gender Identity and Discourse Analysis*. Amsterdam: Benjamins, pp. 43–67.

Tannen, D. (1994), *Talking from 9 to 5: Women and Men in the Workplace: Language, Sex and Power*. New York: Avon.

Thornborrow, J. and Coates, J. (2005a), *The Sociolinguistics of Narrative*. Amsterdam: Benjamins.

— (2005b), 'The sociolingustics of narrative: Identity, performance, culture', in J. Thornborrow and J. Coates (eds), *The Sociolinguistics of Narrative*. Amsterdam: Benjamins, pp. 1–16.

Walsh, C. (2001), *Gender and Discourse: Language and Power in Politics, the Church and Organisations*. London: Longman.

Wenger, E. (1998), *Communities of Practice*. Cambridge: Cambridge University Press.

Wodak, R. (1997), '"I know we won't revolutionise the world with it but...": styles of female leadership in institutions', in H. Kotthoff and R. Wodak (eds), *Communicating Gender in Social Context*. Amsterdam: Benjamins, pp. 355–70.

10 Masculine identities on an academic writing programme

Siân Preece

Introduction

Darvesh: When we started this uni (.) there was (.) how many?/ about six of us int there?
Lalit: yea:h
Darvesh: and we just (.) knock about/ we ourselves an' that
Salman: yeah
Darvesh: and I mean (.) there was a couple of people who used to come up to us/ but other people just used to look/ but they never actually used to come up and say "all right" to us/ 'cos they DID JUST used to get intimidated by a group of lads (.) innit? (Group Discussion).

The opening extract is taken from group work that was audio-recorded in a first-year undergraduate academic writing classroom at Millennium University,[1] one of London's post-1992 higher education institutions. Here we see Darvesh[2] (aged 20), Lalit (aged 19) and Salman (aged 25), three British Asian[3] male undergraduates from working-class families, discussing their transition into higher education. Darvesh's utterance suggests that at the heart of their concerns is the establishment of new social relationships with their peers, the maintenance of 'face' (Goffman 1972) and the performance of 'acceptable' masculinity (Coates 2003) in the peer group. Through adopting the position of a tough 'group of lads' that 'knock about' as a tight-knit unit, Darvesh claims that they have discouraged most other first years from attempting to establish social relations with them. This laddish position appears to help them all maintain face by masking the difficulties that they are experiencing in forming social relationships as 'newcomers' (Lave and Wenger 1991) to higher education. For while Darvesh, Lalit and Salman attempt to convey the impression of a group of tough, confident lads, their talk also suggests that they find themselves positioned as outsiders, as 'Other' to those they gaze at 'inside' the mainstream student body.

Wondering how to establish new social relations in the alien world of higher education, however, is not their only concern. In common with all 'newcomers', Darvesh and his peers are also faced with the demands of an academic community, of keeping up with their studies and coursework and coping satisfactorily with the (literacy) practices of their discipline. Much is at stake, therefore, during this transitory period. Not only do Darvesh and his peers need to establish new social relationships, but also develop and display their subject knowledge through satisfactorily meeting a range of learning outcomes for their first-year modules. This raises issues for those of us involved in working with university 'newcomers', such as Darvesh and his peers, as to how we can assist in the difficult and frequently painful process of social and academic 'integration' (Tinto 1975; Draper 2003) within the constraints of mass higher education. For as Valerie Walkerdine (1990) comments, while new identifications may create opportunities, they also carry risks of dislocations from familiar relationships, detaching us from our closest ties with family and friends.

In this chapter, therefore, I set out to explore 'newcomer' identity and identifications with a group of male undergraduates undergoing the transition into their academic community. Through examining the performance of gendered identities among these male participants in an academic writing classroom, I consider their orientation to some of the practices of the academic community and the settling in process. I argue that in the classroom data, hegemonic masculinity (Connell 2000) is primarily constituted through the participants 'doing being a lad'. Adopting laddish positions not only serves the immediate function of acting 'cool', acting tough and/or having a laugh among peers, but also acts as a way of masking vulnerabilities and resisting institutional practices perceived as face-threatening and/or alienating.

For much of the time, these laddish performances create the impression of 'walking a tightrope' between the frequently conflicting demands of the academic community and those of their peers in which few, if any, of the male participants appeared able to construct a masculine identity through a 'smooth insertion' (Connell 1989: 300) into academia. For many, there seemed to be a clash between public 'social registration' (Hewitt 1992: 34) in a culturally hybrid urban youth culture, and private desires, usually well-concealed from male peers, for membership within higher education 'communities of practice' (Lave and Wenger 1991).

In the following sections, I will explore these issues by first outlining the setting for the research and then discussing the way I have approached identity. Following this, I will illustrate the constitution of gendered identities among three of the male participants by analysing an extract of classroom talk. Finally, I will raise some of the issues facing educators working with higher education 'newcomers' from similar backgrounds to those in this chapter.

Setting

The data for this chapter come from a language and gender research project investigating issues of undergraduate 'newcomer' identities and identifications within the context of widening participation[4] in British universities. As part of its strategy both to widen participation and improve undergraduate retention, Millennium had established a first-year module in academic writing for students educated primarily in English, which was designed to improve first-year undergraduates' chances of coping successfully with their written work and their prospects in the university. This academic writing programme forms the setting for the research project.

All the data were collected in the physical setting of Millennium, over a two-year period while the participants were primarily occupied with studying for their first degree. While the research includes male and female participants and is concerned with questions of identity for both, my discussion in this chapter focuses on some of the male participants in the study. While the data come from field notes, audio-recorded group work in the classroom, question-naires and interviews, the data on which my discussion is based come from some of the audio-recorded group-work discussions of all-male peer groups in the classroom setting.

As Millennium actively recruits from London schools and Further Education (FE) colleges, the majority of the participants in the research had grown up and been educated in the 'polycultural' (Hewitt 1992) setting of London, which Hewitt describes as encompassing 'cultural entities that are not ... discrete and complete ... not "intrinsically equal"; and ... active together and ... bound up with change' (1992: 30). Many were the first in their family to attend university and also to consider applying for professional posts in major institutions following graduation. Many were from working-class backgrounds and all but one from ethnic minority communities. At the time of the research, the participants were mostly in their late teens and early twenties and had entered Millennium with vocational qualifications, such as General National Vocational Qualifications (GNVQs), and A-levels obtained with low grades. There were also a small number of mature participants who had often entered the institution through Access courses.[5]

Apart from one participant in the research, all were 'multilingual' in that their language repertoire embraced both varieties of English and one or more of the 'community' languages in Britain (Martin-Jones and Jones 2000). However, despite experiencing their lives through a variety of languages, most did not have a great command of the spoken and/or written forms of these languages. In fact, most claimed that their greatest affiliation and expertise was in 'slang', a variety of London English used with their peers. When discussing English language practices, the participants frequently constructed a 'slang/posh' dichotomy in which talking 'slang' referred to the vernacular English language practices used with peers whereas talking 'posh' referred to attempts to use '*literate English*' (Wallace 2002), defined as a variety of spoken and written English 'most like formal written English ... (encountered) in broadsheet newspapers, quality novels and (serious) non-fiction texts' (Wallace 2002: 105), favoured by academic communities. Throughout the data, the participants displayed a strong identification with talking 'slang' whereas they were much more ambivalent about learning to talk and, by implication, act 'posh'.

The participants' reported language practices, in relation to their home, peers and formal education, are in keeping with the body of research established by Harris, Rampton and Leung with similar, but younger, participants from ethnic minority communities (see e.g. Rampton 1990, 2005; Harris 1997; Leung and Cable 1997; Leung *et al.* 1997; Leung and Franson 2001; Harris *et al.* 2002). In common with their findings, the participants in this study displayed high levels of affiliation to and expertise in the local vernacular English, generally low levels of expertise, both spoken and written, in heritage language(s), and varying degrees of expertise in using English in academic settings. Commenting on British 'bilingual' adolescents, Leung *et al.* concluded that many were 'most comfortable linguistically with ... a local urban spoken English vernacular, or a non-standard variety of this kind' (1997: 554). This also seemed to be the case for many of the participants in this study.

While varieties of vernacular English used by inner-city British youth have been referred to as 'local multi-ethnic vernacular' or 'community English' (Hewitt 1992), I prefer to use the term 'peer group English', as the language practices with which the majority of the participants felt most at ease and were best able to express themselves had developed in peer-group social settings. Among the male participants, expertise in 'peer group English' appeared particularly important in terms of facilitating displays of affiliation to the peer group as a 'community of practice' and as a method of 'jockeying for position' (Edley and Wetherell 1997) in peer group social relationships. There is evidence throughout the classroom data of the male participants using witty repartee, telling jokes, trashing absent others and academic community practices, using taboo language and engaging in verbal 'battering' of marginalized male peers. These oral displays worked to co-construct laddish bonhomie and, conversely, police talk in which acting tough, acting 'cool' and/or having a laugh came under threat. Expertise in 'peer group English', therefore, assisted the male partici-pants in positioning themselves as 'legitimate speakers' (Bourdieu 1977) with peers and in aligning themselves with laddish masculinity. As Pierre Bourdieu comments, language is not simply a tool of communication but an 'instrument of power' (1977: 648).

Underpinning the research is the belief that learning, including language learning, and identity are intimately bound up with each other. As Lave and Wenger claim:

> Learning involves the whole person; it implies not only a relation to specific activities, but a relation to social communities – it implies becoming a full participant, a member, a kind of person. In this view, learning only partly – and often incidentally – implies becoming able to be involved in new activities, to perform new tasks and functions, to master new understandings. Activities, task, functions, and understandings do not exist in isolation; they are part of broader systems of relations in which they have meaning. These systems of relations arise out of and are reproduced and developed within social communities, which are part systems of relations among persons. The person is defined by as well as defines these relations. Learning thus implies becoming a different person with respect to the possibilities enabled by these systems of relations. To ignore this aspect of learning is to overlook the fact that learning involves the construction of identities (1991: 53).

However, in the debate on mass higher education, there has been little focus on issues of identities or identifications. Instead, dominant discourses on widening participation have focused on ways of equipping students categorized as 'non-traditional' with skills to ensure their success not only in higher education, but also in preparation for work in the knowledge economy. Drawing on Foucault's definition of discourse as 'practices which systematically form the object of which they speak' (1974: 49), it seems that discursive practices frequently constitute 'skills' in mass higher education as sets of observable and measurable competencies that can be 'atomised' (Lea and Street 2000) and taught separately from subject content. One way in which 'newcomer' competencies have been observed and measured at Millennium is through an academic literacy screening test during induction. Based on screening results, first-year undergraduates are either required to take or exempted from a module in academic writing. Despite the best efforts of lecturers involved in this programme, who view the teaching of academic literacy practices as more than simply a matter of equipping students with skills, the module is commonly discussed among staff and students in terms of 'remedial' English and a way of 'fixing' problems with students' academic writing. For the participants in this chapter, therefore, the academic writing classroom became a site for negotiating this ascribed 'deficit' and 'remedial' identity, as I will illustrate later in this chapter. In the following section, the issue of 'identity' will be considered.

Identity

I view identity as both discursively constituted and constructed in interactions with others. As such identity is both fluid and multifaceted. Foucault's conceptualization of individuals as 'discoursing subjects' (1991: 58) embodied within the socially constructed discourses to which they have access, is helpful in considering the construction of identity as a dynamic process rather than as a set of essentialized characteristics or variables. The relationship between the 'discoursing subject' and discourse appears to be symbiotic, in the sense that Foucault claimed that human relations primarily reside within discourse and discourse relies on these relationships to be brought into being and maintained. Foucault theorized that while the 'discoursing subject' had a 'place' and 'function' in discourse, they also had the 'possibilities of displacements ... and functional mutation' (58). In other words, while individuals produce and reproduce their discursive 'subject position', defined by Weedon (1997) as 'ways of being an individual', they also can adapt, subvert and resist this positioning by adopting alternative subject positions within other discourses to which they have access. Consequently, while the 'discoursing subject' is no longer seen as an autonomous author of its world in the Enlightenment sense, neither is it simply a product of discourse. Identity is therefore conceived of as a process, making it susceptible to intervention and change.

Baxter discusses the way individuals are *'multiply'* positioned in discourses, often as simultaneously occupying both powerful and powerless positions within competing discourses (2003: 32). Although in negotiating identity, or a sense of self, the individual experiences conflicts resulting from exposure to different and unfamiliar discourses, as Baxter points out, this process offers the possibility for considering the ways in which individuals adopt, and, in cases of social justice, may be encouraged to adopt, 'subject/speaker' positions which are resistant to relatively 'powerless ways of being' (2003: 33).

Through this process of positioning and repositioning, individuals negotiate a sense of self that is subjected to discursive norms regulating what are and are not culturally 'acceptable' (Coates 2003) and 'intelligible' (Butler 1990) ways of doing gender. In this sense, gender is not an attribute or property of an individual but accomplished through repeated acts. Here, I am following Butler (1990) in her argument that gender is 'performative' and that gendered identity is 'performatively constituted'. According to Butler, it is only through this continual enactment that gender can masquerade as substance. As she comments, 'gender is the repeated stylization of the body, a set of repeated acts within a highly rigid regulatory frame that congeal over time to produce the appearance of substance, a natural sort of being' (1990: 33). Elsewhere Cameron and Kulick argue that 'performativity' views individuals as 'materializing' gender through the constant repetition of conscious and unconscious acts that signify masculinity and femininity within a particular cultural location. Identity comes about therefore as an effect of these practices, not as a '"natural" expression of our essential selves' (2003: 150).

Within a 'performative' view of identity, gender cannot be considered as a separate variable or as constituted in isolation. Rather gender interacts with other 'axes of power relations' (Butler 1990), such as ethnicity, 'race', class, life stage and occupation, within particular settings. While there may be more than one way of enacting gendered identities in any given context, dominant discursive practices regulate norms concerning 'appropriate' ways of doing 'acceptable' masculinity and femininity.

Weedon comments on the power of discursive practices to 'constitute the meaning of the physical body, psychic energy, the emotions and desire' (1997: 109), arguing that these practices are associated with an individual's psychological state and memories. She also comments that individuals are likely to be drawn to discursive subject positions which they identify as fulfilling their interests. These identifications do not arise in a vacuum but in societies strongly oriented to the social practices of discourses which constitute the world in terms of binary oppositions, in which powerful discourses work by offering 'discoursing subjects' seductive messages of coherence and a 'meaningful role' in life.

Elsewhere, Cameron and Kulick elaborate on the psychic dimensions of identification, pointing out its origins in psychoanalysis and its use to discuss the 'processes through which individuals assimilate an aspect or property of an other, and are, in that process transformed' (2003: 139). They argue that while 'identity' is still largely conceived of as a conscious 'claim-staking' of a particular sociological position, 'identification' is related to subconscious desires and fears about ourselves in relation to others. Arguing that identifications are structured by 'rejections, refusals and disavowals' as well as 'affirmations', Cameron and Kulick comment that:

> Identifications are not imagined to constitute a coherent relational system. In other words, the processes that constitute an individual as a certain kind of subject are not harmonious. Rather they are conflicting and contradictory, undermining conscious attempts to produce and maintain subjective coherence and consistency. It follows that a person's claim to a

particular *identity* could be disrupted or contradicted by *identifications* s/he is unaware
or unconscious of (2003: 139).

Consequently, the constitution of identity does not appear to be a free-for-all,
or a trivial and ephemeral affair in which 'discoursing subjects' 'mix and match'
designer identities. Instead, the processes through which identity is constituted
appear constrained by discursive practices to which 'discoursing subjects' have
access, linked to the psychological and emotional feelings that 'discoursing
subjects' consciously and subconsciously experience from constant repetition of
these practices and framed within social and historical contexts in which there
are material inequalities.

In order to apply these abstract theories of identity to the research reported
in this chapter, I have drawn on the 'communities of practice' framework.
Lave and Wenger view a 'community of practice' as a 'set of relations among
persons, activity, and world, over time and in relation with other tangential and
overlapping communities of practice' (1991: 98). Through the social interactions within a community of practice, preferred practices, beliefs and ways of
talking emerge and develop which are oriented to discourses prevalent in wider
society. According to Eckert and McConnell-Ginet, membership of communities
of practice not only provides a way of participating in society, but also enables
individuals to 'forge a sense of their place and possibilities in society' (2003:
57). Through participating in a range of 'communities of practice', each of
differing significance, individuals gradually develop a sense of 'who they are',
their identity and place within the social order. As Eckert and McConnell-Ginet
comment, identity becomes constituted in the 'process of balancing the self ...
across these communities of practice' (2003: 58).

Three influential groupings for the participants in this chapter were their
undergraduate peers, the university (as represented by academic staff and the
overall student body) and their families. As the participants met regularly with
others in these groupings to engage in activities involved with aspects of family
and student life, I have found it helpful to consider each as a 'community of
practice' with practices and beliefs about the world that overlap and conflict.
Within the setting of the academic writing classroom, the participants grapple
with these overlaps and conflicts in trying to make sense of 'who they are' and
what is required of them within the alien setting of higher education. In the next
section, I will illustrate some of these conflicts in an extract of talk in which
three male participants are negotiating a sense of self in relation to the reading
and writing practices favoured by the academic community.

Masculinities in the academic writing classroom

The process of successfully 'balancing the self' between the academic community
and the peer group was perhaps more difficult to achieve in the academic writing
classroom than in the participants' main disciplinary area due to the number of
seemingly conflicting subject positions and practices that the participants needed
to negotiate. In common with all first-year undergraduates, the participants

were positioned as novices and 'newcomers' within higher education who were expected to aspire to an intellectual and academic identity. Additionally, they were ascribed an autonomous and adult identity, in which they were expected to take responsibility for, and be able to cope largely unassisted with, their academic, personal and social life. Besides these issues of common concern, the participants in this chapter also needed to cope with their institutional 'deficit' positioning that had arisen through being placed on the academic writing programme. This was made more problematic by the frequent referral to 'remedial' English in their department, posting lists of referred students on departmental notice boards and separating the writing classes from disciplinary subject content. These practices worked to stigmatize the participants and also to undermine the writing course lecturers, who did not subscribe to the view that they were teaching 'remedial' lessons.

In contrast to their relatively powerless institutional positioning, the peer group offered powerfully seductive positions from which to speak in the academic writing classroom, positions which were not available in the wider academic community. Instead of adopting the identity ascribed to them, as 'newcomers' and 'deficit', through performances of a sometimes tough and sometimes humorous laddish masculinity, they were able to adopt a 'cool' and streetwise persona as part of a generation 'on the move'.[6] As Cameron (2001) points out, all talk is artfully designed to project a particular persona within a setting and to project a particular 'face' (Goffman 1972). Under the gaze of their male peers, much of the talk seemed concerned with performing 'acceptable' masculinity (Coates 2003), which the male participants appeared to associate with doing 'being one of the lads'. In a discussion of 'lad' culture, Whelehan comments on the power of the term 'lad' to conjure up images associated with adolescent male behaviour and denote men's 'natural state of being'. As she comments, we are 'implicitly asked to accept (laddish culture), laugh along with it or reject it at (our) peril' (2000: 9).

In the all-male peer groups, 'cool' laddish youthfulness was associated with peer group language practices which positioned vernacular English, or 'peer group English' as the preferred way of talking and a marker of in-group identity. For most of the male participants, their status as expert users of 'peer group English' was in sharp contrast to the position of non-competent or 'deficit' users of the 'posh' English of academic communities. Additionally, identification with laddish peer group practices prevented talk that could be conceived of as 'feminine' or 'feminized' in some way. This discouraged admissions of difficulty and vulnerability, particularly as these could be used to position the speaker as 'incompetent', 'stupid', 'wimpy' or 'gay', or discussions of academic work as enjoyable or fulfilling, as these could be used to ascribe an 'intellectual' or 'boffin' identity.

Some of these difficulties are illustrated in the following extract of talk among three male participants, all of whom are from working-class backgrounds. In the extract, they are discussing their identification with academic literacy practices and whether they can conceive of themselves as readers and writers of academic texts. This group is composed of Sanjay (aged 19), a British Asian from a Gujarati-speaking family, Mustafa (aged 20), a British Iranian from a

Farsi-speaking family and Osmaan (aged 25), a British Asian from an Urdu-speaking family. In this peer group, Osmaan made frequent efforts to do 'serious' talk with his peers. However, he was not able to sustain this for long before Mustafa and Sanjay resorted to trashing the academic community and its practices, telling jokes, having a laugh and making face-threatening retorts. While Osmaan sometimes went along with these laddish practices, he was more usually silenced. His interests and concerns were frequently marginalized while his status as 'mature' was often problematized.

'All the usual shit'

M=Mustafa, O=Osmaan, S=Sanjay

```
1--------------------------------------------------------------------------------
M:    to what extent do you think (.) of yourself as a reader and writer of academic
O:
S:
2--------------------------------------------------------------------------------
M:    texts (.) say why/ <reading aloud> (4)
O:                                        er:: I don't know/ I'd say that I don't
S:
3--------------------------------------------------------------------------------
M:
O:    (.) I sometimes have difficulty (.) reading and understanding/ I have to write
S:
4--------------------------------------------------------------------------------
M:
O:    sometimes/ I have to break it down/ read it again [(.) then I understand it (.)
S:                                                       [yeah? <scornful tone, laughs>
5--------------------------------------------------------------------------------
M:
O:    simple man (.) there's no- no shyness about it (1) y'know what I mean?/ just
S:
6--------------------------------------------------------------------------------
M:
O:    to make sure that I understand it fully/ I need to break it down sometimes/ and
S:
7--------------------------------------------------------------------------------
M:
O:    then=    some academic texts can be really like (.) high in (.) grammar and
S:       =okay
8--------------------------------------------------------------------------------
M:
O:    everything so/                          exactly/ hopefully by the
S:                   that's why we're doing this course/
9--------------------------------------------------------------------------------
M:                                   erm (2) I think first year's okay/ but (.) we
O:    end of this course that will be gone/
S:
10-------------------------------------------------------------------------------
M:    we'll have to wait and see second year/ (2)
O:
S:                                   I think me/ I don't I don't need
```

```
11-----------------------------------------------------------------------------------
M:
O:                                                                    yeah? (2) some
S:      to do this class anyway yeah/ I don't know why I'm in it/
12-----------------------------------------------------------------------------------
M:
O:      mistake or something went wrong innit?
S:                                           something went wrong/ <laughs>
13-----------------------------------------------------------------------------------
M:
O:
S:      reading wise I think I understand all the texts/ my English is quite good I'd
14-----------------------------------------------------------------------------------
M:
O:
S:      say (1) I can read (.) all the papers and all the usual shit (3) erm (2) work's
15-----------------------------------------------------------------------------------
M:      it's just this shit/     = <laughs>
O:
S:      okay/            yeah=       er: that's what I thought/ that's it (4)
16-----------------------------------------------------------------------------------
<recording turned off>
-------------------------------------------------------------------------------------
```

At the outset of this part of the discussion, Mustafa takes control of the floor by positioning himself as the interviewer and posing a question concerning their identification with academic texts. The four-second pause following his utterance is suggestive of a face-threatening moment as Osmaan and Sanjay decide how to respond. Eventually, Osmaan decides to reveal his difficulties with reading and understanding academic texts to his peers. His extensive hedging (staves 2–3) can be seen as an attempt to mitigate what he knows is a potentially face-threatening disclosure. Nevertheless, his admission of difficulties is not greeted sympathetically as the intonation of Sanjay's 'yeah' and his laughter (stave 4) appear scornful. Perhaps Sanjay is not only resisting Osmaan's admission of vulnerability, but also casting aspersions on his intelligence, suggesting that as he is older, Osmaan should know by now. As Osmaan interrupts what he was saying to respond to Sanjay (stave 5), it suggests that he felt the need for some defensive and tough talk at this juncture. This strategy appears successful as in the following turn, Sanjay concedes to Osmaan (stave 7). Osmaan continues to repair and strengthen his position in the group by distancing himself from the 'high' language of academic texts, thus implying his affiliation to the preferred language practices of his peers (staves 7–8). Osmaan's strategy seems to be working as Sanjay cooperates with him by using his point about 'high' language to justify their participation in the academic writing programme (stave 8). Osmaan then adopts the dominant institutional positioning of the course as existing to 'fix' their language problems (staves 8–9).

At this stage, however, this more positive identification with institutional practices disintegrates. Mustafa's highly ambivalent utterance (staves 9–10) signals lack of support for Osmaan's attempts to identify with institutional practices and creates an opening for Sanjay's defiant statement in which he resists his placement on the academic writing programme (staves 10–11). Rather than challenge Sanjay's contradictory talk, Osmaan saves face by suggesting that there has been an institutional 'mistake' (staves 11–12). Sanjay reproduces the idea of a mistake and then adopts a tough laddish position in which he makes a strong statement about his competence, serving to resist his institutional 'deficit' positioning, and uses taboo language to trash the texts favoured by the academic community (stave 14). His swearing not only degrades his academic work, but also suggests that this is of little value, and it is done solely as a chore. Mustafa collaborates in this tough talk by repeating Sanjay's trashing utterance while Osmaan remains silent. Sanjay has the final word on this issue as neither Mustafa nor Osmaan break the lengthy pause following his final pronouncement (stave 15). Osmaan's attempts to instigate a discussion about their strategies for coping with academic texts has effectively been silenced.

As Frosh *et al.* point out, hegemonic peer group masculinity among young men does not countenance 'stupidity' (2002: 81). In order to maintain a laddish position, it therefore appears necessary to avoid any talk which could be constructed as displaying weakness. As a mature student, Osmaan was prepared to admit difficulties and seek support from his peers although his hedging suggested his awareness of this as face-threatening. While it seemed that his initial persistence would persuade his peers to cooperate in this discussion, his efforts were frustrated by Mustafa's ambivalence and Sanjay's resistance. Sanjay and Mustafa effectively created a situation in which Osmaan was made to feel uncomfortable and gained no support or benefits from participating in the group work. Sanjay and Mustafa's collaboration enabled them to conceal difficulties through ambiguous statements and tough talk. Sanjay also adopted a powerful 'Macho Lad' (Mac an Ghaill 1994) position to resist his powerless institutional 'deficit' positioning, in which he was categorized as requiring academic writing support.

Resistance was one way in which the male participants reacted to being positioned by the institution as needing to take the academic writing programme, which, as previously mentioned, was interpreted as taking 'remedial' English classes. According to literature on the construction of masculinities (e.g. Connell 1989; Mac an Ghaill 1994), the construction of an anti-establishment masculinity is encouraged through the streaming of adolescent males in schools into groups ascribed as low ability. This can exacerbate the performance of 'Macho Lad' masculinity as a response to feelings of 'domination, alienation and infantilism' (Mac an Ghaill 1994: 57). It seems possible that Sanjay was also experiencing some of these feelings of alienation and infantilism but lacked the maturity of Osmaan in dealing with them and in making effective use of opportunities for learning in the writing classroom.

The performance of tough laddish masculinity, through trashing talk and inappropriate classroom behaviour, was one way in which some male partici-pants resisted their institutional positioning. Others resisted through presenting themselves as light-hearted and jokey lads concerned with 'having a laugh' who were disinterested in high achievement. Both these laddish positions prevented sustained participation in the classroom and often disrupted learning for all.

While the institutional deficit positioning often appeared to be a highly sensitive issue among the male participants, the all-male peer groups also seemed a problematic space in which to focus on personal difficulties and concerns, or on making a strong identification with academic work. While some of the male participants were prepared to engage in serious discussion on the issues involved in academic reading and writing, this was not generally viewed as a way of doing 'acceptable' masculinity with peers. Instead attention to a hegemonic laddish 'face' appeared to create a scenario in which it was highly problematic to admit difficulties, seek help or engage fully in academic work. This appeared compounded by institutional practices concerning screening and selecting students for the writing programme and the separation of the programme from the mainstream curriculum.

Conclusion

The preceding extract highlights the tensions between the male participants' perceptions of the academic community and its practices as 'posh' and 'mature', denoting primarily a middle-aged, middle-class and perhaps a rather feminized 'middle Englander' identity, and peer group practices construed as 'cool', denoting largely a youthful, streetwise, working-class and culturally hybrid British 'lad'. These tensions frequently resulted in talk which gave the impression of 'walking a tightrope' between conflicting demands, desires and subject positions. For many of the male participants, this appeared to reduce the potential of the classroom as a site for developing greater identification with and expertise in the language and literacy practices of higher education or of negotiating a greater sense of academic identity as 'newcomers' to higher education. As Coates comments, the attention to hegemonic masculinity acts as an 'imperative to avoid vulnerability' (2003: 198). Subjected to the gaze of their peers, many of the males appeared reluctant either to reveal vulnerabilities or to identify with an oppositional community. Instead, much of the classroom data suggested that the male participants were using their time to accomplish a laddish identity.

Some of the all-male data is reminiscent of Willis's seminal study of working-class adolescent males in schools, in which Willis concluded that for '"the lads" time is something they want to claim for themselves now as an aspect of their immediate identity and self-direction. Time is used for the preservation of a state – being with "the lads" – not for the achievement of a goal – qualifications' (1977: 29). However, unlike Willis's 'lads', I view the male participants in this study as struggling with conflicting positions and desires. Laddish positions offered powerful places from which to speak in the peer group, positions which were not available in the academic community. In many instances, doing being a lad also seemed to engender well-being and affable peer group relations. However, these presentations of a laddish self made it difficult to display identification with doing being 'intellectual' or develop expertise in academic literacy practices. While this resistance to academic identity can be seen partly as a 'strategic response to wider social and cultural trends' (Benwell and Stokoe 2002: 450), it is more doubtful whether, as Benwell and Stokoe have suggested, it enabled the male participants to 'manage to redeem the scholarly enterprise whilst maintaining the social need to orient to other forms of identity' (2002: 450). Many of the male participants in this chapter, who entered university from widening participation backgrounds and with less of the 'cultural capital' (Bourdieu 1984) needed to cope with the system than their middle-class peers, were not able to manage the balancing act that this entailed. Instead, their attempts to balance conflicting demands often came at great personal cost of dropping out, being excluded, taking longer to complete studies and/or underperforming.

I suggest that this raises a number of issues for continuing reflection and discussion among higher education lecturers working in similar contexts, such as how to avoid stigmatizing 'newcomer' undergraduates who need to develop their expertise in academic literacy practices, particularly those who are on academic writing programmes and how to facilitate higher education environments that are more attuned to the development of 'newcomer' identities, particularly in widening participant contexts. Another matter is how to utilize and value the knowledge, experiences and language practices of the upcoming generations of multilingual British youth, who will increasingly form the undergraduate population in urban universities, so that their time at university is an empowering experience in which they develop their ability to 'perceive critically *the way they exist* in the world *with which* and *in which* they find themselves'[7] (Freire 1996: 64).

Transcription conventions

The conventions used in this chapter are based on Coates (2003) and are as follows:
A slash / shows the end of a chunk of talk.
A hyphen - illustrates an incomplete word or utterance.
A question mark ? indicates question intonation.
A colon : indicates elongation of a vowel sound.
"Words in double quotation marks" indicate the speaker is adopting the voice of a person who is not physically present.
Pauses of less than one second are shown with a full stop inside brackets (.).
Pauses of one second and longer are timed to the nearest second and the number of seconds is put in brackets (3).
A dotted line marks the beginning of a stave

Reading the transcription between the dotted lines shows the interplay of the voices at that part of the conversation (like the instruments in a musical score).

[square brackets on top of each other indicate the point where
[speakers overlap.
An equals sign at the end of one utterance = and the start of the next speaker's utterance shows that there was no audible gap between speakers.
<phrases or words in angled brackets> are additional comments by myself as the transcriber on what is happening at the time or the way in which something is said.
WORDS or syllables in CAPital letters are spoken with extra emphasis.

Notes

1 A pseudonym.
2 All participant names are pseudonyms.
3 In this chapter, British Asian refers to people of South Asian heritage. See Block (2006) for a discussion of London-based British Asian communities.
4 This is a Labour Government initiative to increase the number of university graduates in families with no history of higher education and/or who live in areas of Britain with a low percentage of graduates.
5 See Preece and Godfrey (2004) for profile of cohort on the academic writing programme.
6 Quote arising from field notes.
7 Italics in original.

References

Baxter, J. (2003), *Positioning Gender in Discourse: a Feminist Methodology.* Basingstoke: Palgrave MacMillan.
Benwell, B. and Stokoe, E. H. (2002), 'Constructing discussion tasks in university tutorials: shifting dynamics and identities', *Discourse Studies,* 4, (4), 429–53.
Block, D. (2006), *Multilingual Identities in a Global City: London Stories.* London: Palgrave.
Bourdieu, P. (1977), 'The economics of linguistic exchanges', *Social Science Information,* 16, (6), 648–68.
— (1984), *Distinction: a Social Critique of the Judgement of Taste* (translated R. Nice). London and New York: Routledge.
Butler, J. (1990), *Gender Trouble: Feminism and the Subversion of Identity.* London and New York: Routledge.
Cameron, D. (2001), *Working with Spoken Discourse.* London: Sage.
Cameron, D. and Kulick, D. (2003), *Language and Sexuality.* Cambridge: Cambridge University Press.
Coates, J. (2003), *Men Talk.* Oxford: Blackwell.
Connell, R. W. (1989), 'Cool guys, swots and wimps: the inter-play of masculinity and education', *Oxford Review of Education,* 15, (3), 291–303.
— (2000), *The Men and the Boys.* Cambridge: Polity Press in association with Blackwell Publishers.
Draper, S. (2003), 'Tinto's model of student retention', www.psy.gla.ac.uk/~steve/localed/tinto. html (last accessed 20 September 2005).
Eckert, P. and McConnell-Ginet, S. (2003), *Language and Gender.* Cambridge: Cambridge University Press.
Edley, N. and Wetherell, M. (1997), 'Jockeying for position: the construction of masculine identities', *Discourse and Society,* 8, (2), 203–17.
Foucault, M. (1974), *The Archaeology of Knowledge.* London: Tavistock.
— (1991), 'Politics and the study of discourse', in G. Burchell, C. Gordon and P. Miller (eds), *The Foucault Effect: Studies in Governmentality.* Chicago: University of Chicago Press, pp. 53–72.
Freire, P. (1996), *Pedagogy of the Oppressed* (translated M. Ramos). London: Penguin.
Frosh, S., Phoenix, A. and Pattman, R. (2002), *Young Masculinities: Understanding Boys in Contemporary Society.* Basingstoke: Palgrave.
Goffman, E. (1972), *Interaction Ritual: Essays on Face-To-Face Behaviour.* Harmondsworth: Penguin.
Harris, R. (1997). 'Romantic bilingualism: time for a change?', in C. Leung and C. Cable (eds), *English as an Additional Language: Changing Perspectives.* Watford: NALDIC, pp. 14–27.

Harris, R., Leung, C. and Rampton, B. (2002), 'Globalization, diaspora and language education in England', in D. Block and D. Cameron (eds), *Globalization and Language Teaching*. London and New York: Routledge, pp. 29–46.

Hewitt, R. (1992), 'Language, youth and the destabilisation of ethnicity', in C. Palmgren, K. Lovgren and G. Bolin (eds), *Ethnicity in Youth Culture*. Stockholm: Stockholm University, pp. 27–41.

Lave, J. and Wenger, E. (1991), *Situated Learning: Legitimate Peripheral Participation*. Cambridge: Cambridge University Press.

Lea, M. R. and Street, B. V. (2000), 'Student writing and staff feedback in higher education: an academic literacies approach', in M. R. Lea and B. Stierer (eds), *Student Writing in Higher Education: New Contexts*. Buckingham: Society for Research into Higher Education and Open University Press, pp. 32–46.

Leung, C. and Cable, C. (eds) (1997), *English as an Additional Language: Changing Perspectives*. Watford: NALDIC.

Leung, C. and Franson, C. (2001), 'Curriculum identity and professional development: system-wide questions', in B. Mohan, C. Leung and C. Davison (eds) *English as a Second Language in the Mainstream: Teaching, Learning and Identity*. Harlow: Longman and Pearson Education, pp. 199–214.

Leung, C., Harris, R. and Rampton, B. (1997), 'The idealised native-speaker, reified ethnicities and classroom realities', *TESOL Quarterly*, 31, 545–60.

Mac an Ghaill, M. (1994), *The Making of Men: Masculinities, Sexualities and Schooling*. Buckingham: Open University Press.

Martin-Jones, M. and Jones, K. (eds) (2000), *Multilingual Literacies: Reading and Writing Different Worlds*. Amsterdam: John Benjamins.

Preece, S. and Godfrey, J. (2004), 'Academic literacy practice and widening participation: first year undergraduates on an academic writing programme', *Widening Participation and Lifelong Learning*, 6, (1), 6–14.

Rampton, B. (1990), 'Displacing the 'native speaker': expertise, affiliation and inheritance', *ELT Journal*, 44, 97–101.

— (2005), *Crossing: Language and Ethnicity Among Adolescents* (2nd edn). Manchester: St Jerome Press.

Tinto, V. (1975), 'Dropout from higher education: a theoretical synthesis of recent research', *Review of Educational Research*, 45, 89–125.

Walkerdine, V. (1990), *School Girl Fictions*. London and New York: Verso.

Wallace, C. (2002), 'Local literacies and global literacy', in D. Block and D. Cameron (eds), *Globalization and Language Teaching*. London and New York: Routledge, pp. 101–14.

Weedon, C. (1997), *Feminist Practice and Poststructuralist Theory* (2nd edn). Oxford: Blackwells.

Whelehan, I. (2000), *Overloaded: Popular Culture and the Future of Feminism*. London: Women's Press.

Willis, P. E. (1977), *Learning to Labour: How Working Class Kids Get Working Class Jobs*. Farnborough: Saxon House.

11 Ethnolinguistic identity in a Dutch Islamic primary classroom

Massimiliano Spotti

Introduction

As a result of politically, economically and socially motivated immigration, the Netherlands has undergone considerable demographic changes since the second half of the twentieth century (cf. Lucassen and Penninx 1994) leading to, in 2001, almost 3 million inhabitants with at least one parent born outside the country (CBS 2002). Cultural and linguistic diversity among the Dutch population has therefore become an object of public and political debate which mostly focuses on the need for integration of immigrant minority group members – namely Turkish, Moroccan, Surinamese and Antillean – within mainstream Dutch society. Education, both in the primary and secondary sectors, constitutes no exception to such diversity as well as to the call for integration. In 2001, in fact, 15.2 per cent of all pupils enrolled at Dutch primary schools were registered as being members of 'cultural minorities' either because they were offspring of regularly admitted refugees or because they were born to a family with at least one parent originally from outside the Netherlands (Ministerie van OCW 2002). Diversity is also found in the language repertoires that pupils bring along from home to school (Broeder and Extra 1998; Extra *et al.* 2001) which markedly contrast the monolingual character of mainstream (primary) schooling and that are often coupled with low proficiency in the Dutch language (CBS 2001). Within this context, (primary) teachers are challenged in their everyday practice by the cultural and linguistic heterogeneity among their pupils. On the basis of the observed discontinuity between the culturally and linguistically heterogeneous character of immigrant minority pupils and the more homogeneous character of primary education (cf. Gogolin and Kroon 2000; Bezemer 2003) as well as in the light of the little knowledge at our disposal in dealing with the construction of immigrant minority pupils' ethnic and linguistic affiliation in the field of (Dutch) primary education, this study presents an analysis and interpretation of the discourse gathered from the pupils of Form 6/7/8 at a Dutch Islamic primary school classroom. The study tries to unravel the complexities of these pupils' ongoing cultural and linguistic affiliations and the role, if any, that these affiliations play in their identity construction both within and outside the classroom.

Conceptual framework

In coming to grips with the workings of immigrant minority pupils' identity construction, sensitizing concepts (Blumer 1954) have been sought as a general frame of reference to the understanding of identity formation through cultural and linguistic practices. This led to gather a loose series of concepts that served as starting points:

> [i]n thinking about a class of data of which the social researcher has no definite idea and provides an initial guide to her research. Such concepts usually are provisional and may be dropped as more viable and definite concepts emerge in the course of her research.
>
> (Van der Hoonaard 1997: 2)

For present purposes, the sensitizing concepts encountered are outlined, and their usefulness in studying immigrant minority pupils' identity construction is described. While definitive concepts provide prescriptions of what to see, sensitizing concepts merely make the researcher alert to the direction in which to look when gathering, analysing and interpreting data. They thus neither intend to reflect any ready-made conception prior to data collection, nor to constitute an exhaustive review of the literature available in the field. Rather, the following is a short retrospective account of the knowledge that has been formed while coming to grips with the data.

At the outset of the present study, Williams' notion of 'dominant, residual and emergent' cultural repertoires served as a point of departure. As Williams (1977) suggests, any analysis of cultural and linguistic affiliations must struggle in defining dominant, residual and emergent cultural elements in people's lives. This is so because the meanings constituting a culture are continuously being created, moulded and negotiated by people while they interact with others (cf. Gee 1999, for a complete explanation). Trying to identify what is emerging from the inter-mingling of dominant and residual cultural elements in someone's discourse should therefore not be limited to seeing what is merely novel in someone's cultural and linguistic affiliations. Rather, it involves grasping how different cultural elements that a person may possess are then combined and used and how they may give way to new meanings that the person may attach to his cultural and linguistic belongings. For instance, the meanings conveyed by the use of a specific mode of expression, such as a Turkish accent in speaking German or a marked Punjabi style when uttering a greeting in English, could then be re-conducted to 'acts of identity' (Le Page and Tabouret-Keller 1985) where in the latter case the speaker subscribes his identity as a youngster of Punjabi descent living in Britain. Even though Auer (2005) warns against any rushed equation of hybrid language use as a hybrid act of identity ascription, acts of identity of the socio-linguistic type become occurrences that may be limited to the contingency of a certain community of practice. However, acts of identity may also open up a door on how 'cultures of hybridity' (Mercer 2000) forged among overlapping diaspora populations, as for instance the Turkish or the Maghrebian populations residing in Europe, have constructed ethnic, cultural and linguistic affiliations that their members use when their identities are called in cause.

Methodology

This study, situated in an ethnographic empirical-interpretative tradition (cf. Erickson 1986; Kroon and Sturm, 2000), observes three pragmatic rules: openness of the researcher, openness of the subject of research and openness of perspectives when analysing data. The general methodology employed is therefore heuristic in nature, trying to gather how the identities of the pupils in Form 6/7/8 are constructed from multiple perspectives, i.e. teachers, pupils and classroom interactions. In order to gather pupils' discourse practices, four overlapping methods of data collection were employed: a home language survey (Broeder and Extra 1998), an ethno-cultural questionnaire (Jongenburger and Aarssen 2001), a written project compiled by the pupils themselves about their cultural and linguistic affiliations (Leung *et al.* 1997) as well as a focused group discussion carried out with the pupils. The advantage of using overlapping methods of data collection is that they allow the overcoming of the social desirability problem. In fact, even though such a problem may be encountered with any type of informant, children in particular may present different accounts of events to different individuals, including the researcher, based on their understanding of what statements would be acceptable to that particular individual. It follows that by employing overlapping methods of data collection, an internal validity check is drawn on pupils' responses that '[...] form a mosaic of explanations and reasons rather than mutually exclusive accounts' (Davies 1982: 58). The collected pupils' corpus is then approached through grounded theory (Corbin and Strauss 1990) involving a cyclic process in which theoretical insights are tested against the data for the continuous construction of a plausible theory and interpretation. This is achieved through collecting large amounts of texts – written and/or spoken – engaging with them in a process of coding and re-coding until categories emerge. To achieve the category status, the concept developed must have an explanatory power and advocates the advantage of explaining the data by and through the data, providing safeguards against the researcher's imposition of agendas of analysis. The narrow relationship between the themes that were introduced in the questionnaire, developed in the written projects and 'dug into' during the focused group discussions is indeed reflexive of the research focus. On the other hand, it is the own workings of the pupils that have led to the production of discourse practices that once analysed led to category forming.

While questionnaires and written projects were carried out at the beginning of every school day, group interviews took place outside the classroom on two afternoons. The interviews, conducted in Dutch, lasted between 45 minutes and an hour for each of the two groups and none of the informants opted out. Both structure and content of the interviews were left as open-ended as possible, using those concepts that emerged from the pupils' questionnaires and written projects to start off the group discussion. The excerpts presented are in English and although the Dutch used by these pupils was at times grammatically incorrect, this is not reflected in the English transliterations where the goal is to make the content as accessible as possible to the reader. The researcher and pupils' names are indicated in full and the data source within the corpus is indicated for every reported utterance, i.e. WP for written project and by a code assigned to each pupil.

The city, the school, the classroom and the pupils

Duivenberg, the city where the data were collected, is one of the Netherlands' ten largest cities and in 2001, it had a population of approximately 200,000 inhabitants. Following its census data, there are approximately 28,000 first and second generation non-Western allochtonous inhabitants while another 13,000 have allochtonous Western origins (Duivenberg 2002). The largest immigrant minority groups with non-Western origins are the Turkish and the Moroccan ones, followed by the Antillean and the Surinamese groups. In the same year, Duivenberg contains 48 primary schools among which we find 'Mdrasa Islamic Primary. This school, built in 1995, has been labelled a *voorrangsschool* (priority school) with more than 70 per cent of its pupils as *doelgroepleerlingen* (target group pupils). Following the directives spelt out in the 2001 *Gemeentelijk Onderwijsachterstands Beleid* (Municipal Policy for Educational Disadvantage) being a priority school implies the receipt of extra financial help from Duivenberg's municipality toward the improvement of pupils' educational achievement, with a specific focus on Dutch language also through extra-curricular programmes. According to the information given by the school head, the 255 pupils regularly enrolled during the school year 2000–2001 are all Muslims. According to the criteria of pupils' birth country, the Somali group is the largest with 110 pupils, followed by the Turkish with 70 pupils and the Moroccan with 40 pupils. The remaining 35 pupils are classified as 'others'. Pupils are divided into ten clusters and the school has opted to create pedagogically and didactically heterogeneous groups. As for any other denominational primary school in the Netherlands, the school curriculum at 'Mdrasa Islamic Primary meets the statutory requirements laid out in the core objectives of the primary school curriculum (Kerndoelen 1998). The language of instruction used during the lessons for the mainstream classroom is Dutch and the class teachers all qualified at Dutch teacher training institutions. The special nature of Islamic schooling at 'Mdrasa is mainly expressed through religious teaching, consisting mostly in the reading of the Qur'an, implemented from a minimum of one up to three hours per week. In addition, pupils have two and a half hours of community language teaching in (standard) Arabic, Turkish or Somali. 'Mdrasa Islamic Primary was visited by the inspectorate of education for the first time in 1998 and the visit report that followed stressed that the achievement results of pupils were 'non-sufficient', the teaching material was not up to standards and the didactic management of teachers was not effective (Inspectie van het Onderwijs 1998: 15).

In May 2001 Form 6/7/8 has a total of 18 pupils, 7 boys and 11 girls, who all have a 1.9[1] educational weight. Pupils' ages range from 10 to 13 years old due to some pupils needing one extra school year to complete their primary education career. Following the rules of Islam the classroom layout sees no mixing between the two sexes given that pupils are grouped in gender clusters with the girls spread out in three groups close to the teacher table while the boys are located in two groups at the back of the classroom. For Dutch language teaching and mathematics, Form 6 pupils moved to work with Form 5 in a different classroom while Forms 7 and 8 (a total of 13 pupils) stayed in the current classroom. Out of the 18 pupils of Form 6/7/8, 9 pupils were born in the Netherlands, 5 in Somalia, 2 in Iraq, 1 in Turkey from Kurdish parents and 1 in Italy from Somali parents. In Form 6/7/8, all pupils report to have and use at least one or more languages as well as or instead of Dutch in the household. Turkish is the most frequent and most used home language followed by Somali and Arabic. The last is reported as used not only by pupils with Moroccan or Berber background but also by Turkish and Somali ones. Other self-reported home languages also include English and Italian, both used by Somali pupils. In Table 11.1 the results of the home language survey of Form 6/7/8 are reported:

Table 11.1 Home language(s), gender and names of the pupils

Home language(s)	Boys	Girls
Dutch and Turkish	Davud	Menekse
	Osman	Sumeyra
	Nebi	Hulya
		Zeynep
Dutch and Somali	Abshir	
	Abdi-Aziz	
Dutch and Arabic		Doua
		Iman
Dutch, Arabic and Berber		Khadija
Dutch, Arabic and Turkish		Tuba
Dutch, Somali and Arabic		Zahra
		Amel
Dutch, Somali and English	Ibrahim	
Dutch, Somali and Italian	Mohamud	Fatima

Speakers of a language other than Dutch

There are several motivations that inform these pupils' choice to opt for the Dutch language as a code for verbal exchanges with, among others, their younger siblings. For instance, in response to the question of which language they prefer, Sumeyra and Ibrahim state:

Sumeyra: I prefer Dutch because it is the language that is good for the children. (WP 011)

Ibrahim: I prefer to speak Dutch with my little sisters and little brothers. (WP 04)

The two citations above express the general trend reconstructed from the pupils' data that express the positive value attached to the Dutch language as beneficial for child rearing. Further, these pupils' choice for the Dutch language also refers to their language practice with younger siblings, their reported contacts with Dutch peer networks, and the use of Dutch in the classroom; all constitute key factors corroborating a sense of in-group cohesion with the 'host community'. Further, for most of the pupils of Form 6/7/8, speaking Dutch is regarded as a marker of achievement in comparison with older family members. In fact, once asked to give more reflexive answers to the question if they perceive any difference between them and their family members, Hulya states:

Hulya: I can speak better Dutch than my older brother. (WP 06)

And Menekse reports:

Menekse: They [*her family*: MS] don't speak good Dutch. (...) and with my mother, she
               helped me with my homework once, but she can't speak very good Dutch, like
               I do. (GD 088)

During the focused group discussion, the Dutch language not only emerges as a marker of difference from elderly family members, it also embeds a form of 'resistance' that these pupils may employ to challenge parental authority, as Menekse states:

Menekse: Well, my father can speak very good Dutch, and then I think as he can speak
               really good Dutch, I can maybe speak a better Dutch than him (...). (GD 089)

In contrast, Hulya's motive for choosing Dutch is exclusion:

Hulya: Dutch sometimes so to make sure that mum cannot understand (...) for the
               fun of it (...). (WP 06)

The contesting of parental authority through the Dutch language does not only happen when the Dutch language skills of the parents are poor – as for the case of Menekse's mother or when Hulya makes sure that 'mum cannot understand'. Rather, the challenge to parental authority also happens when a parent reports to be highly proficient in Dutch, as for the case of Menekse's father. The reconstructed categories overlap strongly with the generational shift of group image that is common to second-generation members of immigrant minority groups in the Netherlands (Vermeulen and Penninx 2000). This shift consists of 'second-generation' members striving toward what is termed as the 'creation of a new existence' (Ellemers *et al.* 1999: 198), leading young immigrant minority group members to attempt to improve their positions and to obtain status in the future. Among these attempts, there is not only an orientation toward more middle-class values but also an increased use and attainment in Dutch that, as shown above, plays a role in constructing identities in comparison with family members. This view is also supplemented by studies of the acculturation process stemming from the field of cross-cultural psychology (Cuéllar 2000) showing that it is easier for immigrant minority group members to modify certain cultural practices, including language, to converge towards the mainstream culture. These possible modifications are seen as long-term investments that are expected to pay off in terms of economic and social improvement. As a result, within the family, the traditional position of parents' authority can be challenged, or even reversed, depending on the mastering of a certain code.

Further, as it emerges from the home language survey, all pupils of Form 6/7/8 claim to use their immigrant minority languages. However, these languages are kept out of the classroom. As Mazloum, Ayse and Amel demonstrate:

Mazloum: At school I speak Dutch with Miss, with the children that come from other countries. (WP 016)

Ayse: In class, we speak only Dutch. (WP 015)

Amel: In this class, it feels that I can use only one language. (GD 010)

These claims recognize the legitimacy and need of the Dutch language as the language of the classroom at 'Mdrasa Islamic Primary. On the other hand, the school site seems to offer spaces for the pupils to contest the 'dominance' of Dutch. For instance, in response to the question of what language or languages they used in school, Sumeyra and Ibrahim report:

Sumeyra: Arabic in the playground with my friends. (WP 06)

Ibrahim: Somali when I get angry and I have to shout at someone in the playground. (WP 04)

Discursive practices of this kind show the pupils' agency in finding spaces in which to construct their identities that find their actualization through, among other things, linguistic practices. Thereby these pupils employ linguistic codes with their peers according to the spatial interstice in which they find themselves. This does not only count for the school environment but also for the home environment where several pupils report, in fact, a widespread immigrant minority language use. To the question whether they speak any other language beside Dutch at home, they responded as follows:

Fatima: Yes, we speak only Somali to each other. (WP 03)

Hulya: Turkish with my grandmother and grandfather and with my parents too. (WP 06)

Osman: We always speak Turkish at home. (WP 012)

These responses suggest that the Dutch language is mostly preferred for utilitarian purposes and in public domains, such as the classroom, while immigrant minority languages are present in the domestic sphere (Arends-Tóth 2003: 126). Although used in the home environment for communicating with elder family members, the vast majority of the pupils in this study do not express a positive form of attachment to their home languages. For instance, to the question what language is the least liked, Fatima states:

Fatima: Somali because it is a bit difficult. (WP 03)

Fatima: Sometimes my mother wants to know what time it is, as I cannot say it well in Somali, then I tell her mixed. (WP 03)

The same goes for Ibrahim, a pupil with Somali parents, asserting:

Ibrahim: I prefer Dutch because I cannot write well in Somali. (WP 05)

Along this line, Mazloum and Hulya, whose reported home language are Arabic and Turkish, respectively, state:

Mazloum: I prefer Dutch as I cannot make very good sentences and write in Arabic. (WP 016)

Hulya: I don't like Turkish because I cannot speak good Turkish. (WP 06)

Such weak self-reported affiliation to immigrant minority languages is not only instanced through limitations in language competence and performance but also by the value attached to these languages on the 'linguistic market' (Bourdieu 1977). For instance, when asked what language they like the least, Osman and Zahra state:

Osman: Turkish because I do not need it that often. (WP 012)

Zahra: Somali because it is not important. (WP 09)

Even though, in Form 6/7/8, there is one pupil out of the eighteen that expressed strong attachment to his immigrant minority language, the main trend reconstructed from the pupils' data corpus results in them being 'linguistically' most comfortable and confident with Dutch. At the same time, though, they retain a weaker but yet ongoing relationship with one or more immigrant minority languages, e.g. Turkish, Somali or Berber, in particular within the family environment.

Pupils' agency does not emerge only when dealing with their language repertoires but also when dealing with their cultural affiliations. In the following section, given their exhaustive accounts, the stories gathered from three pupils from Form 6/7/8 have been selected to attempt to reconstruct their cultural belonging.

The story of Hulya

Hulya, born in the Netherlands of Turkish parents, shows in her discourse practices how migration has affected a large chunk of her family, as she states:

Hulya: I live here and my aunt does too, and also my oldest cousin lives here. My grandma lives in France and my other six uncles live also in France. And the rest of my family lives in Rotterdam, Turkey, Germany, The Hague. (WP 06)

Her family are spread across the Netherlands and other European countries, without a specific place regarded as the 'home land'. However, when asked to explain her sense of belonging to a country, Hulya asserts:

> Hulya: I am Dutch because I speak good Dutch. (WP 06)

Hulya's statement indicates a key dimension of the legitimacy attached to the Dutch language and the level of proficiency achieved in that language, i.e. speaking it 'good' that is an essential qualifier for her self-categorization as 'Dutch'. Further, in the focused group discussion, Hulya confirms this view:

> Max: Okay (...) and what do you think that other people think when you speak
>   Dutch?
> Hulya: Depending on how you speak, it tells whether one is a foreigner or not. (GD
>   067 – 068)

Even though this may be a reference to non-native accents rather than proficiency, the position claimed in Hulya's discourse overlaps with Pierce's work (1995) which, by drawing on data collected from a longitudinal study of language learning experience of immigrant women in Canada, shows the relevance of proficiency in the majority's language in gaining or being denied access to certain social networks. As for the case of Hulya who states: 'depending on how you speak, it tells whether one is a foreigner or not', learners construct their identity and their positioning within groups of belonging. On the other hand, Hulya's perception of her ethnic belonging is not as clear-cut as it seems in the first place, as she states when asked to which group she feels to belong:

> Hulya: I am Turkish and they are Somali or Arabic. (WP 06)

Further, her position is corroborated with the way others ascribe her identity as that of 'a foreigner'; due to cultural elements that Hulya does not see belonging to mainstream Dutch society:

> Hulya: Yes, I think also that they see me as a foreigner.
> Max: But why? I mean you were born in the Netherlands and you speak very good
>   Dutch.
> Hulya: Yes, but I have another culture. I have a headscarf on and they live free lives,
>   they have another culture, they do different things than us. That is why I think
>   they regard us as very much different. (GD 070 – 072)

Even though attaching a strong value to speaking the Dutch language 'good' so to have status in the Dutch community, Hulya conveys in her discourse a strong ethnic allegiance to the Turkish community once confronted with her classroom peers that she ascribes to cultures that are other than her own. Furthermore, even though indirectly, she also expresses an attachment to the Muslim community when stating 'I have another culture' and giving as a symbol of her cultural affiliation the act of wearing a headscarf opposed to the 'free lives' that 'they', i.e. the Dutch, lead.

The story of Ayse

Ayse, a girl born in Turkey to Kurdish parents who moved to the Netherlands ten days after her birth, explains:

Ayse: Of course I am for my own land because I was born there and that is my country. (WP 015)

The initial appeal to the right conferred by a form of *jus soli* positions Ayse's identity as part of an imagined community because she was born on Turkish soil. Ayse, however, does not specify whether her own land affiliation refers actually to being Turkish or Kurdish. This doubt about her affiliation to the Turkish or the Kurdish group is solved when answering the question about where she felt she belonged:

Ayse: I feel myself Dutch when I am outside with my friends and at school. I feel Turkish when at home and with my parents. (WP 015)

While there is no mentioning throughout her written project and in the group discussion of a Kurdish identity, which could lead one to think that Ayse feels herself to be part of an imagined Turkish community due to the low status that the Kurdish minority has in Turkish eyes. Ayse's self-reported identification process seems to overlap with the results gathered by Verkuyten and Thijs (1999) who have shown that many youngsters of Turkish origin feel more Turkish once in the home environment rather than when outside. In the same way, Ayse's statement above proposes a shifting feeling of belonging that hampers the clear-cut affiliation she presented in the first utterance, given that an affiliation 'brought along' from the home environment is substituted by an affiliation 'brought about' in the classroom as well as with her peers (Zimmerman 1998).

The story of Mohamud

Mohamud is a boy born on Italian soil to Somali parents who then moved to the Netherlands when he was one year old. When asked about his feelings of belonging to an unspecified 'own land', Mohamud replies:

Mohamud: For Somalia because that is my country. (WP 07)

His belonging to Somalia is taken further when in response to the question of what makes him feel different in the classroom, he states:

Mohamud: Yes, because I have a Somali culture and they do not. (WP 07)

In his discourse, Mohamud expresses that someone 'has' a certain culture, as for his case the Somali culture. Later on in the discussion, Mohamud makes explicit what underlies his feeling of bearing upon those Somali cultural habits he claims to 'have' in his previous statement. As he asserts:

Mohamud: (...) as you move from your own country, you come to another country, you
keep on being of the land that you truly are from, you don't change because
you live here. You keep simply to where you have come from.
Max: What do you mean exactly?
Mohamud: (...) Although you are here, you belong still to where you came from, here you
still are a sort of guest, it is not your own home. I mean it is because you live
here, but it does not become your own country, (...). (GD 060 – 062)

As it appears to emerge from Mohamud's statements, the sense of belonging he
proposes retains strong meanings attached to his origins, as instanced with the
use of the adverb 'truly' in the utterance 'you keep on being of the land that you
truly are from'. Mohamud's discourse appears to be bearing traces of his own
cultural origins constructing a form of identification that goes beyond time and
space reified in a 'strategic essentialism' (cf. Spivak and Harasym 1990). Such
affiliation with Somalia, i.e. 'the land where one comes from', appears therefore
prolonged in time through the adverb 'still' which also works toward emphasizing
the feeling Mohamud reports of 'being a guest'. As he states: 'although you are
here, you belong still to where you came from, here you still are a sort of guest'
and further: 'you don't change because you live here. You keep simply to where
you have come from'. As Gilroy describes it (1987: 287), Mohamud presents
'forms of community consciousness and solidarity that maintain identification
outside the national time/space, in order to live inside with a difference'.

Discussion and conclusions

This chapter has offered a reading of the identity construction of immigrant
minority pupils of Form 6/7/8 at 'Mdrasa Islamic Primary. The reconstructed
categories are representative of the responses at all class levels and show that
even though pupils invest in being better at Dutch than their family members
and use Dutch with their younger siblings, because Dutch constitutes a marker
of social distinctiveness, as well as being aware of the low value that their home
languages have on the linguistic market, these pupils are still confronted with the
ascribed identity of being a 'foreigner' and by the differences between the values
and norms of Dutch culture and the norms coming from their home cultures.

Furthermore, the stories gathered from Hulya, Ayse and Mohamud – chosen
from others because they provide fuller accounts of subscribed identity constructions – have been reported. From these pupils' discourse practices a sense of
displacement seems to emerge where belonging to their parental country and to
its cultural habits is intermingled with being Dutch not only because of being
born and raised in the Netherlands, but also because they report that they speak
Dutch 'good'. On the other hand, as shown in Mohamud's account, a pervading
willed essentialism is also present and it is shown through the statements that
picture the Dutch language and the Netherlands as incidental facts of life due to
the migratory route of their parents. As a result, a strong, yet quasi-nostalgic,
affiliation remains to the land 'where one truly comes from'.

Even though we do not know whether the linguistic and cultural affiliations of
these pupils will be transitory or permanent in their life and although we cannot

simply replace the notion of monolingual national standard varieties with the styles of bilinguals as new styles of communication that 'naturally' express the condition in which their identities are constructed (cf. Auer 2005), these pupils' discourse practices concerning their belonging to the parental country of birth as well as the proficiency in the Dutch language open up the question of how to move beyond their designation as allochtonous pupils or as pupils with a language other than Dutch. Consequently, it appears necessary to address these pupils not as 'passive inheritors of views of nations as culturally homogeneous communities of sentiment' (Gilroy 1987: 59) where their cultural and linguistic repertoires remain untapped or ought to fit; rather, following Bourne (2003), these pupils have to be seen as active participants of urban communities that are engaged in a new process of cultural and linguistic meaning making through which they redefine what it means to belong to a certain nation.

Notes

1   A pupil with father, mother or child minder who has an education at *Voorbereidend Middelbaar Beroepsonderwijs* (Preparatory Secondary Vocational Education) level and who also has, in the position of the parent with the primary source of income, someone who is an unskilled worker or who has no steady income. The pupil also has one parent who can be included in the target group for the integration policy for ethnic minority members or who comes from a non-English speaking country outside Europe, with the exception of Indonesia.

References

Arends-Tóth, J. (2003), *Psychological Acculturation of Turkish Migrants in the Netherlands: Issues in Theory and Assessment*. Amsterdam: Dutch University Press.

Auer, P. (2005), 'A postscript: Code-switching and social identity', *Journal of Pragmatics*, 37, 403–10.

Bezemer, J. (2003), *Dealing with Multilingualism in Education – A Case Study of a Dutch Primary School Classroom*. Amsterdam: Aksant.

Blumer, H. (1954), 'What's wrong with Social Theory?', *American Sociological Review*, 19, 3–10.

Bourdieu, P. (1977), 'The Economics of Linguistic Exchanges', *Social Science Information* 16, 645–68.

Bourne, J. (2003), 'Remedial or radical? Second language support for curriculum learning', in J. Bourne and E. Reid (eds), *World Yearbook of Education 2003: Language Education*. London: Kogan-Page, pp. 21–34.

Broeder, P. and Extra, G. (1998), *Language, Ethnicity and Education: Case Studies on Immigrant Minority Groups and Immigrant Minority Languages*. Clevedon: Multilingual Matters.

CBS (Centraal Bureau voor de Statistiek) (2001), *Allochtonen in Nederland 2000*. Voorburg/ Heerlen: Centraal Bureau voor de Statistiek.

CBS (Centraal Bureau voor de Statistiek) (2002), *Allochtonen in Nederland 2001*. Voorburg/ Heerlen: Centraal Bureau voor de Statistiek.

Corbin, C. and Strauss, A. (1990), 'Grounded theory research: Procedures, canons and evaluative criteria', *Qualitative Sociology*, 13, (1), 3–21.

Cuéllar, I. (2000), 'Acculturation as a moderator of personality and psychological assessment', in R. H. Dana (ed.), *Handbook of Cross-cultural and Multicultural Personality*

Assessment. Mahwah, NJ: Erlbaum, pp. 113–29.

Davies, B. (1982), *Life in the Classroom and Playground: The Accounts of Primary School Children.* London: Routledge & Kegan Paul.

Duivenberg (2002), *Rapportage Volkshuisvestingsmonitor Gemeente Duivenberg.* Office for Statistics and Information: Duivenberg City Council.

Ellemers, N., Spears, R. and Doosje, B. (1999), *Social Identity: Context, Commitment, Content.* Oxford: Blackwell.

Erickson, F. (1986), 'Qualitative methods in research on teaching', in M. Wittrock (ed.), *Handbook of Research on Teaching.* New York: Macmillan, pp. 119–61.

Extra, G., Aarts, R., Van der Avoird, T., Broeder, P., and Yağmur, K. (2001), *Meertaligheid in Den Haag. De Status van Allochtone Talen Thuis en op School.* Amsterdam: European Cultural Foundation.

Gee, J. P. (1999), *An Introduction to Discourse Analysis – Theory and Method.* London: Routledge.

Gilroy, P. (1987), *There ain't no Black in the Union Jack.* London: Routledge.

Gogolin, I. and Kroon, S. (2000) (Hrsg), *'Mann Schreibt, wie Mann Spricht'. Ergbenisse einer International-vergleichenden Fallstudie über Unterricht in Vielsrachingen Klassen.* Münster: Waxmann.

Inspectie van het Onderwijs (1998), *Verslag schoolbezoek regulier schooltoezicht.* Duivenberg: Inspectie van het Onderwijs.

Jongenburger, W. and Aarssen J. (2001), 'Linguistic and cultural exchange and appropriation: A survey study in a multi-ethnic neighbourhood in the Netherlands', *Journal of Multilingual and Multicultural Development,* 22, (4), 293–308.

Kerndoelen (1998), 'Besluit kerndoelen basisonderwijs 1998', *Staatsblad,* 1998, 354.

Kroon, S. and Sturm, J. (2000), 'Comparative case study research in education: Methodological issues in an empirical-interpretive perspective', *Zeitschrijft für Erziehungwissenschaft,* 3, (4), 559–76.

Le Page, R., and Tabouret-Keller, A. (1985), *Acts of Identity: Creole-based Approaches to Language and Ethnicity.* Cambridge: Cambridge University Press.

Leung, C., Harris, R. and Rampton, B. (1997), 'The idealised native speaker, reified ethnicities and classroom realities', *TESOL Quarterly,* 3, (18), 543–60.

Lucassen, J. and Penninx, R. (1994), *Nieuwkomers, Nakomelingen, Nederlanders. Immigranten in Nederland 1550–1993.* Amsterdam: Het Spinhuis.

Ministerie van OCW (Onderwijs, Cultuur en Wetenschappen) (2002), *Primair Onderwijs in cijfers 1997–2001.* Zoetermeer: Ministerie van Onderwijs, Cultuur en Wetenschappen.

Pierce, B. N. (1995), 'Social identity, investment and language learning', *TESOL Quarterly,* 29, 9–31.

Spivak, G. C. and Harasym, S. (1990), *The Post-colonial Critic: Interviews, Strategies Dialogues.* London: Routledge.

Van den Hoonaard, W. C. (1997), *Working with Sensitizing Concepts: Analytical Field Research.* Newbury Park, CA: Sage.

Verkuyten, M. and Thijs, J. (1999), 'Nederlandse en Turkse jongeren over multiculturalisme: Cultuurbehoud, aanpassing, identificatie en groepsdiscriminatie', *Tijdschrift voor Sociologie en Sociaal Onderzoek,* 46, 407–25.

Vermeulen, H. and Penninx, R. (2000), *Immigrant Integration: the Dutch Case.* Amsterdam: Het Spinhuis.

Williams, R. (1977), *Marxism and Literature.* Oxford: Oxford University Press.

Zimmerman, D. (1998), 'Identity, context and interaction', in C. Antaki and S. Widdicombe (eds), *Identities in Talk.* London: Sage, pp. 75–110.

12 Negotiating identities in a multilingual science class

Roberta J. Vann, Katherine Richardson Bruna and Moisés D. Perales Escudero

Introduction

Iowa, the largest pork producer in the United States, is also known for its high rate of literacy, and until recently its lack of ethnic diversity. Like many other agricultural areas in North America, this Midwestern state is being transformed demographically, with a 212 per cent increase in the number of school-aged children with limited English proficiency in the 1990s (Iowa Department of Education, English Language Learners Report 2001).[1] Of the approximately 15,000 limited English proficiency students in Iowa schools representing nearly a 100 different languages during the 2004–2005 academic year, about 11,000 (approximately 70 per cent) were Spanish speakers (Iowa Department of Education, Basic Educational Data Survey 2005). Most of their families are from Mexico or El Salvador and have come to Iowa to work in agriculture-related jobs, primarily meat processing.

The central meeting places for cultural interaction in these newly transformed communities are the schools, where teachers of all subjects increasingly face classrooms that are culturally and linguistically diverse and consequent instructional issues as students learn not only a new language, but also new socio-academic identities (Cummins 1994). Yet, few teachers are prepared to deal with these challenges. While 41 per cent of all US public school teachers report having English language learners in their classes, only 2.5 per cent have credentials in English as a Second Language (ESL) or bilingual education (National Center for Educational Statistics 2000). Although researchers have pointed out teacher needs in integrating language and socio-academic identity development in subject areas (Baker and Saul 1994; Rollnick and Rutherford 1996; Stoddart *et al.* 2002), few studies have analysed the face-to-face exchanges between teachers and students in these new sociolinguistic borderlands. What happens linguistically when teachers encounter new immigrants in their classrooms; that is, when 'culture travellers step over cultural lines to launch new identities' (Ochs 1993: 301). The purpose of this paper is to examine this phenomenon in a secondary school multilingual classroom. Utilizing discourse from a larger data set, we provide an example of identity negotiation and suggest that such slices of discourse, when analysed through the lens of interactional sociolinguistics, provide insights valuable to both research and pedagogy.

Theoretical framework

Identities in classroom discourse

A growing body of work focuses on the ways in which learners negotiate their identities in the context of acquiring a second/foreign language; see, for example, Norton Pierce (1995); McKay and Wong (1996); Norton (2000); Pavlenko and Blackledge (2004); and Hawkins (2005). Much of this work has been ethnographic and focused on observations, interviews, questionnaires and written discourse collected from the learners rather than on micro-analysis of oral classroom interactions. Of the studies that have utilized discourse analysis, most have focused on codeswitching; for example, Bailey's (2002) study of multiple identities among Dominican Americans. Though codeswitching occurs in our data, our focus is on other aspects of interaction that provide linguistic clues to how identities are negotiated in the classroom.

The groundwork for studies of classroom interaction was laid by Courtney Cazden (1988). She argues that certain features of schools make communication central to a greater extent than it is in other social institutions where language is used, such as hospitals. First, in schools spoken language is the medium through which much learning takes place and though which students demonstrate what they have learned. Secondly, unlike other social institutions, teachers control much of that talk, both to 'avoid collisions' (Cazden 1988: 3) and enhance learning. Thirdly, spoken language is part of the identities of all learners and the differences learners and teachers bring to the classroom can impair or enhance learning. While Cazden's notion of identity highlights what the student *brings into* the classroom, we want to spotlight the linguistic means students use for negotiating identities with a teacher *while in class* and the clues these can provide for enhanced learning.

Frame and face

Erving Goffman developed two important concepts, those of *frame* and *face*, that we utilize in our analysis. Building upon Bateson's (1954, 1972) concept of frame, the idea that no communicative move could be understood without reference to a metacommunicative message about what was going on, Goffman (1974) created a structural model for applying frame theory that has been utilized by sociolinguists, most notably Tannen (1993), though not, that we are aware, for classroom analysis. We believe this concept has much to add to discourse analysis in classroom settings especially in studying identity construction, and we utilize it in our analysis. We also borrow Goffman's concept of *face*, (Goffman 1967) which Brown and Levinson (1987) use in their theory of politeness.

We agree with Cazden (1988) that much of what teachers do in their daily interactions with students is potentially face-threatening, thus making Brown and Levinson's politeness theory an ideal way to gain insight into teacher–student interaction and examine the ongoing construction and transformation of identity in the classroom. In Brown and Levinson's model, interactional discourse is full of face-threatening acts (FTAs) that are mediated by politeness strategies, ones that appeal to the hearer's positive face, the need to be accepted, or one's negative face, one's right to not be imposed upon. Classroom examples of FTAs include asking a question, making a request, disagreeing or reprimanding. The relative seriousness of such acts is determined by the social distance between interlocutors, power differentials and the gravity of the particular act in the social and cultural context. Interlocutors can soften these FTAs by their use of positive or negative politeness strategies. Positive politeness is designed to appeal to one's desire to be part of a social relationship and to be liked by others, whereas negative politeness strategies appeal to one's right to privacy, autonomy and respect. The choice of negative or positive politeness strategies provides a powerful indicator of the identities one is claiming for oneself and others.

Identities, social acts and stances

'Identity' has been used in a variety of ways in sociolinguistic and specifically identity-related research; for example, some researchers differentiate social identities, such as gender, social status, and age – from discourse identities (Georgakopolou 2002). However, for the purposes of this discussion, we want to adopt Ochs' (1993: 288) broader definition of social identity, as 'a cover term for a range of social personae, including social statuses, roles, positions, relationships, and institutional and other relevant community identities one may attempt to claim or assign in the course of social life'.

Though perhaps obvious, it is important to underline our assumption that these identities are fluid rather than fixed and mediated primarily through interactions where they can be created, negotiated and resisted, often in a matter of a few turns. This happens, according to Ochs (1993: 288) when '...speakers attempt to establish certain identities for themselves and others through verbally performing certain *social acts* and verbally displaying certain *stances*'. A social act is a socially recognized goal-directed behaviour such as a request, a contradiction, an interruption or a question; a stance is a socially recognized point of view or attitude such as the certainty one expresses in a proposition or the display of affective emotions.

Aims of the research
Others have pointed out the important role of teacher-orchestrated group discussion as a critical site for changing students' role and identities (Michaels and Sohmer 2002). This paper presents an example of such a teacher-led discussion in a multilingual classroom which illustrates how linguistic interactions between teacher and students and between students are used to signal, ratify and resist discourse frames and identities. While such negotiation is

intrinsic to human encounters, we agree with Pavlenko and Blackledge (2004: 18) that 'identity becomes interesting when it is contested or in crisis'. Certainly in cases where students are being newly initiated into the practices of a hetero-geneous classroom community, where languages and cultures are, at most, partially shared and where values about gender and power roles are likely not shared, we see the greater likelihood for the negotiation of identities as well as more possibilities for misunderstanding. The classroom here is an example of such a place.

Setting

The data on which we base our discussion here comes from our investigation of a 9th grade multilingual class called 'English Learner Science'. It is one of seven classes we visited as part of a larger exploratory study in which we video-taped classroom interactions in multilingual science classes. The class is located in a large high school where about 25 per cent of the students are non-native speakers of English of whom the majority are Spanish speakers from Mexico or of Mexican descent. The community is the location of a large meat-packing plant where many of the students' families work; the teacher tells us that many students also plan to work in the plant after finishing school.

In this class the teacher introduces a unit that involves dissecting a foetal pig, a common exercise in secondary biology classes in the United States and one that is typically the culmination of a series of dissecting activities on smaller animals such as worms and frogs. We observe here participant relational dynamics, shifts in framing of the pig dissection task and negotiations and displays of social identity.

Framing: the teacher posits students as friends and future meat-packers

The class opens with the teacher standing in front of 15 students, all Spanish speakers except for two recently arrived Sudanese. Students range from non-English speaking, including the Sudanese, to emerging fluent. The teacher, a middle-aged Iowa woman, stands with a preserved foetal pig on a table in front of her and begins by connecting with the work in the meat-packing plant that several students have told her they wanted to do when they left school. All names of persons and places are pseudonyms. Translations appear in italics and brackets. Other commentary appears in parentheses.

Extract 1

Teacher: (1)   Manuel más cerca *Manuel closer* José (.) come closer (.) come closer.
                (students move around the classroom)
         (2)   ok (.) we have been (.) talking
                [students continue to talk]
         (3)   shhh... nosotros antes hablar los sistemas de la cuerpo
         (4)   *shhh...we before talk the body systems*(.) and then we took a
         (5)   and we started working on something else (.) I PROMISED
         (6)   you (.) that I was going to teach you how to DI:ssect (.) an animal

(7)   (.) the animals that we are going to dissect (.) are pigs because all
(8)   of you guys keep saying (.) oh I can't wait to go down to Benson (.)
(9)   so I can make money (.) well if you're gonna learn about a pig
(10)   before you go to work at (.) we're gonna start talking
(11)   about a pig and we're going to start talking about what is on the
(12)   inside of a pig (.) this is what you are going to be doing (.) this is a
(13)   TRUE baby pig

During the opening above, students noisily move about the room. As the teacher talks she uses intensifiers (Brown and Levinson 1987), including speaking in a higher volume than her conversational voice, projecting over students' own conversations in Spanish, and using a series of solidarity-building and involvement strategies to connect with her audience and engage students in the topic at hand. She begins by repeating her invitation to 'come closer, come closer' (1). Noteworthy is her use of a direct imperative here rather than possible alternatives which would have oriented the discourse to more formal and socially distant stance via negative politeness strategies such as: 'Could you come closer? Or do you want to come closer so you can see?' The alternative use of a direct, bald-on-record *come closer* (1) (Brown and Levinson 1987: 98–9) serves the dual services of directly eliciting attention and indicating that the speaker wants to project common ground and cooperation: she has the students' interests in mind, in this case, wanting them to be able to see something of interest. The repetition of *come closer* (1) is followed by other repetitions, e.g. the name of the meat-packing plant (8), the word *dissect*, (6–7) and the word *pig* repeated five times (7,9,11,12,13) in this turn along with the exaggerated emphasis on words such as *'promised'* (5) and *'dissect'* (6) and *'true'* (13) serve as both involvement strategies (Tannen 1989) and emphatics.

The teacher displays solidarity in switching from her native English to Spanish, the in-group language of most, but not all, of her students. While she begins with *'we have been talking'* (2), in English, when students appear to ignore her, she tries to quiet them with 'shhh' and then switches to a Spanish version (3) of her opening sentence, which she then translates into English (4). With the students now listening, the teacher continues in English for the rest of her turn. Thus after gaining student attention, she moves from the solidarity-signifying home language of most of her students to English, the less familiar academic language, but she continues to invoke solidarity. This includes showing that she has the interests and desires of the students in mind and seeking the students' cooperation is by repeating an earlier promise: *I promised you that I was going to teach you how to dissect an animal* (5–6) and indicating that she is about to fulfil this promise (9–12), an act which carries the presupposition that this is something the students keenly desire, as she supports with the reported words of the students themselves, i.e. (8–9) *'all of you guys keep saying oh I can't wait to go down to Benson's so I can make money'*. This use of constructed dialogue – especially the act of using the audience's 'own words' is both a powerful involvement strategy (Tannen 1989) and one which elicits solidarity by communicating that the speaker knows what the hearer wants and wants to involve the hearer in an act that is directly related to his/her self-interest. Note also within the direct speech, the solidarity-evoking use of exaggeration here (Brown and

Levinson 1987) – that *all* the students want to go down to the local meat-packing plant so they can make money and that they *can't wait* to do so (7–9).

The teacher's presentation reflects not only her institutional status as a teacher, but her locally constructed identity as one who knows her students well, attends to their needs and seeks to be in community with them, one who keeps her promises and delivers what they want and need; that is, she is attending to the relational aspects of communication. At the same time, she sets up a frame for the activity in accord with the particular identity she sets for *all* the students: they are future workers in a meat-packing plant and so will be interested in learning about a pig. For that purpose she has provided a *real pig*. Not only is it a real animal, not a mere model, as the teacher indicates that the student will expect, but it is a pig, the animal most closely associated with meat-packing in this area. In the next two excerpts, we see both the influence of this frame and students use of strategies to *alter* the identity in which they have been cast.

Students respond to real pig-meat-packing frame

The teacher's introduction of dissection of a pig as preparation for meat-packing rather than as the typical school biology exercise that it is in the United States is particularly salient for this group of students because of their family ties to meat-processing in the community and their prior experience with farm animals in Mexico. Because rabbits rather than pigs are typically dissected in Mexican schools, pigs for the Mexican students are most likely associated not with scientific labs or with biology classes, but with farm animals, packing plants and food on the table.

In the segment that follows, two male students demonstrate their involvement in the frame:

Extract 2

MS1:	(14)	Es un puerco [*it's a pig*]
Teacher:	(15)	este es una puerco (.) poquito (.) [*it is a pig (.) little (.)*] has been (.)dissected (.)
	(16)	they have opened up (.) the entire system(.) what we're gonna do
	(17)	and this is what we (.) will be actually doing as well (.) this is
	(18)	NO model (.) this is a real foetal pig...
	(19)	este es una verdad [*this is a truth*]
MS2:	(20)	(*laughter*) cómo lo agarraron pues? [*well, how did they catch it?*]
Teacher:	(21)	it is

The first student who speaks (14) confirms for other students the veracity of the teacher's remarks: it is indeed a pig. This notion of this being a 'real' activity connected with real world actions becomes a pervasive theme in the teacher's subsequent turn (15–19) in which she starts by connecting with the student's phrase but adds qualifiers emphasizing the dissection aspect and reiterates that the pig is *real*, thus connecting the task with the outside world of remunerative work, the presupposition being that she believes school lessons are less engaging to her students than something connected with the working world she assumes they all want to enter.

This stance is negotiated by the second student, signalled by his laughter and his question (20) *cómo lo agarraron pues* [*well, how did they catch it?*] that he intends his question as a break with the established classroom talk, while showing involvement in the task and the teacher's proposal. Note that as he aligns himself with the real-world meat-packing frame, he interjects his own knowledge about baby pigs: they are difficult to catch. If Mrs C has brought them a real pig, then how was it caught? The student's initial laughter in turn provides a contextualization cue (Gumperz 1982) indicating the nature of his communicative act for others: this is meant to be a joke which constructs the speaker as witty and knowledgeable rather than a true question that would cast doubt on what the teacher said; other students show their appreciation of his wit with their laughter, thus co-constructing his identity at this moment. The teacher does not join in the joking repartee, starting to say something, but breaking off, the first sign of a shift in her solidarity with the students and perhaps an indication that she views the comment as off-topic. So, we see the two students who have taken the floor showing signs of accepting the frame and identity the teacher presented: This-is-a-real-pig-and-we-are-learning-about-it-in-order-to-butcher-them; and within that context one student positioning himself in the role of clever communicator who both demonstrates his sense of humour and his own practical real-world knowledge that young pigs are difficult to catch. At the same time we see the teacher break with her earlier identity of solidarity, a stance that her status as teacher makes it possible for her to do. Though we cannot determine what the teacher was thinking, when there is no uptake of a student's attempts at humour, this might conventionally be viewed as the teacher seeing the student as off-topic and/or inappropriate; in any event, she does not assist in the construction of his identity. While the teacher ignores the humorous interlude, students follow with a series of other questions connecting with the theme of veracity. Through these questions we observe a subtle shift to more scientific talk as well as further signs that one student, Augusto, is being co-constructed as a leader who, like the teacher, is a powerful controller of the turn rights of others in the class.

Students construct and resist identities

An outside observer walking into the class might view the students as unmotivated and not invested in learning. The room is noisy, students jump out of their seats, hop up to sharpen pencils, look at snapshots classmates have brought, answer the teacher's ringing phone and do other off-task activities. Yet, students' interactions clearly indicate their involvement in the task as we see in the opening question below:

Extract 3

MS3:	(22)	y cómo se conserva allí? [*and how is it preserved there*]
Augusto:	(23)	tiene la mitad [*half of it is there*]
Teacher:	(24)	it is in a chemical tiene como el cincuenta por ciento de alcohol y
	(25)	lo demás de agua [*it has about fifty per cent alcohol and the rest is*
	(26)	*water*] it is in a chemical (.) the pigs that we'll be working on (.)
	(27)	are going to be small pigs (.) like this (.) we'll be working on them in a
	(28)	TRAY (.) just like a doctor (.). igual un doctor (.) [*same a doctor*] you
	(29)	will have a SCALPEL (.) and you
	(30)	will be doing the CUTTING
Augusto:	(31)	un bisturí (.) esos son muy peligrosos no jueguen con
	(32)	esos [*scalpel(.) those are very dangerous do not play with those*]

In the segment above another male student poses a serious scientifically oriented question reflecting the structure of the earlier student question: '*how was it caught?*' Yet, student 3's question (22): '*how is it preserved*'? differs in projecting an identity that is engaged and intellectually curious. Since the question is posed to the teacher, she is the expected respondent. But instead, another student, Augusto, contradicts his peer, telling him in Spanish that he has not spoken truthfully; only *half*, not *all* of the pig has been preserved (23). Such an unmitigated criticism is not only a face-threatening act (Brown and Levinson 1987), but one that is accepted by both the student who was corrected and the teacher, thus confirming that Augusto has certain powerful floor rights. In the next turn, (24–26), the teacher answers Student 3's question, telling him that it is a chemical, before she moves back to reinforcing the size and location of the pigs (27–28). What is interesting here is that scientific turn of the student's question appears to have been perceived by Augusto as a move threatening his power as the class leader. The teacher, however, reacts to the student's question by modifying her earlier frame. We see her now recontextualize the activity (28), not as factory work, but *like* the work of a doctor, telling the students in English that *like doctors* they will use a scalpel. But even as the teacher raises this prospect, Augusto speaks in Spanish to his classmates, (31–32), not translating what the teacher said about their work being like that of doctors, but positioning himself as a leader more capable and intelligent than his peers, warning them in a bald and unmitigated form: *no juegeun con esos* (do not play with those) of the dangers of playing with a scalpel, a statement which presupposes that he identities his peers as potentially childlike and unworldly, and that he is justified in warning them as a father might do.

As the class continues, we see some students showing uptake of the science frame in which the teacher had suggested that students about to do dissection shared a role similar in respect to doctors. After an exchange not included here about whether or not the pig was alive, a student asks a serious scientific question related to the doctor frame about how the internal organs of humans and pigs compare:

Extract 4

MS 4:   (43)   y cuando abres un puerco también es como cuando abres una
           (44)   persona? [*and when you open a pig is it also like when you open
                   a person?*]

Rather than answering directly or asking the class to reflect on the question, the teacher turns to Augusto with whom she engages in a rhythmic presentational dialogue as the other students watch:

Extract 5

Teacher: (45)   you can see (.) if you look at this book (.) that a pig (.) has the
            (46)   same systems that we have (.) does the pig (.) have a heart?
Augusto: (47)   yes
Augusto: (48)   does the pig have blood?
Augusto: (49)   yes lungs
Teacher: (50)   so (.) if it has a heart (.) and it has blood (.) then it has a
            (51)   circulatory system (.) right?
Augusto: (52)   right

Note that Augusto not only participates in the dialogue, but asks and answers his own question in lines 48 and 49. In fact, during the class period, Augusto takes the floor some 96 times without the teacher directly calling on him. In comparison, the teacher directly calls on students, including Augusto, 38 times. Male students, most often Augusto, instead tend to call out answers. In the following sequence we see how power comes into play when the teacher calls on a male student other than Augusto:

Extract 6

Teacher: (159)   because they've been preserved... Eduardo qué significa la palabra
            (160)   preserved? [*what does the word preserved mean?*]
Eduardo: (161)   qué? [*what*]
Teacher: (162)   qué significar es la palabra preserved? (*what mean is the word
                     preserve?*)
Eduardo: (163)   preservar [*preserve*]
Teacher: (164)   qué es? qué significar? [*what is it? what mean?*]
Eduardo: (165)   no sé (.)mejor a Augusto el sabe [*I don't know (.) you'd better ask
                     Augusto he knows*]
Students: (166)   laughter
Teacher: (167)   pero tú saber también saber porque tú es inteligente [*but you know
                     also know because you are intelligent*]
Eduardo: (168)   pues este como este (.) como (.) está ese puerquito ahí [*well this
                     like this like that piglet is there*]
Students: (169)   (laughter)

Here Eduardo advises the teacher to call on his classmate, Augusto, a potentially face-threatening act to both Eduardo himself, as not being intelligent enough to answer, and to the teacher as someone needing advice from a student. When the teacher insists that Eduardo too is intelligent (167), rather than directly contradicting her – a social act that might signal disrespect, he agrees, but downgrades his own intelligence by making a self-effacing and witty response, comparing himself to the baby pig (168). Norrick (1993) and Boxer (2002) both suggest that such self-denigrating humour can work to display identity and develop relations among interlocutors. Indeed here, Eduardo's self-denigration provokes appreciative laughter from his peers, suggesting that he has managed in a matter of two turns to resist the identity the teacher has proposed – as academically capable – and to present himself, while not academically intelligent like Augusto, as, nevertheless, both a self-effacing and sharp-witted community member who has also shown public support of Augusto, thus co-constructing Augusto as the class leader with floor and topic control rights that surpass those of himself and other classmates.

Gender identity construction

Aside from the teacher, in this class few women hold the floor, instead sitting in pairs and speaking quietly in asides to one another, in this way seeming to present themselves as bystanders. The teacher seldom challenges this identity, calling on women less than half as frequently as she calls on males (12:26). Women nevertheless engage in constructing their own identities in relation to the frame the teacher has proposed. Below we see evidence of the power of the earlier meat-packer/butcher role for one young woman and her desire to resist that identity:

Extract 7

Teacher:	(124)	(*T is passing out books*) here are some more books that have more
	(125)	information (.) and I want you TODAY (.) because we're actually
	(126)	gonna start dissecting on Monday (.) Each person in here will be
	(127)	responsible for dissecting their own individual pig. so whether
→	(128)	are a boy or a girl you will have to dissect a pig
Rosa:	(129)	a mí me da cosa [*it scares me*]
Teacher:	(130)	todo ustedes a Lunes necesito hacer una disección de tu mismo
	(131)	puerco [*all you at Monday I need to make a dissection of your same pig*]
Rafael:	(132)	(*to Rosa*) tu lo vas a hacer? [*are you going to do it?*] (*Rosa shakes her head*)
AMS6:	(133)	yo no carnicero [*I no butcher*]

Here the teacher draws attention to the role of gender; her statement (127) *so whether you are a boy or a girl you will have to dissect a pig* is new information. Presumably she would not need to say this if she did not expect that this was counter to the expectations of at least some of her students, though when she codeswitches to Spanish she is less gender specific, using *todos ustedes* (all of you). When her classmate, Rafael, expresses interest in whether his female classmate will participate (132), Rosa resists by shaking her head (132) the identity that for her is entailed in dissection. Similarly, we hear the words *yo no carnicero (I no butcher)* by another student (133) as a strong denial of the identity at least some students feel as being set up for them by the teacher and confirming their attention to the original meat-packing frame.

In the whole class sequence that follows, we see a rare instance where the teacher calls on a female student. The sequence below comes towards the end of the class, following a small group interaction with the teacher in which one student revealed that he had dissected a rabbit in Mexico and wondered how similar a rabbit and pig were internally:

Extract 8

Teacher:	(428)	Rosa qué pensar (.) son igual o no? [*Rosa what think (.) are they the same or not?*]
Rosa	(429)	no
Teacher:	(430)	why not
Rosa:	(431)	él se está riendo [*he is laughing*]
Teacher:	(432)	because what (*looks to students that are being noisy*) excuse me
	(433)	(*looks back at Rosa*) because what (*looks at a group of male students*)
Augusto:	(434)	Mrs.
Teacher:	(435)	Augusto
Augusto:	(436)	I think there is a little difference as I know a lot of kinds of animals that eat like grass or something
Teacher:	(437)	(*looks at students who are being noisy* excuse me (.) (*looks at Augusto*) Augusto
Augusto:	(438)	that they first that they have two conducts in their trachea or I don't
	(439)	know they have two different conducts one is for the food that they
	(440)	eat and then after time that they eat they have the other one so the
	(441)	food comes again up and they start like (mimes chewing) like
Teacher:	(442)	ok what's that called when the food comes back up? that's called regurgitation
Augusto:	(443)	I saw that in cows in horses that they do that after time they are like (*mimes chewing*)
Teacher:	(444)	ok have you seen cows puer uh vacas and caballos cuando ellos [*pi...uh cows and horses when they*]
	(445)	(*mimes chewing*) pero este la comida de salir [*but this the food to leave*] (*mimes vomiting*)
	(446)	called regurgitation
Augusto:	(447)	no se han fijado que cuando ya comen después de rato cada vez
	(448)	están mastica y mastica sin estar comiendo sino que la [*they haven't noticed that when a little bit after they eat each time they are chewing and chewing without eating but instead the*]
Teacher:	(449)	Rosa what is that called when the food is brought back up from the stomach ? (.) cómo se llama [*what do you call it*](.) re everybody re
Students:	(450)	re
Teacher:	(451)	gur
Students:	(452)	gur
Teacher:	(453)	gi
Students:	(454)	gi
Teacher:	(455)	tation
Students:	(456)	tation
Teacher:	(457)	regurgitation
Students:	(458)	regurgitation

Teacher: (459)   that's what I always say as I throw up (*mimes throwing up*) vómito
                   [*I vomit*] regurgitation (.)

In the segment above the teacher twice attempts to call on a female student, but becomes derailed when the targeted young woman gives as her reason for not answering, the fact that a male classmate is laughing at her (431). As the teacher starts to question why, Augusto seizes the opportunity to speak by soliciting the teacher (434) and Mrs C. assists him in extending his turn by silencing other students who are being disruptive (437). Augusto's remark about the dual digestive systems of some animals (438–441) leads to an extended drill-and-practice on the word regurgitation, (450–459), notably not related to the original student question regarding the similarity of pigs and rabbits. Again, we observe Augusto's successful attempt to gain the floor and change the topic, even after another student had been selected by the teacher. We see this manoeuvre, which we view as an assertion of his identity as leader, affirmed by the linguistic moves of his teacher and his classmates, continue throughout the remainder of the class; meanwhile, Rosa and her female peers continue to have their outsider stance affirmed not only by their fellow students, but by the teacher as well as she allows turns and topics to be grabbed by more powerful members.

Summary and discussion

As we reflect on the interaction we have observed, several points seem worth highlighting. First, we are reminded of the extent to which identity negoti-ation is multi-layered and multi-faceted. As Tannen (1993: 22) pointed out, speech events represent '...the overlapping and intertwining of many relations concerning the context as well as content of communication'. Our data illustrate how in the classroom context social categories ascribed to the interlocutors such as 'woman,' or 'Spanish speaker' intertwine with individual characteristics such as a sense of humour or intelligence to influence the roles students take in a particular class. As students are encouraged or discouraged from connecting with their own prior knowledge, from answering questions, or from sharing ideas, their own identities and their potential to think of themselves as having the skills to be successful students is affirmed or disavowed.

Secondly, we note that frames influence the directions subsequent interactions take and the identities that result from these interactions; in turn, the interac-tions influence framing and reframing. As we saw, after science-oriented student questions at certain points, the teacher began to move away from her initial frame of dissection-as-preparation-for-meat-packing. Nevertheless, this initial frame played an important role in shaping the identities students maintained in this class, with one student proclaiming that he wouldn't participate because he was not a 'butcher'. For this student and for others, being a butcher or working in a meat-packing plant continued to be entailed in the academic task of dissection.

Thirdly, we observe the powerful role of the teacher as 1) the initial and primary framer of classroom activities; and 2) the controller of floor rights and topic and we note the potential for these roles in socializing students. As classrooms become increasingly heterogeneous communities (Lave and Wenger 1991) our findings here underscore the need for sociolinguists with an interest in pedagogy to continue to explore alternative kinds of discourse to create more egalitarian classroom communities where speakers of all languages have the possibility of joining in the discussion. For example, in this class, not only did a male Spanish speaker (Augusto) with advanced English skills dominate the discussion, but some members, notably the two Sudanese students and most women, were non-participants. Interestingly, as we can see from the transcript, the teacher attempted to build solidarity with students by codeswitching to Spanish and trying to connect class tasks to student interests outside the classroom. In fact, her accommodation to the cultural norms of this classroom community may have led her to allow male domination, since, as we saw, there is evidence that the class assisted in this pattern of interaction.

Fourthly, this classroom provides us with a rich example of the power students have to negotiate their own and the identities of others. Here we saw first-hand what students have reported to other researchers, that is, that peers with power can be instrumental in excluding students from discussion (Leki 2001).

In addition to noting the specific ways in which frames, teachers and students shape the construction of identity in the classroom, it is clear that as Morita (2004) notes, the negotiation of identities is not necessarily a smooth, cooperative effort. More interestingly, portions of this transcript suggest that what *appears* to be cooperative discourse on the surface may in fact be promoting identities of incompetence in some learners as we saw in Eduardo's good-natured suggestion to the teacher to call on someone else.

Our analysis demonstrates what others have suggested: identities are fluid, multi-layered and contradictory, and constructed through linguistic interaction (Pavlenko and Blackledge 2004; Bloome *et al.* 2005). What is noteworthy is the power of interactional sociolinguistic discourse analysis to reveal this, suggesting that this form of analysis may provide insights into a a deeper understanding of classroom discourse.[2]

Conclusion and research implications

The interactions we observed in a multilingual 9th grade science classroom in a new borderland, the Midwestern United States, illustrate that classrooms of young adults can yield powerful examples of discourse used to negotiate one's identities and those of others. These segments also demonstrate ways in which the construction of self is 1) cued by others, through the frames they offer and the identities of themselves and others they project; and 2) negotiated and strategically deployed to achieve social needs, such as the need to be liked and respected. As other researchers have argued (Zimmerman 1998; Georgakopoulou 2002), such discourse identities create their own context, '... not just the proximal turn-by-turn context, but also the distal context for social activities...' (Georgakoupoulou 2002: 445). This suggests the power of relatively short segments of interaction to influence the future actions of interlocutors.

We have limited ourselves to presenting the identity construction that participants *themselves* make visible in local contexts. This is not to suggest that the interactional history of the participants is not important. Indeed, we gain hints from our transcript of the power of the interactional history of this community: the comments from some students prior to this class about wanting to work in the local meat-packing plant seem to have influenced the teacher's decision to set up the task in a particular way. Similarly, Augusto's role as class leader was clearly not entirely constructed in this particular class, nor were the gender expectations to which both the students and the teacher alluded. Without a doubt, a fuller perspective could be gained from an integration of interactional history, examining, for example, the leadership roles Augusto may have outside the school with his classmates. Nevertheless, interactional sociolinguistic discourse analysis provides a valuable tool for analysing classroom interaction; this approach may be especially useful for those interested in the communication challenges of classrooms set on sociolinguistic borderlands where identities are likely to be under construction.

Notes

1 The relationship of newcomers to longer-term Iowa residents is complex. The state officially encourages in-migration. Thousands of Vietnamese refugees were welcomed to Iowa in the late 1970s, with more settling there than in any other state in the US. In 2001, Governor Villsack, concerned with an ageing population and a steady out-migration of young people, suggested that he wanted Iowa to be the new Ellis Island, welcoming immigrants from around the world. On the other hand, sudden changes in the population have not been without negative repercussion, including the passage of a bill in 2002 making English the official language of Iowa.

2 Not all classes we visited showed the clear evidence of identity negotiation that we describe here. Negotiation of identity, though present, was discouraged in several ways. For example, in one bilingual class, the teacher simply lectured in English and at the end of each segment a bilingual translated the lecture into Spanish with no interaction with students. In all other classes that we observed where students had a variety of mother tongues, English was the sole lingua franca and we saw little evidence of modification for bilingual students. In one case where a student attempted to negotiate identity by asking if he could use Spanish in his written assignment, the teacher simply answered no, thus denying him symbolic capital in the language in which he was fluent (Omoniyi 2004) and literate. In another case, where the topic was natural disasters and would presumably have allowed student discussion and contribution, the instructor, who admitted not knowing where individual students were from, elicited no input. In these situations where there was no open discussion, one might argue that the teachers imposed an all too-familiar student identity for non-native speakers: that of passive listeners with no possibility of contributing to a community of learning. In these cases there was little possibility for student negotiation of identity, except to resist being a student. When open discussion did occur in bilingual classrooms, as Cazden (1988) would predict, teachers typically asked questions they knew the answers to, one student responded, and the teacher evaluated that response.

References

Bailey, B. (2002), *Language, Race and Negotiation of Identity: A Study of Dominican Americans*. New York: LFB Scholarly Publishing.

Baker, L. and Saul, W. (1994), 'Considering science and language arts connections: A study of teacher cognition', *Journal of Research in Science Teaching*, 31, (9), 1023–37.

Bateson, G. (1954, 1972), 'A theory of play and fantasy', in *Steps to an Ecology of the Mind*. New York: Ballantine Books.

Bloome, D., Carter, S. P., Christian, B. M., Otto, S. and Shuart-Faris, N. (2005), *Discourse Analysis and the Study of Classroom Language and Literacy Events: A Microethnographic Perspective*. Mahwah, NJ: Lawrence Erlbaum Associates.

Boxer, D. (2002), *Applying Sociolinguistics: Domains and Face-to-Face Interaction*. Amsterdam/Philadelphia: John Benjamins.

Brown, P. and Levinson, S. C. (1987), *Politeness: Some Universals in Language Usage*. Cambridge: Cambridge University Press.

Cazden, C. (1988), *Classroom Discourse: The Language of Teaching and Learning*. Portsmouth, NH: Heinemann.

Cummins, J. (1994), 'Knowledge, power and identity in teaching English as a second language', in F. Genesee (ed.), *Educating Second Language Children: The Whole Child, the Whole Curriculum, the Whole Community*. Cambridge: Cambridge University Press, pp. 33–58.

Georgakopoulou, A. (2002), 'Narrative and identity management: Discourse and social identities in a tale of tomorrow', *Research on Language and Social Interaction*, 35, (4), pp. 427–51.

Goffman, E. (1967), *Interaction Ritual: Essays in Face-to-Face Behavior*. Chicago: Aldine.
— (1974), *Frame Analysis*. New York: Harper and Row.

Gumperz, J. (1982), *Discourse Strategies*. Cambridge: Cambridge University Press.

Hawkins, M. (2005), 'Becoming a student: Identity work and academic literacies in early schooling', *TESOL Quarterly*, 39, (1), 59–82.

Iowa Department of Education (2001), *English Language Learners Report*. Des Moines, IA: Grimes State Office Building, www.state.ia.us/educate/reports.html.

Iowa Department of Education (2005), *Basic Educational Data Survey*. Des Moines, IA: Grimes State Office Building, www.dom.state.ia.us/planning_performance/reports/Education.doc.

Lave, J. and Wenger, E. (1991), *Situated Learning: Legitimate Peripheral Participation*. Cambridge: Cambridge University Press.

Leki, I. (2001), 'A narrow thinking system', *TESOL Quarterly*, 35, (1), 39–67.

McKay, S. L. and Wong, S. C. (1996), 'Multiple discourses, multiple identities: investment and agency in second-language learning among Chinese adolescent immigrant students', *Harvard Educational Review*, 66, (3), 577–608.

Michaels, S. and Sohmer, R. (2002), 'Discourses that promote new academic identities', in D. Li (ed.), *Discourses in Search of Members*. Lanham, MD: University Press of America, pp. 171–219.

Morita, N. (2004), 'Negotiating participation and identity in second language academic communities', *TESOL Quarterly*, 38, (4), 573–603.

National Center for Education Statistics (2000), *NAEP 1999 trends in academic progress: Three decades of student performance* (Report No. NCES 2000-469). Washington, DC: US Government Printing Office.

Norrick, N. (1993), *Conversational Joking: Humor in Everyday Talk*. Bloomington, IN: Indiana University Press.

Norton, B. (2000), *Identity and Language Learning: Gender, Ethnicity and Educational Change*. London: Longman.

Norton Peirce, B. (1995), 'Social identity, investment, and language learning', *TESOL Quarterly*, 29, (1), 9–29.

Ochs, E. (1993), 'Constructing social identity: a language socialization perspective', *Research on Language and Social Interaction*, 26, (3), 287–306.

Omoniyi, T. (2004), *Sociolinguistics of Borderlands*. Trenton, NJ: African World Press.

Pavlenko, A. and Blackledge, A. (eds) (2004), *Negotiation of Identities in Multilingual Contexts*. Clevedon: Multilingual Matters.

Rollnick, M. and Rutherford, M. (1996), 'The use of the mother tongue and the learning and expression of science concepts—A classroom-based study', *International Journal of Science Education*, 18, (1), 91–104.

Stoddart, T., Pinal, A., Latzke, M. and Canaday, D. (2002), 'Integrating inquiry science and language', *Journal of Research on Science Teaching*, 39, (8), 664–87.

Tannen, D. (1989), *Talking Voices: Repetition, Dialogue, and Imagery in Conversational Discourse*. Cambridge: Cambridge University Press.

Tannen, D. (ed.) (1993), *Framing in Discourse*. Oxford: Oxford University Press.

Zimmerman D. H. (1998), 'Identity, context, and interaction', in C. Antaki and S. Widdicombe (eds), *Identities in Talk*. London: Sage, pp. 87–106.

13 Standard Irish English as a marker of Irish identity

Goodith White

Introduction

If you type the words 'Irish identity' into a Google search, you are presented with a number of websites which link notions of Irish identity almost exclusively to the Irish language. The search term 'language and identity' on Irish government websites similarly produces references to the part played by the Irish language in the political, economic and cultural life of the Republic, or to recent legislation which seeks to ensure that Irish continues to be used in these spheres. The English language barely merits a mention. What are we to make of these electronic connections? Do they truly reflect 'Irish identity' and the fact that it is inextricably linked to the Irish language? Or do we decide that such websites are representative of an 'older, nationalist version' of Irish identity (Arrowsmith 2004) which is irrelevant in the face of Ireland's more recent participation in a global culture and economy? In seeking to make a case for standard Irish English as a marker of Irish identity, I will first attempt to establish what 'Irish identity' might mean at the present time, and why an Irish variety of English might be an appropriate vehicle for expressing that identity, before moving on to describe some of the characteristics of that variety and attitudes towards it in the Republic of Ireland, using evidence from a corpus, a map task and a questionnaire.

Problems with defining national identity

The current poststructuralist take on identity as primarily individual, unstable and ambivalent (see for example, Block, this volume) poses problems for discussing individual participation in a group identity such as 'national identity'. If we reject essentialism, which would describe the members of such a group as similar in their attributes and behaviour due to shared cultural and/or biological characteristics, on the grounds that it fails to account for or recognize the full range of human diversity, we are left with a picture of individuals dropping in and out of an affiliation to a national identity as and when it becomes salient for them personally, using linguistic behaviour as one means of claiming connection to that identity (Le Page and Tabouret-Keller 1985:'181). We would also have to recognize that national identity, like other geographically located collective identities, while generally contained within real political and geographical borders, is also to some extent 'imagined' by the individuals who feel allegiance to it (Anderson 1991). This makes it highly likely that individuals will differ in how they experience and define 'national identity', and that some aspects of that identity might be more important for individuals within particular contexts. For example, different aspects of Irish identity might be more salient for a Dubliner watching a Gaelic football match at Croke Park and the same Dubliner on a package holiday in Ibiza, or for someone from a rural village in County Mayo in these two contexts.

The fact that it is difficult to define national identity and that it differs in focus and expression for individuals in different contexts does not mean that it resists description entirely or that it does not have some recognizable characteristics. National identity appears, for the time being at least, to be resilient in the face of supranational projects such as the European Union and the pressures of globalization and localization:

> The growth of supra-national trading blocks, of trans-national companies, of new forms of media and communication technology, of international peace-keeping forces have led to much talk of the demise of nationalism. But, to adapt Mark Twain, one might say that reports of its death have been exaggerated. Nationalism remains one of the most potent organising forces on earth...
>
> (Wright 2000: 10–11)

Thiesse (1999: 6) talks of 'the power of the idea of the nation as a community of solidarity, in which individuals are guaranteed a place not solely dictated by their economic status'. Fishman (1971: 18) describes how nationalism can combat the anomie caused by the break up of traditional communities and the decline of religious faith. The term 'national identity' has been defined in countless, often contradictory ways, but one widely-cited, comprehensive and ideologically unbiased conceptualization may be useful here. Smith (1991: 14) describes five 'fundamental features' of national identity, at least as it is conceived in present-day Western terms: a historic territory, or homeland; common myths and historical memories; a common, mass culture; common legal rights and duties; and a common economy. The first three features seem to be necessary for a cultural concept of national identity, the other two seem to be more concerned with the existence of national identity in a political sense (Suleiman 2003: 6–7). I will argue in the course of this chapter that these features have historical resonance for describing Irish national identity in the past, but may be problematic in some ways for providing a present day framework for describing Irish identity.

Language plays a vital role in forming, promoting and maintaining national identity. Suleiman (2003: 29) points out that language, as a primary means of socialization, enables individuals to participate in a community of speakers in the present and also to connect past, present and future by means of cultural transmission. Joseph (2004: 94) reminds us that the reverse is also true, that national identities shape national languages, and that these national languages are not a 'given', but are constructed and modified 'as part of the ideological work of nationalism-building'. He cites the example of the British Isles: 'for centuries their linguistic pattern was a patchwork of local dialects, Germanic or Celtic in origin. Only in modern times did individuals motivated by national-istic ambitions of various sorts set out to establish "languages" for the nations of England, Ireland, Scotland and Wales'. We are familiar with the processes of selection, elaboration, codification and maintenance which 'national' languages undergo in order to make them more adequate tools of communication within a newly formed polity, as described by Haugen (1972) and Milroy and Milroy (1999), among others. Such 'standardized' forms act as tools of both inclusion and exclusion (Downes 1998: 36; Wright 2000: 7). They enable the members of a national community to communicate with each other easily, and to build solidarity and cooperation, but they are also owned by elites within the community, who control access to the standard language through education and are responsible for the creation and maintenance of notions of correctness.

The roles of English and Irish as identity markers in the Republic

After the Republic of Ireland gained independence in 1921, all of the effort to shape a national language through such processes was focused on Irish, not English. The constitution of 1937 clearly states the relative positions of Irish and English within the new state: 'The Irish language as the national language is the first official language'; 'The English language is recognised as a second official language'. English was thus established as subordinate in status to Irish, which received all the available monetary resources for investigation, description and expansion. The Irish Free State embarked on the construction of an 'authentic' national identity which depicted itself to the world as 'not English', but instead, wholly 'Irish'. It involved the invention, revitalization, preservation and evocation of the 'common myths and historical memories' mentioned by Smith (1991) and cited earlier in this chapter. The state emphasized its political and cultural differences from England, Britishness and the Empire, and promoted an image of Ireland as a rural, Catholic, Irish speaking society. The Prime Minister, Eamonn De Valera, famously described this vision of Irish national identity in a St Patrick's Day speech in 1943 as based on a rural landscape 'bright with cosy homesteads ... and the laughter of happy maidens'. This view of 'Irish identity', so concerned with differentiating itself from the colonial yoke, conveniently excised the fact that English had been long established in Ireland, that English as well as Irish had been used by members of the nineteenth-century nationalist movement, and that writers such as W. B. Yeats and John Synge had argued that literature written in Irish English could be a valid means of expressing Irish identity (Kiberd 1996: 155). It excluded historical events and sections of society (e.g. the urban, the Protestant, the huge Irish diaspora worldwide) which inter-fered with a homogeneous picture of Irish identity.

The failure of nationalist economic policies forced Ireland from the 1960s onwards to move into a global market (Pašeta, 2003: 131–4) and, conse-quent upon this movement outwards into the world, to develop a different, more diffuse notion of national identity (or perhaps, more accurately, to value elements of the heterogeneity that had always been there). Arrowsmith (2004: 468) describes this as 'a new, more inclusive and cosmopolitan version of Irishness' and Harte (1997: 20) talks about 'the mongrel identity of a diasporic people' far removed from the former 'conception of national identity based on notions of territoriality and exclusion'. Arrowsmith even goes so far as to suggest that the Republic has moved into a 'post-nationalist' era. Post-nationalism has been characterized (e.g. by Delanty 1996, 1997; Harte, 1997) as based on multiple identities, not focused on the territorial nation state, referring to the present rather than the past, acknowledging cultural difference, seeking to establish commonalities rather than excluding difference, and based on a new way of inventing the nation around cultural rather than political discourses (Delanty and O'Mahoney 1998). This notion of national identity is very different from that proposed by Smith (1991), but perhaps it better describes present-day Ireland, with its entry into the global economy, its worldwide diaspora of people who claim the right to appropriate some aspect of Irish identity, and the increasing multiculturality of Ireland itself, now that it is an attractive destination for inward migration.

What part do Irish and English, and more particularly Irish English, play in expressing all the aspects of this heterogeneous national identity, encompassing a number of different ethnolinguistic communities both within Ireland and abroad? It is obvious that no one language can totally serve that purpose but I will suggest that a standard variety of Irish English should be recognized as playing some role at least in articulating many of those parts of national identity which are held in common. Standard Irish English, whose features I will describe in greater detail later in this chapter, is more suited to this role than more localized dialectal varieties of Irish English, since it has a prestige which regional dialects lack, and is a variety which is used by educated speakers across the Republic. I will also suggest that a recognition that standard Irish English plays some part in expressing Irish national identity serves to focus attention on real language use in the present, as opposed to a myth of current language use based on reference to the past.

What do we know about the use of Irish and English in the past and the present? Considering the case of Irish first, Kallen (1988) describes how in 1800, monoglot Irish speakers and bilinguals outnumbered monoglot English speakers by 3.5 million to 1.5 million. Although census figures are not completely reliable, there seems to have been a dip in reported Irish usage to 17.6 per cent of the total population in 1911 following a century marked by the Potato Famine and emigration, and then a rise by 1971 to 28.3 per cent, possibly reflecting the fact that Irish rose in prestige after independence, and considerable governmental efforts were devoted to encouraging the use of Irish in a wide range of public contexts. As for the current situation, although McArthur (2003: 115–16) may claim that 'Ireland today is an overwhelmingly English-speaking country in which only 2% at most use Irish on a regular basis' it is important to recognize that Irish continues to play an important symbolic role in expressing Irish identity, even if, as Edwards (1985) points out, actual Irish language use for most people may be confined to the maintenance of a small number of Irish words to designate national or political institutions (e.g. *Bord Failté, Dáile Éireann, Tánaiste, Sinn Fein, Radio Telefís Éireann, Gardai, Iarnród Éireann*) or cultural items (e.g. *craic, brogue, boreen, ceilidh*). The Irish language continues to be diffused through music, radio and TV stations (e.g. TG4, which claims 800,000 viewers per day), it is a designated official language of the EU effective from 1 January 2007 and a subject of study at all levels of education. Some parents choose to send their children to schools which teach all subjects through the medium of Irish (*Gaelscola*). The 2002 census shows that 42.8 per cent of the population claim some knowledge of Irish, although the percentages are, as to be expected, higher in the school-age section of the population who have to study Irish as a compulsory subject and these figures do not give any detail about proficiency in the language or contexts of use. As a marker of identity it could be argued that the use of the Irish language expresses how the Irish are different and separate from the rest of the world; as such, it does not easily fit into Delanty and O'Mahoney's (1998) characterization of 'post-nationalism' as focusing on commonalities which are shared by all members of a heterogeneous nation, which in the Republic's case would include recent immigrants and other non-Irish speaking sections of the population as well as the Irish diaspora. It might be that some variety of English would best serve to express this post-nationalist identity. Most tellingly, Davis (2003) cites the results of a questionnaire given to 31,000 people in 23 countries throughout Europe, North America and the Western Pacific. Only 14.5 per cent of Irish respondents (the smallest proportion of any country polled) felt that it was very important to be able to speak their national language (Irish) in order to be considered 'truly Irish'. Davis explains this response as an acknowledgement by respondents that they themselves do not have proficiency in Irish and therefore cannot use it as a necessary criterion for belonging to the Irish nation.

If we consider the role played by English, it is only really in the nineteenth century that it began to be used widely, and before this it was associated 'with the colonial administration, in opposition to the native culture and political structure' (Kallen 1988: 130). In the nineteenth century English became the language of school education, the language of betterment and emigration, the language associated with 'secular progressive culture' (McArthur 2003: 115), despite also being the language of the colonizer. We have seen in previous sections of this chapter how, in the years immediately following independence, it was politically subordinated to the development and encouragement of Irish, although it is fair to say that Irish revivalists never saw any possibility of Irish replacing English as the dominant language of Ireland; they were more concerned with preventing Irish from dying out and aiding the development of bilingualism in English and Irish. However, the cold fact is that Irish is not really of practical use for communication with other countries in a global economy in the twenty-first century, and English, as the world's principal lingua franca (Graddol 1997, 1999; Crystal, 2003) is more suitable for this purpose. It could be argued that it is English which has now become the means of transmitting Irish culture in the 'global village'. The 'Irish pub' (with English speaking bar staff) has been commodified and exported as a representation of Irishness to cities and towns worldwide (McGovern 1999). Novels and plays written in English (Irish English) and focusing on Irish issues, by writers such as Frank McCourt, Dermot Bolger, Roddy Doyle, Brian Friel and William Trevor, win international prizes; they also export 'Irishness' through the medium of English.

Standard Irish English

If Irish still plays an important, but largely symbolic role in expressing certain aspects of present day Irish identity, why am I arguing that standard Irish English, rather than say standard British English, general American English or even English as an International Language (e.g. McKay 2002) does the main work of communicating this identity worldwide? I suggest two main reasons, one to do with the Republic's colonial past, the other to do with the effects of globalization. Taking the colonial past argument first, Kachru's (1985) model of the historical spread of English has been acknowledged, both by others and by Kachru himself (e.g. Kachru 1992; Kachru and Nelson 2001) as problematic in a number of ways, in particular its assumption of homogeneous language use by all the individuals in a particular country, but it does provide a useful paradigm for comparing the ways in which English spread to different polities and attitudes towards different varieties of English. Kachru (1985) describes the spread of English in terms of three concentric circles, namely the 'Inner Circle', the 'Outer Circle' and the 'Expanding Circle' roughly equated with L1, L2 and EFL speakers respectively. He places Ireland in the 'Inner Circle', which encompasses the countries to which English first spread between the late twelfth and early eighteenth centuries. These countries, he says, now refer for notions of correctness to one of the traditional standard Englishes (i.e. standard British English or general American English). It is true that in the past, most speakers of English in the Republic considered standard British English to be the 'correct' and desirable variety to aim for, even if it did not match the English that was actually used in the Republic. As Croghan (1986: 265) remarks:

> From the 19th century the Irish adopted not only the English language as the first language of the majority of the people, but they also adopted the political culture of language from England which included the myth that Hiberno-English was deviant.

In fact, Ireland is more correctly placed, not in Kachru's 'Inner Circle' but in the 'Outer Circle', those countries which were colonized by English speakers, and where a major language (or languages) was already in place before colonization. If we see Ireland as part of this group of territories, it seems logical that it would no longer regard standard British English as the yardstick against which language use should be judged. Most former colonies of Britain are now in the process of establishing their own standard varieties of English (e.g. standard Indian English, standard Singaporean English, Jamaican National Language, and so on) and of creating norms of usage which are in some respects different from those of the traditional standard varieties, although the norms may overlap in other respects, as shown, for example, in the diagram of these emerging standard varieties provided by McArthur (1998: 97), which he characterizes as:

a wheel with a hub, spokes and a rim. The hub is called *World Standard English*, within an encircling band of regional varieties, such as the standard and other forms of *African English*, *American English*, *Canadian English* and *Irish English*.

These regional standard varieties do not carry the colonial taint of standard British English, of which Killian (1986: 271) has remarked in the context of attitudes in Ireland:

> English is both valued (for being a language that could provide economic freedom) and scorned (for being a colonial language), more frequently than not in the same breath.

As in McArthur's diagram, the new standard regional varieties exist alongside the traditional standard varieties of English (standard British English, general American English), as well as standard varieties of indigenous languages and a spectrum of dialects. The former colonies maintain international communication through the medium of a regional standard variety of English which is internationally intelligible but which also has features which express a local identity.

As far as the second argument is concerned, postmodernist theory would argue that the preservation/creation of a local identity in the face of globalization is necessary, and provides a kind of refuge from the ever-changing collage of experiences which make up the global village. As Arnett (2002: 787) says:

> Most people now develop a bi-cultural identity, in which part of their identity is rooted in their local culture while another part stems from an awareness of their relation to the global culture.

One way in which we manage to reconcile our citizenship of the global village and these more local allegiances is through our use of language, and in the case of Ireland, a standard variety of Irish English fits the bill, rather than standard British English with its colonial overtones, or Irish, which may express some aspects of Irish identity, but does not, unlike standard Irish English, easily permit users to link their local identity with a global one.

So why has Irish English (often referred to in pre-1990 writings as 'Hiberno-English') never been valued for its role as a marker of national identity in the Republic until fairly recently? Why, as Croghan has pointed out (1980: 17), has there 'never been an official or popular understanding that Hiberno-English is the real language of Ireland'? I would argue that part of the reason lies in the fact that the colonized accepted the myth that their English usage was inferior and deviant when measured against the norms of standard British English, and that this intellectual 'colonization' with regard to language attitudes persisted long after political independence in 1921. Another reason lies in the ways in which some linguists persisted in viewing regional varieties of English which differed from standard British English as inferior because, for example, their distinctive linguistic features had not been codified in the form of grammar books and dictionaries, or because these linguists had not yet appreciated the ways in which English was developing new standard varieties worldwide. Harris

(1991: 39) for example, clearly working within the older tradition of measuring English use in Ireland against the norms of standard British English, and also with traditional notions of 'standardness', says:

> There exists no fully independent Irish English vernacular ... the written model is more or less indistinguishable from that of standard British English ... when used in formal contexts ... spoken English tends to follow the norms of the written standard in matters of grammar and lexis.

Linguistic features of standard Irish English

Recent corpus-based approaches to standard language have rather changed definitions of what standard language consists of. They incorporate examples of real language use, spoken as well as written, thus shifting the focus of standard language away from an exclusively written form. Corpora such as the International Corpus of English (ICE),[1] collected in 15 countries which have established or emerging national standard varieties of English, start from the premise that standard language consists of whatever language is produced by standard language users, rather than judging language against pre-established norms of correctness. One of the aims of the ICE corpus was to compare similarities and differences between established and emerging standard varieties of English worldwide (Greenbaum 1990), and standard Irish English was one of the national varieties which was included in the corpus.

In the mid-1990s, I collected a small corpus of English (31,554 words) from mainly young educated standard language users in the Republic. The data in this corpus was collected under the same conditions and with the same aims as the ICE-Ireland corpus. My corpus (Corpus of Southern Irish English, hence-forward referred to as CSIE) reveals that there are differences from standard British English in the syntactical and lexical choices of the English language users in the Republic and the differences are found in formal spoken situations such as lectures and radio and TV broadcasts, as well as in more informal conversations. It is not easy to dismiss this variety of Irish English as some kind of 'brogue-speak' (Croghan 1986: 265) used by rural, uneducated speakers, and I have argued elsewhere (White 2003) that it has now attained many of the traditional characteristics of a standard form of English in its own right (e.g. prestige, codification) and to be attracting government spending and public interest. The Arts and Humanities Research Council funding granted in 2001 to the ICE-Ireland project, after eight years of effort, points to a new governmental willingness to recognize the existence and value of Irish English. Over the last ten years a number of dictionaries of Irish English words have been published, ranging from the scholarly to the populist: (Beecher 1991; Christensen 1996; O'Muirithe 1996a, 1996b; Share 1997; Dolan 1998) as have descriptions of Irish English grammar, both fuller descriptions: (Harris 1991, 1993; Kallen 1994, 1997; Filppula 1999) and discussions of particular structures, or of the varieties of English found in particular areas: (e.g. Moylan 1996; Dolan and O'Muirithe 1996). This contrasts with the slow and piecemeal trickle before the 1990s; of wordlists described by Van Ryckeghem (1997) or the occasional appearance of descriptions, either of English in the Republic as a whole, for example, Bliss (1979), Barry (1981); or of particular dialects of Irish English, for example, Henry (1957). This growing interest on the part of the general public in the Republic in reading about their own indigenous varieties of English, both standard and 'dialectal', seems to be a sign of the growth of those regional and local allegiances mentioned earlier in this chapter.

I found that some features which have been associated with dialectal varieties of Irish English, particularly by Filppula (1999), either did not occur in my corpus or occurred very infrequently, e.g.

- *Do be + ing* (as in 'I do be listening to the Irish here') (Filppula 1999)
- Subordinating *and* (as in 'And how was it she never stays with you and she's plenty room'?) (CSIE)
- Lack of plural subject-verb concord with noun subjects (as in 'My mother and father was reared in Dublin') (Filppula 1999)
- Definite article used in contexts where it would not be found in standard British English (as in 'The carpet's not the best for dancing') (CSIE)

Other features, however, which do not appear in standard British English were quite frequent in the CSIE corpus of standard Irish English users. Standard Irish English can, for instance, realize the temporal and aspectual meanings linked to the use of the present perfect in standard British English in a number of other ways:

1. An action which started in the past and continues in the present (as in 'I'm up since quarter to seven') (CSIE)
2. An event or activity which occurred and was completed in the past, but which has an effect on the present (as in 'A new fella is after taking over one of the pubs at home') (CSIE)
3. An event experienced at an indefinite point in the past (as in 'We was ever here, I think') (Filppula 1999)
4. Something completed or achieved as a result of an action in the past – different constructions with transitive and intransitive verbs (as in 'I've my flashcards done' or 'the next team up are chosen particularly for their unique accentual variation') (CSIE)

While there were a large number of occasions when the use of the present perfect conformed to standard British English patterns (68) these Irish English alternatives persisted (17), and accounted for 20 per cent of all possible occurrences. It is remarkable that these present perfect alternatives persist in the face of strong counter influences from American English and standard British English. Similarly, it is surprising that indirect questions with subject-verb inversion, another feature associated with Irish English, persist in spite of the pressure exerted by neighbouring standard varieties , e.g. 'I don't know is it my favourite', 'If somebody asked me how many hours a week do I have, I would say twenty-eight' (CSIE). Out of seven opportunities for this feature to occur in the corpus, three conform to the standard British English pattern for reported questions, e.g. 'I was asked whether I'd move in or not' and four correspond to the subject-verb inversion mentioned earlier.

Standard Irish English also differs from neighbouring varieties pragmatically. *Like* in clause-final position is very frequent in the CSIE corpus, and appears to be performing several interpersonal functions, such as expressing evaluative judgements (e.g. 'It's handier like'), making changes of topic less abrupt, and clarifying in a polite, non-threatening way (e.g. 'You know, where you draw the lines and do the letters like'). *So* can be used to organize transitions in talk, for example to signal the beginning of a turn in speaking, (e.g. 'OK so. When I was a child I used to visit my grandmother every Sunday'); or as a politeness device, to soften or hedge what has been said (e.g. 'Oh sure he's no bother so'). *Now* is frequently used on its own by shop assistants as a signal that they are ready to serve a customer. The initial greeting of the weather forecaster on RTE 1 (an Irish television channel) every evening before he gave the forecast, 'Good night', is also surprising to standard British English users, since in British English this phrase would be used to close, not to open, a speech event.

Attitudes towards standard Irish English within the Republic

In addition to the linguistic evidence provided by the CSIE corpus for the use of a standard form of Irish English in the Republic which differs in a number of ways from standard British English, it is also useful to examine attitudes towards standard Irish English. One well established method is to ask subjects to draw a map of the area they live in, and to elicit attitudes concerning the language use of particular groups of geographically located speakers on that map (e.g. Hartley and Preston 1999; Preston 2002). In the early 1990s, the popular belief, at least among people I encountered when I lived there, was that the varieties of English in Ireland which most closely resembled standard British English were the most correct, and that Irish English as a whole was in the process of converging on standard British English. However, as we have seen from the corpus, this appears not to be the case, and the map task also tells a different story. One of the questions which the participants were asked concerned which variety of English they considered to be the best. A selection of their replies is given below:

Question: Which is the best variety of English?

Responses:

'The best English is spoken in Dublin, but it's RTE, Dublin suburbs, Gay Byrne, not DART speak'

'The best Hiberno-English is spoken in the West, with an Irish flavour'

'The best English isn't spoken in Dublin – that's beginning to sound too English. The best is in Galway City – it's cleaner, less accent than the south. The worst is Kildare' 'the easiest to understand is Dun Laoghaire'

'the best English is cultured Cork'

'the best English is spoken in the Gaeltachts where English was learnt as a second language'

'a vaguely northern accent has become quite prestigious'

While many of the comments focused on accent rather than linguistic form, it is significant that none of the 58 respondents, drawn from a wide geographical area and a range of age, chose standard British English as the best variety, and that their replies centred on a number of varieties of Irish English.

Evidence from a questionnaire administered to 20 teachers of ESOL (English to Speakers of Other Languages) and 23 teachers of English as a first language in the Republic of Ireland reveal an interesting mismatch between teachers' attitudes to language use and what they actually do in the classroom. When asked the question 'Which variety of English do you think you draw on when you correct students' errors, or give them rules about language use?' the majority of both groups of teachers replied that standard British English was the 'gold standard' to which they referred (16 out of the 20 ESOL teachers, 19 out of 23 first language teachers). However, when they were given examples of Irish English usage, some of which were dialectal features which the corpus had indicated might be falling out of use, and others which appeared to belong to standard Irish English and to differ from standard British English norms, they viewed a number of the standard Irish English examples as correct:

Table 13.1 ESOL teachers' opinions of norms

Structure/lexical item	Acceptable in speaking		Acceptable in writing	
	yes	no	yes	no
I'm after selling the house	12	7	1	18
I wish you'd stop giving out to me	17	3	*12	8
There's some good pubs in Cork	10	10	1	10
I tend to sleep it out on these cold winter mornings	9	9	3	12
The nights do be getting cold	5	15	*0	*20
Will I help you with the washing up?	19	1	*12	8
My brother has the car sold	6	14	0	20
He asked me was I from Galway?	11	9	2	18
Who's your actual teacher here, like?	10	9	1	18

Table 13.2 English as a first language teachers' opinions of norms

Structure/lexical item	Acceptable in speaking		Acceptable in writing	
	yes	no	yes	no
I'm after selling the house	10	13	5	18
I wish you'd stop giving out to me	21	2	*15	8
There's some good pubs in Cork	9	14	4	18
I tend to sleep it out on these cold winter mornings	16	4	11	9
The nights do be getting cold	2	21	*0	*23
Will I help you with the washing up?	23	0	*18	5
My brother has the car sold	11	11	10	13
He asked me was I from Galway?	18	5	11	11
Who's your actual teacher here, like?	9	13	2	19

As can be seen from the tables, not all the teachers commented on all of the examples. However, as the highlighted items (*) show, while structures such as 'do be + ing', which did not appear in the CSIE corpus, are stigmatized, probably because they are felt to be dialectal and are associated with older, rural and uneducated speakers, both groups would not correct 'Will I help you with the washing up?' and 'I wish you'd stop giving out to me' (which would certainly cause intelligibility problems outside the Republic). The first language English teachers are a lot more tolerant of Irish English alternatives to the standard British English present perfect and also to subject-verb inversion in indirect questions. This could be attributed to the fact that the ESOL teachers are often engaged in preparing students for English language examinations which are written in Britain and which tend to use standard British English norms. Nevertheless, the exercise proves that teachers in the Republic of Ireland, as important gatekeepers of standard language, are no longer referring exclusively to standard British English for norms.

Conclusion

This chapter has attempted to demonstrate that the time has come to consider a standard form of Irish English as an important means of marking Irish identity, and to re-evaluate the historical roles played by standard British English and Irish in doing this work. The 'postnational' condition of Irish identity, its position in a globalized economy, the recent output of writing on and in Irish English, the views of both members of the public and teachers in the Republic and data from a corpus of standard language users in Ireland all appear to prove the hypothesis that language users in the Republic have a strong allegiance to their own regional standard form of English, and that it might be an appropriate present-day vehicle for expressing national identity.

Notes

1   Further details of the components of the International Corpus of English can be found at: www.ucl.ac.uk/english-usage/ice.

References

Anderson, B. (1991) (revised edn), *Imagined Communities: Reflections on the Origin and Spread of Nationalism*. London: Verso.

Arnett, J. J. (2002), 'The psychology of globalisation', *American Psychologist*, 57, (10), 774–83.

Arrowsmith , A. (2004), 'Plastic Paddies vs Master Racers: "Soccer and Irish identity"', *International Journal of Cultural Studies*, 7 (4), 460–79.

Barry, M. V. (1981), *Aspects of English Dialects in Ireland*. Belfast: Institute of Irish Studies.

Beecher, S. (1991), *A Dictionary of Cork Slang*. Cork: The Collins Press.

Bliss, A. J. (1979), *Spoken English in Ireland 1600–1740*. Dublin: Dolmen

Christensen, L. (1996), *A First Glossary of Hiberno-English*. Odense: Odense University Press.

Croghan, M. (1980), 'Demythologising Hiberno-English', *Working Papers in Irish Studies*, 90, (1), Northeastern University, Boston, USA.

— (1986), 'The Brogue : Language as political culture', in J. Harris *et al.* (eds), *Perspectives on the English Language in Ireland : Proceedings of the First Symposium on Hiberno-English*. Centre for Language and Communication Studies, Trinity College, Dublin.

Crystal, D. (2003), *English as a Global Language* (2nd edn). Cambridge: Cambridge University Press.

Davis, T. C. (2003), 'The Irish and their nation: A survey of recent attitudes', *The Global Review of Ethnopolitics*, 2, 2, 17–36.

Delanty, G. (1996), 'Habermas and post-national identity: Theoretical perspectives on the conflict in Northern Ireland', *Irish Political Studies*, 11, 20–32.

— (1997), 'Towards a postnational Europe? The future of democracy and the crisis of the nation state', in P. Nemo (ed.), *The European Union and the Nation State*. Paris: Groupe ESCP Press, pp. 161–86.

Delanty, G. and O'Mahony, P. (1998), *Rethinking Irish History: Nationalism, Identity and Ideology*. London: Macmillan.

Dolan, T. P. (ed.) (1998), *A Dictionary of Hiberno-English: the Irish Use of English*. Dublin: Gill & Macmillan.

Dolan, T. P. and O'Muirithe, D. (1996), *The Dialect of Forth and Bargy, Co. Wexford, Ireland*. Dublin: Four Courts Press.

Downes, W. (1998) (2nd edn), *Language and Society*. Cambridge: Cambridge University Press.

Edwards, J. (1985), *Language, Society and Identity*. Oxford: Blackwell.

Filppula, M. (1999), *The Grammar of Irish English: Language in Hibernian Style*. London: Routledge.

Fishman, J. A. (1971), 'Language and nationalism', J. A. Fishman, *Language and Ethnicity in Minority Sociolinguistic Perspective*. Clevedon: Multilingual Matters.

Graddol, D. (1997), *The Future of English?* London: The British Council.
— (1999), 'The decline of the native speaker', in D. Graddol and U. H. Meinhof (eds), *English in a Changing World*. Milton Keynes: AILA.
Greenbaum, S. (1990), 'Standard English and the International Corpus of English', *World Englishes*, 9, (1), 79–83.
Harris, J. (1991), 'Ireland', J. Cheshire (ed.), *English Around the World: Sociolinguistic Perspectives*. Cambridge: Cambridge University Press.
— (1993), 'The Grammar of Irish English', in J. Milroy and L. Milroy (eds), *Real English*. Harlow: Longman.
Harte, L. (1997), 'A kind of scab: Irish identity in the writings of Dermot Bolger and Joseph O'Connor', *Irish Studies Review*, 20, 17–22.
Hartley, L. C. and Preston, D. R. (1999), 'The names of US English: Valley girl, cowboy, yankee, normal, nasal and ignorant', in T. Bex. and R. J. Watts (eds), *Standard English: The Widening Debate*. London: Routledge, pp. 207–38.
Haugen, E. (1972), 'Dialect, language, nation', in J. B. Pride and J. Holmes (eds), *Sociolinguistics: Selected Readings*. Harmondsworth: Penguin, pp. 97–111.
Henry, P. L. (1957), *An Anglo-Irish Dialect of North Roscommon. Phonology, Accidence, Syntax*. Zurich: Aschman and Scheller.
Joseph, J. (2004), *Language and Identity: National, Ethnic, Religious*. Basingstoke: Palgrave Macmillan.
Kachru, B. (1985), 'Standards, codification and sociolinguistic realism: The English language in the outer circle', in R. Quirk and H. Widdowson (eds), *English in the World*. Cambridge: Cambridge University Press.
— (1992), 'World Englishes: Approaches, issues and resources', *Language Teaching*, 25, 1–14.
Kachru, B. and Nelson, C. (2001), 'World Englishes', in A. Burns and C. Coffin (eds), *Analysing English in a Global Context*. London and New York: Routledge, pp. 9–25.
Kallen, J. L. (1988), 'The English Language in Ireland', *International Journal of the Sociology of Language*, 70, 127–42.
— (1994), 'English in Ireland', in R. Burchfield (ed.), *The Cambridge History of the English Language, Volume V, English in Britain and Overseas: Origins and Development*. Cambridge: Cambridge University Press, pp. 148–96.
Kallen, J. L. (ed) (1997), *Focus on Ireland*. Amsterdam: Benjamins.
Kiberd, D. (1996), *Inventing Ireland: The Literature of the Modern Nation*, London: Vintage.
Killian, P. (1986), 'English in Ireland: An attitudinal study', in J. Harris *et al.* (eds), *Perspectives on the English language in Ireland: Proceedings of the first symposium on Hiberno-English*. Centre for Language and Communication Studies, Trinity College, Dublin.
Le Page, R. B. and Tabouret-Keller, A. (1985), *Acts of Identity: Creole-based Approaches to Language and Identity*. Cambridge: Cambridge University Press.
McArthur, T. (1997), *The English Languages*, Cambridge: Cambridge Unioversity Press.
— (2003), *The Oxford Guide to World English*. Oxford: Oxford University Press.
McGovern, M. (1999), 'The craic market: Irish theme bars and the commodification of Irishness in contemporary Britain'. Paper delivered to the Sociological Association of Ireland, Annual Conference, Belfast.
McKay, S. L. (2002), *Teaching English as an International Language*. Oxford: Oxford University Press.
Milroy, J. and Milroy, L. (1999) (3rd edn), *Authority in Language: Investigating Standard English*. London: Routledge.
Moylan, S. (1996), *The Language of Kilkenny*. Dublin: Geography Publications.
O'Muirithe, D. (1996a), *A Dictionary of Anglo-Irish: Words and Phrases from Gaelic in the English of Ireland*. Dublin: Four Courts Press.
— (1996b), *The Words We Use*. Dublin : Four Courts Press.
Pašeta, S. (2003), *Modern Ireland: A Very Short Introduction*. Oxford: Oxford University Press.

Preston, D. (2002), 'Language with an attitude', in J. K. Chambers, P. Trudgill and N. Schilling-Estes (eds), *The Handbook of Language Variation and Change*. Oxford: Blackwell, pp. 40–66.

Share, B. (1997), *Slanguage: A Dictionary of Irish Slang*. Gill and Macmillan Ltd: Dublin.

Smith, A. (1991), *National Identity*. Harmondsworth: Penguin Books.

Suleiman, Y. (2003), *The Arabic Language and National Identity*. Washington DC: Georgetown University Press.

Thiesse, A. (1999), 'Inventing national identity', *Le Monde Diplomatique*, June 1999, available at: mondediplo.com/1999/06/05thiesse.

Van Ryckeghem, B. (1997), 'The lexicon of Hiberno-English', in J. Kallen (ed.), *Focus on Ireland*. Amsterdam: Benjamins, pp. 171–87.

White, G. (2003), 'Is there such a thing as Irish Standard English?', in G. L. Agullo, A. B. Gonzalez and G. T. Molina (eds), *Languages in a Global World*. Jaen: Associacion Espanola de Linguistica Applicada/University of Jaen, pp. 305–16.

Wright, S. (2000), *Community and Communication: The Role of Language in Nation State Building and European Integration*. Clevedon: Multilingual Matters.

Index

Lightning Source UK Ltd.
Milton Keynes UK
UKOW032121090312

188642UK00002B/149/P